TRIAL BY FIRE

AND

WATER

The Medieval Judicial Ordeal

ROBERT BARTLETT

E P B M

ECHO POINT BOOKS & MEDIA, LLC

Published by Echo Point Books & Media
Brattleboro, Vermont
www.EchoPointBooks.com

ISBN: 978-1-62654-889-3

Cover Image: *Justice of the Emperor Otto: The Ordeal by Fire* by Dirk Bouts

Cover Design by Adrienne Núñez,
Echo Point Books & Media

Editorial and proofreading assistance by Christine Schultz,
Echo Point Books & Media

FOR NORA

Acknowledgements

GRATEFUL thanks are due to James Amelang, Geoffrey Barrow, T. S.Brown, Rees Davies, Alexander Gieszytor, Angus MacKay, and Nicholas Phillipson for providing helpful references; to Michael Angold, Fergus Kelly, and Patrick Wormald for help on the Byzantine, Irish, and Anglo-Saxon material, respectively; to Michael Clanchy for stimulating discussion; to Matthew Hoffmann, William Jordan, R. I. Moore, Andrew Reeve, and Lawrence Stone for their kindness in reading and commenting upon earlier drafts of some of this material; and to my wife.

Earlier versions of some chapters were delivered as talks in St Andrews, Edinburgh, Brooklyn College, Dalhousie University (Halifax), and the University of Pennsylvania. I am grateful for the invitations and for the comments and criticisms offered on those occasions.

Some of the work for this book was done during the tenure of a Davis Center Fellowship at Princeton University.

Contents

	List of Maps and Figures	ix
	Abbreviations	x
1	Introduction	1
2	Early History	4
3	The Workings of the Ordeal in its Heyday	13
	Types of Ordeal	13
	Ordeal, Testimony, and Oath	24
4	The End of the Ordeal and Social Change	34
	The Functionalist Case	34
	The Persistence of the Ordeal	42
	Exemptions	53
	The Case of England	62
5	The End of the Ordeal: Explanations in Terms of Belief	70
	Critics of the Ordeal	70
	Clerical Interests	90
6	Trial by Battle	103
	Trial by Battle: A Sketch	103
	Battle and Ordeal	113
7	Aftermath	127
	Disappearance	127
	Replacement	135
	Recrudescence	144
8	Further Reflections	153
	Select Bibliography	167
	Index	171

Maps and Figures

Map 1. References to Unilateral Ordeals prior to 800   6

Map 2. References to Unilateral Ordeals after 800.   43

Map 3. Exemptions from Unilateral Ordeals granted to Lay Communities, 1050-1200.   58

Figure 1. The Varad Register. Cases involving the ordeal as a percentage of total cases recorded   129

Abbreviations

Books and articles listed in the bibliography are referred to by author's surname and short title.

Györffy, 'Anhang'	György Györffy, *Wirtschaft und Gesellschaft der Ungarn um die Jarhrtausendwende* (Vienna, etc., 1983), 'Anhang Gesetze und Synodalbeschlüsse Ungarns aus dem 11. Jahrhundert', pp. 249-331, based on the text of L. Zavodszky (Budapest, 1904)
JL	*Regesta pontificum Romanorum . . . ad annum . . . 1198*, ed. P. Jaffé, rev. S. Loewenfeld *et al.* (2 vols., Leipzig, 1885-8)
Mansi	*Sacrorum conciliorum nova et amplissima collectio*, ed. G. D. Mansi (2nd ed., 53 vols., Paris, etc., 1901-27)
MGH	Monumenta Germaniae historica
Capit.	*Capitularia regum Francorum*
Conc.	*Concilia*
Const.	*Constitutiones et acta publica imperatorum et regum*
DD	*Diplomata*
Epp.	*Epistolae* (in quarto)
Fontes iuris	*Fontes iuris Germanici antiqui in usum scholarum separatim editi*
LL	*Leges* (in folio)
LL nat. Germ.	*Leges nationum Germanicarum*
SS	*Scriptores* (in folio)
SRG	*Scriptores rerum Germanicarum in usum scholarum separatim editi*
NS	new series
PL	*Patrologiae cursus completus, series latina*, ed. J.-P. Migne (221 vols., Paris, 1844-64)
Po.	*Regesta pontificum Romanorum inde ab annum . . . 1198 ad a.1304*, ed. A. Potthast (2 vols.,Berlin, 1874-5)
RS	*Rerum britannicarum medii aevi scriptores* (251 vols., London, 1858-96), 'Rolls Series'
UB	*Urkundenbuch*
X	*Decretales Gregorii IX*
ZRG	*Zeitschrift der Savigny-Stiftung für Rechtsgeschichte*

I

Introduction

O God, the just judge, who are the author of peace and give fair
judgement, we humbly pray you to deign to bless and sanctify this fiery
iron, which is used in the just examination of doubtful issues. If this
man is innocent of the charge from which he seeks to clear himself, he
will take this fiery iron in his hand and appear unharmed; if he is guilty,
let your most just power declare that truth in him, so that wickedness
may not conquer justice but falsehood always be overcome by the truth.
Through Christ.[1]

WITH these words medieval priests initiated one common form of
trial by ordeal. A man accused of a crime, or a man seeking to claim or
defend his rights, would, after a solemn three-day fast, pick up a hot
iron, walk three paces, and put the iron down. His hand would be
bandaged and sealed, then, after three days, inspected. If it was
'clean'–that is, healing without suppuration or discoloration–he was
innocent or vindicated; if the wound was unclean, he was guilty.

The medieval ordeal is a subject of great intrinsic interest and fasci-
nation. It is one of the more dramatically alien practices of medieval
society and, as such, it demands and yet resists explanation. For those
concerned to make the imaginative leap into a past society, the ordeal
is a hurdle and a challenge. Its 'otherness' represents an explanatory
problem. Just as anthropologists seek to understand the inner
rationale of strange and apparently incomprehensible practices and
beliefs among peoples of other cultures, so here the medievalist is
confronted with the problem of a custom which has no familiar
counterpart in the modern West. Medieval armies, farms, or, even,
churches do not seem obviously opaque–there are modern armies,
farms, and churches which suggest to us how these kinds of thing work
in general. Trial by ordeal has no real counterpart in the modern
world. It is necessary to stretch our minds to understand this custom.

Yet a true grasp of its nature might give a deep and penetrating
insight into the society which practised it. Recent scholarship has

[1] Zeumer, *Formulae*, pp. 700-1.

seized the challenge and a series of distinguished historians have attempted to examine the ordeal as a key or focus for understanding social processes and social change in the medieval period: social change, especially, for the ordeal was abandoned in the thirteenth century and the inherent lure of this exotic custom is increased by the need to explain its disappearance, by the prospect of understanding, through the microcosm of the ordeal, a major social change. Such phrases as 'the ending of sacral society', the atrophy of 'the world of the ordeal', a growing 'impersonality' in society, a 'shift from consensus to authority', spring up in the literature on the subject and illustrate this generalizing urge.[2] Clearly the explanation of the abandonment of the ordeal is as problematic, and yet holds as much promise, as the characterization of the practice itself. Obviously, the two enterprises are related: no satisfactory account can be given of the demise of a practice unless it is clear what the practice *is*.

Trial by hot iron was only one form of ordeal. There were numerous other varieties, some important, some mere monuments to the ingenuity of long-vanished communities (the Navarrese 'ordeal of the candles',[3] for example). The central focus here will be upon the trials of fire and water: holding or walking on hot iron, immersing the hand in boiling water, or complete immersion in a pool or stream. Such practices have two important features in common. They were all unilateral, usually undertaken by only one party in the case; and they all required that the natural elements behave in an unusual way, hot iron or water not burning the innocent, cold water not allowing the guilty to sink. In this respect they differed from another major form of ordeal, the duel or trial by battle, which is discussed in Chapter 6.

Ordeals of fire and water have been employed by peoples in many different parts of the world and throughout history. They crop up in the laws of Hammurabi and in the judicial practice of modern Kenya; men have undergone the ordeal from Iceland to Polynesia, from Japan to Africa.[4] It is enlightening to compare and contrast the form, func-

---

[2] Morris, '*Judicium Dei*', p. 111; Hyams, 'Trial by Ordeal', p. 100; Brown, 'Society and the Supernatural', p. 143 (repr., pp. 323-4).

[3] *Fuero General de Navarra*, 5.3.11-12; 5.7.1 and 3, ed. Pablo Ilarregui and Segundo Lapuerta (Pamplona, 1869, repr. 1964), pp. 181-2, 196; see also Nottarp, *Gottesurteilstudien*, pp. 51-2.

[4] For trial by ordeal in non-European countries, see, for instance, Société Jean Bodin pour l'histoire comparative des institutions, *Recueils*, 18 (1963), *La Preuve*, 3, *Civilisations archaïques, asiatiques et islamiques*, pp. 8-10, 29-31, 49-53, 76, 113, 131, 364-71, 391-2, 411-18, 461-90, 512, 522-3; Patetta, *Le ordalie, passim*; Lea, *Superstition and Force*, pp. 249-69, (1973

tion, and workings of the ordeal in different times and places. Students of trial by ordeal can usefully consider the diverse contexts and environments in which this form of proof flourished. It may even be possible to make large-scale generalizations about the kind of social structure which is most congenial to the ordeal.[5] This book, however, is historical. It concentrates upon the story of trial by ordeal in Christian, European societies, ranging from the laws of the Franks in the early Middle Ages to the last vestiges of the custom in eighteenth- and nineteenth-century America and Europe.

partial reissue, Chap. 1); Nottarp, *Gottesurteilstudien*, pp. 40-3; Roberts, 'Oaths, Autonomic Ordeals and Power'; R. W. Lariviere (ed. and tr.), *The Divyatattva of Raghunandana Bhattacarya: Ordeals in Classical Hindu Law* (New Delhi, 1981).

[5] Roberts, 'Oaths, Autonomic Ordeals and Power'. The confidence to be placed in generalizations such as these depends largely on the accuracy and coherence of the information in the 'Human Relations Area Files' on which they are founded. Some anthropologists are sceptical of this data. A striking adumbration of Roberts' method and conclusions is to be found in a curious psychoanalytically-inspired study of the ordeal , H. Goitein, *Primitive Ordeal and Modern Law* (London, 1923), pp. 134-9.

2

Early History

THE story of the ordeals of fire and water falls into two distinct phases: the period before AD 800, which, because of the scantiness of the evidence, can only be called protohistorical, and the period from 800 onwards, when there is a true explosion of evidence. The protohistorical period lasts about three hundred years, from the time of the earliest reference to trial by ordeal, around AD 500. During this period the sum total of our data is a handful of mentions in the early law codes and a miracle story from Gregory of Tours.

Two things emerge from this material, one quite clearly, one less certainly, but with some degree of probability. Firstly, there is no room for doubt that the only form of unilateral ordeal mentioned in these early records is the ordeal of the cauldron, that is, the ordeal of hot water. For the sixth, seventh, and most of the eighth century there are no references to any other kind of ordeal. The procedure involved, in which an object, usually a stone or a ring, had to be plucked from a bubbling cauldron, is vividly described in Gregory of Tours' *De gloria martyrum*: 'the fire was built up, the cauldron was placed on it, it boiled fiercely, a little ring was tossed into the hot water'. The proband 'drew back his clothes from his arm and plunged his right hand into the cauldron ... the fire roared up and in the bubbling it was not easy for him to grasp the little ring, but at last he drew it out'.[1]

The second point that emerges from this evidence is that there is a strong likelihood that the custom was of Frankish origin. Certainly, the earliest mention of the ordeal of the cauldron is in the first recension of the Salic Law (*c.* 510). Here there are references to men being 'adjudged to the cauldron' or satisfying a charge of contempt of court 'by composition or by the cauldron'. Later, but still sixth-century, additions to the Salic law and, also, the Ripuarian law contain provisions for both slaves and free men—even the royal *anstruciones*, the king's immediate retainers—going to the cauldron on charges of theft; and for the cauldron as the proof in a charge of false witness. Regu-

[1] Cap. 80, ed. Bruno Kisch, MGH, *Scriptores rerum Merovingicarum*, 1 (Hanover, 1885), pp. 542-3.

lations prescribed 'whoever has to justify himself at the cauldron shall hold the staff [the court official's staff of office] with his left hand and draw out with his right'. There seems as good evidence here for a sixth-century Frankish custom as it is possible to get.[2] The case described by Gregory of Tours, the earliest such description in existence, has recently been interpreted as an indication of the early spread of Frankish law among the Gallo-Roman population.[3]

References to the ordeal outside the Frankish world begin in the seventh century (see Map 1). The earliest of these occur in Irish law. Several of the earliest Irish legal treatises, dating to the seventh or eighth centuries, refer to the *fír caire* or *fír fogerrta*, 'the truth (or test or trial) of the cauldron', sometimes also termed *fír De*, 'the truth of God' (a fairly exact equivalent of *iudicium Dei*). This form of proof was used especially in testing the legitimacy of doubtful claimants to the rights and property of the kindred. As we shall see, this was a common function of the ordeal in many other countries too. One passage in these treatises describes how the cauldron, along with other forms of trial, was introduced by St Patrick: 'these things were the tests Patrick established to decide the disputes of the men of Ireland . . . in the new knowledge of the men of Ireland'. The introduction of the ordeal by a Christian Briton is, needless to say, highly improbable.[4]

Now early Irish law is a hard and complex subject and there is little room here for the judgements of an amateur, but it does seem very likely that these seventh- and eighth-century Irish legal references represent a tradition of the ordeal by cauldron quite distinct from the Frankish one. There are few plausible paths of influence or suggestions of common ancestry which would link these two early bodies of

---

[2] *Pactus legis Salicae*, 14.2, 16.5, 53, 56.1-3, 81, 112 and 132; *Lex Salica* 89(88) and 91; ed. Karl August Eckhardt, MGH, *LL nat. Germ.* 4, pts. 1 and 2 (Hanover, 1962-9), 1, pp. 64-5, 74, 200-3, 210-11, 251, 262, 267; 2, pp. 154-7, 158; *Lex Ribuaria*, caps. 30-1, ed. Karl August Eckhardt, *Lex Ribuaria II. Text und Lex Francorum Chamavorum* (Hanover, 1966), pp. 39-40.

[3] Edward James, *The Origins of France* (London, 1982), p. 88.

[4] References to trial by cauldron from the seventh and eighth centuries (accompanied by glosses from the twelfth and thirteenth centuries) can be found in *Ancient Laws of Ireland*, ed. W. N. Hancock, etc., (6 vols., Dublin, etc., 1865-1901), 1, pp. 195-9; 5, pp. 457, 471-3. The corresponding passages in the definitive edition of the Old Irish texts are D. A. Binchy (ed.), *Corpus iuris hibernici* (6 vols., Dulin, 1978), 2, pp. 393-4; 1, pp. 233, 238 (fragments also in 3, p. 916; 5, pp. 1872-3; 6, p. 2232). Another seventh-century reference can be found in E. J. Gwynn (ed.), 'An Old-Irish Tract on the Privileges and Responsibilities of Poets', *Ériu*, 13 (1942), pp. 1-60, 220-36, at p. 22, lines 7-8. A more elaborate tract, containing some evidence for the importation of new ordeals of foreign origin, dating from the ninth century, is edited by Stokes, 'The Irish Ordeals'.

Map 1. References to Unilateral Ordeals prior to 800

legal material (unless we have recourse to the *deus ex machina* of the Indo-European heritage). In this relative isolation from the legal currents of contemporary Europe, however, the situation in Ireland was quite exceptional. Yet, just as they represent a tradition un-influenced by others, so the Irish ordeals were a legal tradition without influence. These laws of the seventh and later centuries mention trial by cauldron (and, later, some other varieties of the ordeal) but Irish trial by ordeal is an autonomous and self-contained story. The tap-root of the ordeal was, it seems, Frankish.

The evidence for this assertion is suggestive rather than conclusive, but the case is quite strong. The first main point is negative, the absence of the trials of fire and water from the law codes of many other peoples. The Burgundian, Alamannic, and Bavarian laws contain no mention of such practices. They do not occur in early Kentish law. The Saxon law, as finally codified in 802, does not have them either. This is all strong presumptive evidence that the trials of fire and water were not of pan-Germanic origin. If they were not pan-Germanic, then, of course, they must have originated among either one or several individual Germanic peoples.[5] The second point is that, apart from the specific case of Ireland, all early non-Frankish occurrences of the ordeal can be plausibly attributed to Frankish influence. Outside of the Frankish and Irish laws, there are four early codes which contain a mention of trial by cauldron: the laws of the West Saxons, the Visigoths, the Lombards, and the Frisians, which each have a single reference. Of these, the laws of Ine, king of the West Saxons, produced around 690, are the earliest. The manuscript tradition of these laws is late and the very existence of the reference to the ordeal here hangs on a palaeographical thread–Liebermann's emendation of *ceape* (market) to *ceace* (cauldron)–but there do seem to be grounds here for seeing an isolated occurrence of the cauldron ordeal in early Anglo-Saxon law.[6] Ine's law is the only mention of ordeal in Anglo-Saxon England before the tenth century. Frankish influence on Anglo-Saxon ordeals in this later period, the tenth and eleventh centuries, is quite certain[7] and it may perhaps be conjectured for the earlier reference too. Two of the seventh-century bishops of the West Saxons were Franks and the early Wessex charters have similarities to those of the Merovingians.[8]

[5] Contrast the opinion of Heinrich Brunner, 'Auf arischer Grundlage erwachsen, waren die Gottesurteile einst eine gemeingermanische institution', *Deutsche Rechtsgeschichte* (2 vols., 1st edn., Leipzig, 1887-92), 2, p. 400. He was only a little more reserved in the second edition (2 vols.; 1, Leipzig, 1906, repr. Berlin, 1961; 2, rev. Claudius von Schwerin, Berlin, 1928, repr. Berlin, 1958), 1, pp. 261-3; 2, pp. 538-9.

[6] Ine's laws, caps. 37 and 62, ed. Liebermann, *Gesetze*, 1, pp. 104-5, 116-17. The earliest manuscript of Ine's laws, dating to the tenth century, reads *ceape* (market), where the later ones, of the earlier twelfth century, have *ceace* (cauldron). The case for the emendation is, nevertheless, strong; see Felix Liebermann, 'Kesselfang bei den Westsachsen im siebenten Jahrhundert', *Sitzungsberichte der königlich preussischen Akademie der Wissenschaften zu Berlin* (1896), pp. 829-35. Eadmer thought that ordeals had taken place in Canterbury since the eighth century (*Vita Bregwini*, PL 159, col. 755, and ed. Bernhard W. Scholz, *Traditio*, 22 (1966), pp. 127-48, at pp. 139-40 (cap. 3)). Lea's reference to an apparently eighth-century mention of the ordeal (*Superstition and Force*, p. 414, 1973 partial reissue, p. 168) is misleading; the source cited there, the *Dialogus Ecgberti*, ed. Benjamin Thorpe, *Ancient Laws and Institutes of England* (2 vols., London, 1840), 2, p. 320, does not, in fact, mention the ordeal.

[7] Hyams, 'Trial by Ordeal', p. 109, citing the work of Patrick Wormald, who will discuss the subject in his forthcoming book on Anglo-Saxon kingship and law; Liebermann, *Gesetze*, 2, pp. 601-2.

[8] Wilhelm Levison, *England and the Continent in the Eighth Century* (Oxford, 1946), pp. 226-8. Contact had existed between Saxons and Franks much earlier too. If the

In the laws of the Visigothic and Lombard kings there are two further references to trial by hot water. Both date to the early eighth century. The Visigothic law supposedly dates to 705, the reign of Wittiza, and, if genuine, may well be the very last law of a Visigothic king (the kingdom was overthrown by the Moslems in 711). It seems to be an innovation designed to deal with a perceived increase in crime: 'however small the amount involved, we order the judge to test the accused by the trial of the cauldron'.[9] Recently, however, the genuineness of this law has come under scholarly attack.[10] If this criticism is correct, then Wittiza's law should be banished from the corpus of early evidence. It may show what Spaniards later thought about the earlier history of trial by ordeal in their country, but it does not tell us anything authentic about Visigothic law. The Lombard case is much more straightforward. A law of Liudprand, king of the Lombards, dating to 723, refers to slaves undergoing trial by cauldron.[11] Both the Lombard law and, if genuine, the Visigothic law are isolated references in kingdoms adjacent to and much influenced by the Frankish realm. The argument that we are here witnessing the diffusion of trial by ordeal is obviously not provable, but is plausible.

The last reference from the protohistorical period, that in the Frisian laws, also supports this interpretation. Frisian law, which was probably codified in the eighth century after Frankish conquest, contains various references to the ordeal of the cauldron, for instance in cases of theft. The most interesting provisions, for the argument advanced here, are those relating to killing in a mêlée. The procedure for dealing with this offence varied regionally, between West Frisia, Mid Frisia, and East Frisia. While West Frisia, conquered earliest by the Franks and under greatest Frankish influence, employed the

Franks were able to bring their cauldrons to the upper Thames valley in the fifth century, there is no reason why they could not also have brought trial by cauldron; see Vera I. Evison, *The Fifth-Century Invasions South of the Thames* (London, 1965), p. 32. Any satisfactory account of the appearance of trial by cauldron in Ine's laws must take account both of the fact that the continental Saxons did not, apparently, have this practice, and also the fact that, if Frankish influence is the explanation, the laws of Kent, an area much more heavily involved than Wessex with Gaul, do not have the ordeal either.

[9] *Leges Visigothorum* 6.1.3, ed. Karl Zeumer, MGH, *LL nat. Germ.* 1 (Hanover and Leipzig, 1902, repr. 1973), pp. 250-1.

[10] Iglesia Ferreirós, 'El proceso del conde Bera', pp. 69-104. He was not the first to point this out; see the remarks of Tomas Muñoz y Romero, *Colección de Fueros Municipales*, 1 (Madrid, 1847), p. 22 n. 34.

[11] *Leges Langobardorum, Liutprandi leges, Anni XI*, 50 (xxi), ed. Franz Beyerle, (2nd edn., Witzenhausen, 1962), p. 122.

ordeal of the cauldron, Mid Frisia used trial by lot, and East Frisia, closest to Saxon custom, the duel.[12] Here the association between Frankish influence and the ordeal of the cauldron seems clear.

In this protohistorical period we thus see two traditions of trial by cauldron in Christian Europe, an isolated Irish one and a major Frankish one. For the future history of the ordeal in Europe, it was this Frankish custom that was to be of importance. Trial by cauldron was, then, an ancient Frankish custom, appearing in the earliest legal records as a device employed in cases of theft, false witness, and contempt of court, used against free men and slaves. As Frankish power and influence spread, so this form of proof was exported into neighbouring regions.

The protohistorical period ends in the reign of Charlemagne. This is partly because there is more surviving evidence from this period, but also because there really was a new emphasis on the ordeal. References in the laws and accounts of actual cases multiply dramatically from the early ninth century. There is a real Carolingian efflorescence of trial by ordeal. From this period on, it is possible to write a true history of trial by fire and water.

During the reign of Charlemagne, three related developments took place. There was a multiplication of different types of ordeal, the dissemination of the practice into new areas, and a novel governmental emphasis on the ordeal. The variety of ordeals that emerged around the year 800 is striking. Not all were ordeals of fire or water. For example, one of the most frequently mentioned was the ordeal of the cross, a bilateral ordeal in which the two contendents stood with their arms outstretched in the shape of a cross until one flagged. This is recorded as early as the reign of Charlemagne's father, Pippin: 'if a woman claims that her husband has never cohabited with her, let them go to the cross, and if it is true, let them be separated'. In 775 a dispute between the bishop of Paris and the abbot of St Denis over the possession of a monastery was settled in this way in the royal chapel. In the first decades of the ninth century the practice was introduced, by capitulary legislation, into Italian, Ripuarian, Salic, and Saxon law. In ecclesiastical cases it was envisaged as a normal alternative to trial by battle. It was even prescribed as the method for deciding disputes over territory between Charlemagne's sons in the division of the empire drawn up in 806. Yet suddenly, in 818 or 819, Lewis the Pious banned

---

[12] *Lex Frisionum*, 3.5-9 and 14, ed. Karl A. Eckhardt and Albert Eckhardt, MGH, *Fontes iuris*, 12 (Hanover, 1982), pp. 44, 56-8.

the practice: 'henceforth let no one presume to employ trial by the cross, lest what was glorified by Christ's passion should be held in contempt by anyone's temerity'. The exact meaning of this is not entirely clear, but the grounds for the condemnation are explicitly religious. The ordeal of the cross, which had flourished under the first two Carolingians, was now quashed by the spiritual sensitivity of the third.[13] In the Carolingian period such new forms of ordeal were being created, hotly debated, and, sometimes, destroyed.

Other new ordeals that emerged in Charlemagne's reign were less subject to fashion. The earliest mention of the ordeal of walking on hot ploughshares is in the Thuringian law, compiled, probably, in 802. 'If a woman is accused of killing her husband by poison,' it states, 'or of procuring his death by some trick, let the woman's nearest relative prove her innocence in battle, or, if she has no champion, let her be sent for trial by the nine red-hot ploughshares.'[14] This is clearly an exceptional judicial procedure for an exceptionally heinous and subversive offence. Perhaps it was a Thuringian custom in origin. If so, Charlemagne and his advisers were favourably impressed with it, for they introduced it into Salic law in the following year, 803, in a capitulary which was to find its way to eleventh-century Italy and twelfth-century England.[15] The ordeal of 'hot burning cultures [i.e. coulters]', as the Jacobean dramatist Webster called it,[16] was never as widespread as the other ordeals of fire and water, but it had a long and continuous history as a form of proof, especially for suspected marital infidelity. A case was recorded in Naples in 1811.[17]

Trial by cold water was probably an innovation of Charlemagne's reign. A substantial number of the liturgical manuscripts which con-

---

[13] MGH, *Capit.* 1, ed. Alfred Boretius (Hanover, 1883), pp. 41, 49, 117-18, 129, 160, 208, 230, 268-9, 279 (and 409, 430, 439, and 449 for copies in Ansegius' collection). The 775 case is in MGH, *DD Karolinorum*, 1, ed. Engelbert Mühlbacher (Hanover, 1906), pp. 146-7. There is also a hagiographic story telling how the Abbess Lioba of Bischofsheim (d. 780) cleared her nuns of the imputation of unchastity, when the dead body of a newborn child was discovered in their grounds, by undertaking the ordeal of the cross, Rudolf of Fulda, *Vita S. Liobae*, cap. 12, ed. George Waitz, MGH, *SS* 15 (Hanover, 1887), p. 127. In general, see F. L. Ganshof, 'L'Épreuve de la croix dans le droit de la monarchie franque', *Studi e materiali di storia delle religioni*, 38 (1967), pp. 217-31.

[14] *Lex Thuringorum*, cap. 52, ed. Claudius von Schwerin, *Leges Saxonum et Lex Thuringorum*, MGH, *Fontes iuris*, 4 (Hanover, 1918), p. 65.

[15] MGH, *Capit.* 1 (as in n. 13), pp. 113 and 448; *Liber Papiensis*, ed. F. Bluhme and A. Boretius, MGH, *LL* 4 (Hanover, 1868), p. 507; *Leges Henrici primi*, 89.1a, ed. L. J. Downer (Oxford, 1972), p. 278.

[16] *The Duchess of Malfi*, III. i.   [17] Patetta, *Le ordalie*, p. 34.

tain rituals for this form of ordeal trace its origin back to the events of 800 in Rome and, despite the obvious suspicions which 'origin accounts' of this kind arouse, many scholars have been convinced that there is a kernel of truth in this story. At the very least, it is certain that both popes and emperors regulated the ordeal of cold water in the early ninth century. The so-called Roman version of the ritual was probably drawn up by Pope Eugenius II in the 820s. In 829 Lewis the Pious commanded 'Let our *missi* prohibit trial by cold water as it has been practised until now', and the implication of the wording must be that he was not banning the practice itself, but one form of it. It is ironically characteristic of the sources for early medieval history that the earliest certain evidence for the existence of trial by cold water should be in the form of an edict condemning it.[18]

Trial by hot iron, the last of the important trials of fire and water, emerges rather shakily into the historical record. A canon of the Council of Reisbach in 800 apparently specified trial by hot iron for soothsayers and necromancers, but the tradition of the canon is very faulty and it might be unwise to regard it as genuine evidence for the Carolingian period.[19] Another supposedly Carolingian mention of this form of ordeal, in a law concerning cases between Christians and Jews, is probably also a forgery.[20] This means that the earliest absolutely reliable reference to the ordeal of carrying hot iron is in the works of Agobard of Lyons in the reign of Lewis the Pious.[21] The liturgical material seems to bear out a picture of the ordeal of hot iron as a late offshoot, since the rituals for this ordeal were probably derived from those of the ordeal of the cauldron.[22]

In the first century of the Carolingian dynasty the available types of ordeal thus multiplied, through a complex process of borrowing from local custom, spontaneous generation, and the modelling of new forms on old. By the mid-ninth century all the ordeals of fire and water had come into vigorous life. The liturgical formulae which survive from this period convey a little of their ritual solemnity. Capitulary

---

[18] Von Schwerin, 'Rituale für Gottesurteile', esp. pp. 42-8; Nottarp, *Gottesurteilstudien*, pp. 323-31; MGH, *Capit.* 2, ed. Alfred Boretius and Victor Krause (Hanover, 1897), p. 16.

[19] MGH, *Conc.* 2, ed. Albert Werminghoff (Hanover, 1906-8), pp. 215-19.

[20] MGH, *Capit.* 1 (as in n. 13), p. 259.

[21] Agobard, *Liber adversus legem Gundobadi* and *Liber contra iudicum dei*. Both date to around 820, according to Egon Boshof, *Erzbischof Agobard von Lyon* (Cologne and Vienna, 1969), pp. 41 n. 10, 43 n. 17.

[22] Von Schwerin, 'Rituale', p. 54.

legislation reveals them spreading into areas, like Saxony, where such practices had earlier been unknown, or Italy, where they had been relatively unimportant. The Carolingians were not simply permissive on this issue. They did not passively approve a spontaneous growth. Their legislation furthered and enforced the ordeal. In 809 Charlemagne ordered 'Let all believe in the ordeal without any doubting' (*Ut omnes judicio Dei credant absque dubitatione*).[23] This enactment not only provides evidence for early scepticism about the ordeal, it also shows us the king's mind on this matter. The credibility of the ordeal was backed by royal command.

[23] MGH, *Capit.* 1 (as in n. 13), p. 150.

3

The Workings of the Ordeal in its Heyday

By the ninth century the ordeal had thus entered its heyday. It was to be a long heyday, lasting four centuries from 800 to 1200. In this period evidence is reasonably abundant. There are laws, rituals, accounts in chronicles and charters, the comments of ecclesiastics. A picture emerges from this material of the workings of the ordeals of fire and water. It is possible to see how they were applied, against whom they were directed, and in what circumstances men had recourse to them. The centuries between the reign of Charlemagne and the pontificate of Innocent III form the age of the ordeal and we are able, to some extent, to analyse the workings of the ordeal in this period.

Types of Ordeal

There were different types of ordeal not only in the sense of the different modes of trial, hot water, cold water, and the rest, but in the sense of different situations which generated ordeals. It is necessary to distinguish, for example, the ordeal as employed in the state trial of Queen Teutberga of Lotharingia in 858, when a Carolingian king wished to rid himself of a barren wife, from, say, the routine application of the ordeal to suspected thieves and murderers in later Anglo-Saxon England. The entire environment and ambience, the pressures and the issues, would be different. It may be worthwhile attempting a rough and ready taxonomy of the ordeal.

The trial of Teutberga is a good, early example of the employment of the ordeal in a case of great political importance. Her husband, King Lothar, wished to get rid of her, marry his mistress, and legitimize their children. He therefore accused his wife of various elaborate sexual offences. She summoned one of her retainers to undergo trial by cauldron on her behalf. In this instance the very existence of Lotharingia as a political entity was at stake. The success of the queen's champion meant that Lothar was unable to legitimize his children, and saw his line become extinct. It is little wonder that Hincmar of Rheims, the chief statesman of Lothar's neighbour and rival, Charles the Bald, should write a long justification of the

employment of the ordeal.[1] Teutberga's trial was not the only occasion
when ordeals played a part in determining the future of the Lotharingian inheritance. In 876, when the Middle Kingdom was disputed
between Charles the Bald and his nephew, Lewis of Saxony, 'Lewis
sent ten men to the ordeal of hot water and ten to the hot iron and ten
to the cold water, in the presence of those who were with him, and all
prayed that God should declare in that trial if he should rightly have a
greater share in the kingdom ... all were found to be unharmed'.[2]
This, of course, was pure propaganda. The really compelling judgement of God was the one that took place soon afterwards on the battle-
field of Andernach–for battles were also 'judgements of God'.[3]

In these cases, we see the political fortunes of ninth-century
Lotharingia being decided or intimated by the results of ordeals. The
point of these political ordeals was that they provided a chance to
assert a claim or vindicate innocence in a dramatic public spectacle.
They moved the interplay of political manœuvres on to a new plane.
The offer to undergo ordeal was a way of heightening the atmosphere,
of concentrating and dramatizing claims, when political issues were
at stake. On occasion, the political ordeal could be a last resort in
wriggling out of a difficult situation. In 991, for example, when the fate
of Arnulf of Rheims was being debated, after his unsuccessful opposition to Hugh Capet, Arnulf's partisans sought desperately for ways of
distancing themselves from their former master and avoiding the
worst consequences of his fall. The priest Adalger, accused of handing
over the city of Rheims to the king's enemies, pleaded that he was only
obeying Arnulf's orders and offered to strengthen his testimony
through the ordeal: 'if any of you doubt this and think I am not worthy
of belief, then believe the fire, the boiling water, the glowing iron ...'.
Similarly, one of Arnulf's chief lieutenants, now hoping to save
himself by testifying against him, said to Arnulf, 'So that faith in my
words may be confirmed for ever, after I have made my charges I will
affirm them with an oath and hand over to the bishops my servant,

---

[1] Hincmar, *De divortio.* A convenient recent account of the case can be found in
Peter R. McKeon, 'The Politics of Divorce and the Seizure of Lotharingia, 857-69',
Hincmar of Laon and Carolingian Politics (Urbana, etc., 1978), pp. 39-56.

[2] *Annales Bertiniani, s.a.*, 876, ed. Felix Grat, Jeanne Vieillard and Suzanne
Clémencet, *Annales de St-Bertin* (Paris, 1964), p. 207.

[3] In the words of the *Annales Vedastini*, 'iudicio Dei cessit victoria Hludowico', ed.
B. de Simson, *Annales Xantenses et Annales Vedastini*, MGH, *SRG* (Hanover and Leipzig,
1909), p. 41. See Kurt Georg Cram, *Judicium belli. Zum Rechtscharakter des Krieges im
deutschen Mittelalter* (Münster and Cologne, 1955), pp. 87-9.

who, by going over the hot ploughshares, will declare, by manifest signs, that God judges you!'[4] As Arnulf's men saw the collapse of their political plans, the ordeal seemed to provide one last chance of saving something from the ruins.

We can see the effects of offering the ordeal in the account of another tenth-century political crisis. In 943 the count of Flanders, who had arranged the killing of the duke of Normandy and was worried that their common overlord, the king of France, might be preparing vengeance, sent messengers to him, who said, 'O lord king, our lord offers his service to you . . . you have heard a false rumour that our lord condoned the death of the duke; he wishes to clear himself before you by the ordeal of fire'. It was only a gesture, but it worked. The king's counsellors advised him, 'You should not prejudge any man who seeks so hard to justify himself to you'. By voluntarily offering to undergo the ordeal, the count had removed the onus of action from his own shoulders and stepped into the role of the aggrieved innocent. The king, 'deceived and blinded' by the gambit (according to the Norman tradition), was no longer a real candidate for avenger of the murder.[5]

The ordeal could thus be a political gambit, volunteered by those on the defensive or by the weaker party. It could also, however, be insisted upon by the stronger. Kings could find the ordeal a useful tool in the pursuit of their ends, and the subjection of rivals to the ordeal might be simply another aspect of the exercise of royal domination. The feelings involved are well expressed in a literary source, the *Saga of Saint Olaf* (written in the thirteenth century, set in the eleventh). Sigurth Thorlakson was accused by King Olaf of the murder of his foster-brother and trial by hot iron was ordered before the bishop. The king clearly viewed this as a test case for royal authority and the defendant was suitably apprehensive. The night before the trial was due to take place, Sigurth addressed his men, 'To say the truth, we have got into great difficulties. . . . This king is crafty and deceitful. . . . It will be very easy for him to falsify this ordeal. I would consider it dangerous to risk that with him. And now there is a light breeze from the mountains along the sound. I advise

---

[4] *Gerberti acta concilii Remensis*, caps. 11 and 30, ed. George H. Pertz, MGH, *SS* 3 (Hanover, 1839), pp. 662-3 and 678.

[5] Dudo of St Quentin, *De moribus et actis primorum Normanniae ducum*, 4.72, ed. Jules Lair, *Mémoires de la Société des Antiquaires de Normandie*, 3rd ser., 3 (1858-65), pp. 228-9. Although the story is probably apocryphal, it is, nevertheless, good eleventh-century evidence for how men envisaged such proceedings.

that we hoist our sail and make for the open sea.'[6] Which is what they did.

Although a literary source, the saga account can be paralleled in many more properly historical sources. Rulers could use the ordeal as a method of crushing their enemies and potential victims knew this. In the very different world of Byzantium, where the ordeal of hot iron was introduced via the crusaders in the mid-thirteenth century, the emperor Theodore II Lascaris used it 'as a means of routing out aristocratic opposition'; just as Sigurth Thorlakson suspected in the case of King Olaf, it was 'an instrument of imperial tyranny'.[7]

Ordeals were also important in the history of the Gregorian Reform, and their role here has been examined by Colin Morris. He describes how the reformers used the ordeal against simoniacs, and how ordeals were employed by both sides in the Investiture Conflict to justify their position; for instance, 'an ordeal about the empire and the papacy' was held in 1083. Professor Morris observes, 'By this means men could seek to justify their actions or submit others to examination, and it was especially appropriate to the needs of great religio-political movements such as the gregorian reform and investiture conflict'. As he rightly points out, 'it is natural that they [ordeals] occur in connection with political charges or accusations'.[8] It *is* natural, and the association of the ordeal with political issues continues unbroken from the ninth century through to the fourteenth, when Frederick of Salm, preceptor of the Rhineland Templars, offered to carry the hot iron to refute the charges against his Order.[9]

The Teutberga case is not only an early example of the use of the ordeal in a matter of great political importance, it also exemplifies another major category in which ordeals were applied, namely questions of sexual purity. The queen was accused of incest and sodomy. Recourse to the ordeal was common when dealing with such charges. In 887, for example, the wife of another Carolingian, Charles the Fat, was accused of adultery and offered to clear herself through the duel or the ordeal of red-hot ploughshares.[10] These cases are the authentic

---

[6] *Olafs saga helga*, cap. 135, tr. Lee A M. Hollander, *Heimskringla* (Austin, 1964), p. 412.

[7] Angold, 'The Interaction of Latins and Byzantines', p. 7.

[8] Morris, '*Judicium Dei*', pp. 103 and 108.

[9] F. Raynouard, *Monuments historiques relatifs à la condamnation des Chevaliers du Temple* (Paris, 1813), p. 269.

[10] Regino, *Chronicon, s.a.* 887, ed. Fr. Kurze, MGH, *SRG* (Hanover, 1890), p. 127. For discussion of the trustworthiness of Regino's testimony, and for references to some of the later legendary material surrounding Richardis, see Ernst Dümmler, *Geschichte des ostfränkischen Reiches* (2nd edn., 3 vols., Leipzig, 1887-8), 3, pp. 284-5.

historical prototypes of what was to be a flourishing literary motif—the story of the queen unjustly accused of adultery, who clears herself by the ordeal. One example is the tale of how Cunigunda, wife of the emperor Henry II, vindicated her innocence by the red-hot ploughshares (although believed by some historians, it is probably hagiographic embroidery). From the twelfth century onwards, the incident is not only recounted in prose and verse, but also vividly illustrated. An illuminated manuscript from Bamberg, which was painted around 1200, shows Cunigunda stepping daintily over nine red-hot ploughshares, a bishop holding each hand. In another picture her penitent husband and his barons kneel before her while she stands on the ploughshares. The ploughshare in fact became her symbolic attribute and many later medieval and sixteenth- and seventeenth-century depictions of her show her clasping one to her breast.[11]

A similar account of the ordeal undergone by Queen Emma, Edward the Confessor's mother, is certainly fictional. It is told at length in the *Winchester Annals* of *c.* 1200. Emma was accused by the villain of the piece, Robert of Jumièges, the Norman archbishop of Canterbury, of adultery with a bishop (a not uncommon conjunction[12]). The queen offered to undergo the ordeal of hot iron; Robert of Jumièges unwillingly agreed, but only if he could specify particularly rigorous conditions: 'let the ill-famed woman walk nine paces, with bare feet, on nine red-hot ploughshares—four to clear herself, five to clear the bishop. If she falters, if she does not press one of the ploughshares fully with her feet, if she is harmed the one least bit, then let her be judged a fornicator.' The queen, resting her hopes

---

[11] The earliest source for Cunigunda's ordeal seems to be Adalbert's *Vita Henrici II imperatoris*, cap. 21, ed. George H. Pertz, MGH, *SS* 4 Hanover, 1841), p. 805 (see also pp. 819-20); this dates to around 1160. The story also appears in the letters of canonization of 1200, recently re-edited by J. Petersohn, 'Die Litterae Papst Innocent III zur Heiligsprechung der Kaiserin Kunigunde (1200)', *Jahrbuch für fränkische Landesforschung*, 37 (1977), pp. 1-25. The manuscript illumination is from the *Vita Cunegundis* of the same date as the canonization and is reproduced by Eberhard Lutze, 'Bamberger Buchmalerei im XII Jahrhundert', *Zeitschrift für Bildende Kunst*, 64 (1930-1), p. 165. For other artistic representations of the scene see J. Braun, *Tracht und Attribute der Heiligen in der deutschen Kunst* (Stuttgart, 1943), cols. 447-50, and *Bibliotheca Sanctorum* (12 vols. and index, Rome, 1961-70), 4, cols. 397-9. See also the early thirteenth-century vernacular poem by Ebernand von Erfurt, *Heinrich und Kunegunde*, ed. R. Bechstein (Quedlinburg, 1860, repr., Amsterdam, 1968).

[12] For instance, the accusation against Richardis, wife of Charles the Fat (as in n. 10), was of adultery with a bishop; Thietmar of Merseburg tells how the bishop of Freising cleared himself, through the eucharastic ordeal, of a suspicion of illicit sexual relations with Judith, the widow of Henry, duke of Bavaria, *Chronicon*, 2.41, ed. Robert Holtzmann, MGH, *SRG* ns (Berlin, 1935), p. 91.

on her innocence and on the help of St Swithun, walked over the ploughshares 'and did not see the fire nor feel the burning'. In gratitude she gave to St Swithun nine manors, one for each ploughshare, and the bishop accused with her did likewise.[13]

Another example is provided by one of the poems of the *Edda*. It tells of a cauldron ordeal after Gudrun, Atli's queen, was accused of adultery by the serving woman Herkja:

> She put her hand into the water
> and gathered up the glittering gems:
> 'My lords, you have seen the sacred trial
> prove me guiltless–and still the water boils.'
>
> Atli's heart laughed in his breast
> because Gudrun's hand had not been harmed:
> 'Now let Herkja go to the kettle,
> she who hoped to hurt my wife.'
>
> No man has seen a pitiful sight
> who has not looked at Herkja's scalded hands;
> then they forced her into a foul swamp–
> Gudrun's grievance was well avenged.[14]

Cunigunda, Emma, and Gudrun were wronged innocents. However, the most famous literary queen undergoing the ordeal on a charge of adultery was very different. Isolde was not accused unjustly–she was an adultress. Nevertheless, by a cunning equivocation in the words of her oath, she was able to clear herself in the ordeal of hot iron. In Gottfried of Strassburg's much quoted lines, 'Thus it was made manifest and confirmed to all the world that Christ in his great virtue is pliant as a windblown sleeve. . . . He is at the beck of every heart for honest deeds or fraud.'[15] Isolde's story thus stands in sharp relief to

---

[13] *Annales de Wintonia* ed. Henry R. Luard, *Annales Monastici* (5 vols., RS, 1864-9), 2, pp. 20-5. The way these stories spread is indicated by the following observation of Paul Christophersen: 'We have good reason to believe that the story told about Emma in England is no other than the story of Richardis and Cunegund with the names and one or two of the details changed', *The Ballad of Sir Aldinger. Its Origin and Analogues* (Oxford, 1952), p. 100. The story was still being sung in fourteenth-century England (*ibid*., p. 34).

[14] 'The Third Lay of Gudrun', tr. Patricia Terry, *Poems of the Vikings. The Elder Edda* (Indianapolis and New York, 1969), p. 204.

[15] Gottfried of Strassburg, *Tristan*, tr. A. T. Hatto (Harmondsworth, 1960), p. 248. See Helaine Newstead, 'The Equivocal Oath in the Tristan Legend', *Mélanges offerts à Rita Lejeune* (2 vols., Gembloux, 1969), 2, pp. 1077-85; Hexter, *Equivocal Oaths*; York, 'Isolt's Ordeal'. For the general theme of 'accused queens' see Christophersen, *Ballad*, (as in n. 13) and M. Schlauch, *Chaucer's Constance and Accused Queens* (New York, 1927).

the other medieval tales of wronged queens; Gottfried's comment provides evidence for a particularly elaborate form of scepticism about the judicial use of ordeals. Isolde's ordeal is mentioned here, however, as another example of how natural it was for medieval story-tellers to move their plot from accusations of adultery to the drama of the ordeal. This charge and this form of proof belonged together.

The literary tradition reflected a more general reality, affecting not only real and fictional queens, but less exalted women too, for the evidence of laws and legal cases shows that ordeals were deemed particularly appropriate in deciding charges of sexual misconduct throughout society. The liturgies containing the ritual of the ordeal envisage 'lechery and adultery' as one of the common offences to be brought to this kind of trial.[16] The law codes of thirteenth-century Scandinavia specify, 'If a woman's husband accuses her of adultery, she must clear herself with the iron'.[17] In the early twelfth century it was to this same proof that the French aristocracy took their suspicions of their wives.[18] The link between sexual misconduct and the hot iron was sometimes so compelling that the ordeal was prescribed exclusively for women of ill-repute, as in the important Castilian law code, the *Fuero de Cuenca*.[19] It was not only women who went to the ordeal on sexual charges. Men, too, might find themselves faced with the hot iron when accused of crimes of this type. The Norwegian provincial law known as the Frostathing law, for example, prescribes that 'if a man is charged with having carnal dealings with cattle of any sort, which is forbidden to all Christians, the bailiff shall bring action against him with witnesses to the fact of common rumour; and let him carry the hot iron or go into outlawry'. Another Norwegian law book prescribes the ordeal against men for charges of sodomy and sexual relations with near kin.[20] Examples could be multiplied.

Ordeals were not only used to try cases of adultery, but also, very frequently, in the related issue of disputed paternity. We have already seen how the early Irish laws prescribe the ordeal of the cauldron in

---

[16] Adolph Franz (ed.), *Das Rituale von St. Florian aus dem zwölften Jahrhundert* (Freiburg im Breisgau, 1904), p. 122. See also Liebermann, *Gesetze*, 1, pp. 404-7, 420; Zeumer, *Formulae*, pp. 610, 614, 624, 650, 659, etc.

[17] *Schönisches Kirchenrecht*, cap. 9, German tr., Claudius von Schwerin, *Dänische Rechte* (Weimar, 1938), p. 203.

[18] e.g. Ivo of Chartres, *epistola* 205, *PL* 162, col. 210.

[19] Caps. 295 and 298, ed. R. de Ureña y Smenjaud (Madrid, 1935), pp. 328 and 330.

[20] *Frostathing Law*, 3.18, *Gulathing Law*, 'Church Law', 24 and 158, tr. Laurence M. Larson, *The Earliest Norwegian Laws* (New York, 1935), pp. 252, 254, 260.

such cases, and this particular application can be documented in virtually every part of Europe. In the late eleventh century, for example, a woman came to Duke Robert Curthose of Normandy with two boys and claimed that these were the offspring of her earlier affair with the duke. 'Because he saw some truth in this, but hesitated to recognize the boys as his, the mother publicly carried the red hot iron, and, escaping without the least burn, proved that she had conceived by the king's son [i.e. Duke Robert].'[21] Amongst the aristocracy of the Middle Ages, when it was common for men to have not only irregular liaisons, but also 'concubines', second-class wives with some rights in customary law, issues of paternity were complicated and important. At the very highest level, the fate of kingdoms might turn on the verdict of an ordeal. In 1218 Inga of Varteig carried the hot iron to prove that her son, born out of wedlock and after the supposed father's death, was indeed the son of King Hakon III. In this way the claim of Hakon IV to the throne of Norway was secured.[22] Scandinavia, with its complex gradation of forms of sexual liaison, the greater freedom apparently allowed to women, and its busy sea-lanes, seems to have generated many such cases, and this is reflected in Scandinavian law; but the practice of the ordeal for disputed paternity was very common, found, for example, in Spanish and German law as well as in Ireland, Normandy, and the North. It was not only royal inheritances whose fate was determined by the ordeal. Around 1070, for instance, a dispute arose over an estate in Bayeux, consisting of houses in the town and meadows outside it, which had originally been built up by a ducal chaplain. The case hinged on the issue of disputed paternity. As a result of the ordeal the chaplain's family lost the property, which, in an arresting development, was then granted to the cleric who had presided over the trial. The resolution of the intimate sexual issue had large public consequences.[23]

Just as men of this time judged that doubts about sexual purity could best be settled by the searing pain of the ordeal iron, so too they felt that this was the right way to determine the orthodoxy of religious beliefs. The very earliest extant acount of an ordeal, that by Gregory of

---

[21] Orderic Vitalis, *Ecclesiastical History*, 10.14, ed. Marjorie Chibnall (6 vols., Oxford, 1969-80), 5, p. 282.
[22] *The Sage of Hakon*, caps. 14, 41-6, tr. George W. Dasent, *Icelandic Sagas*, ed. and tr. Gudbrand Vigfusson and George W. Dasent (4 vols., RS, 1887-94), 4, pp. 22, 42-5.
[23] P. Le Cacheux, 'Une Charte de Jumièges concernant l'épreuve par le fer chaud', *Mélanges de la Société de l'histoire de Normandie* (1927), pp. 203-17.

Tours, describes a trial that was intended to decide between Arian and Catholic doctrine. Several centuries later, in the mid-ninth century, the Saxon monk Gottschalk, who was suspected of heresy because of his doctrine of predestination, offered to undergo an elaborate form of ordeal by fire and water 'in order, in this way, to prove the truth of his profession'.[24]

The dramatic trial of faith, which vindicated the beliefs of the man who underwent it successfully, was a not uncommon incident in medieval life and literature. According to the chronicler Widukind, writing around 970, the Danes were wooed away from their earlier syncretic religion, in which they recognized Christ as a god, but thought that other gods 'revealed themselves to mortals by stronger signs and wonders', to a whole-hearted Christian monotheism by the cleric Poppo, who carried the hot iron to vindicate his faith. Later writers in Denmark, indeed, traced the Danish use of ordeals back to this event.[25] Peter Damian, in his account of Bruno of Querfurt, claims that Bruno converted the Russians by passing through fire unharmed.[26] St Francis volunteered a similar feat before the Sultan of Egypt, who wisely declined the offer.[27] In the constant encounters between Christians and pagans, Moslems, and Jews that took place in the Middle Ages, a successful miracle was as telling as a good piece of disputation. Picking up a burning brand in the name of Jesus was, as Guibert of Nogent observed in the twelfth century, an argument 'more powerful than any clash of words'.[28]

The rituals for the ordeal of hot iron frequently contain the invocation, 'If you are innocent of this charge . . . you may confidently receive this iron in your hand and the Lord, the just judge, will free you, just as he snatched the three children from the burning fire'.[29] The Old Testament reference, to Shadrach, Meshach, and Abednego passing

---

[24] Hrabanus Maurus, *epistola* 44, ed. Ernst Dümmler, MGH, *Epp.* 5 (Berlin, 1899), p 498.

[25] Widukind of Korvei, *Res Gestae Saxonicae*, 3.65, ed. H. E. Lohmann and P. Hirsch, MGH, *SRG* (Hanover, 1935), pp. 140-1; Saxo Grammaticus, *Gesta Danorum*, 10.11.4, ed. J. Olrik and H. Raeder (2 vols., Copenhagen, 1931-57), I, p. 282; for a thorough survey of the ramifications of this tale, see Claudius von Schwerin, 'Das Gottesurteil des Poppos', *ZRG, Germanistische Abteilung*, 58 (1938), pp. 69-107.

[26] *Vita Romualdi*, cap. 27, *PL* 144, col. 978.

[27] Bonaventure, *Legenda maior*, 9.8, *Analecta Franciscana*, 10 (Quaracchi, 1926-31), p. 601. For recent discussion of the historicity and significance of this event see Giulio Basetti Sani, *L'Islam e Francesco d'Assisi* (Florence, 1975), pp. 168-80.

[28] *Tractatus de incarnatione contra Judaeos*, 3.11, *PL* 156, col. 528.

[29] Zeumer, *Formulae*, pp. 696-7.

unharmed through the burning, fiery furnace, linked trial by fire and the vindication of belief, since the reason why the three children were cast into the furnace was that *deos tuos non colunt*–'they do not worship your gods'–and the aftermath of their ordeal was that the king recognized the supremacy of their god. This biblical precedent, strengthened, one might speculate, by experience of the natural ability of fire to purify and concentrate matter, supported the testing of true belief by fire. When the authenticity of relics was in doubt, for example, they would be cast into the fire to be tried.[30] There are stories of how books too–the liturgy of the Mozarabic rite, the religious writings of the Cathars–were tested in this way.[31] And men might volunteer to venture to pass through fire to vindicate their claims to have received a divine message or mission.[32]

Some of these ordeals were entered into voluntarily, and some were not strictly judicial, but in the twelfth century we see the rise of the regular judicial use of the ordeal in one particular trial of belief–cases of heresy. The ordeal was a natural form of proof to apply in such cases and the increase in heresy at this time made its use more common. In 1172 in Arras a cleric accused of heresy was not only burned in his hand, but all over his body, after undergoing the ordeal.

---

[30] Nicole Hermann-Mascard, *Les Reliques des saints* (Paris, 1975), pp. 134-6. There is a well-known English case in which the post-Conquest Norman abbot of Evesham insisted on trying the validity of the relics of the abbey's Anglo-Saxon saints, *Chronicon abbatiae de Evesham*, ed. William D. Macray (RS, 1863), p. 336.

[31] For the legend of the trial of the Mozarabic and Roman rites by fire, see *Crónica Nájerense*, 3.49, ed. A.A Ubieto Arteta *Textos medievales*, 15 (Valencia, 1966), p. 116; Nottarp, *Gottesurteilstudien*, pp. 112-3. On one famous occasion, St Dominic challenged a group of Cathar heretics to a trial of fire, in which the books containing their doctrines were thrown into the flames. The saint's book was unharmed, the heretics' book burned; Jordan of Saxony, *Libellus de principiis Ordinis Praedicatorum*, caps. 24-5, ed. H. C. Scheeben, *Monumenta ordinis Fratrum Praedicatorum historica*, 16 (Rome, 1935), p. 38. There are many depictions of the scene, including that by Nicola Pisano on Dominic's tomb at Bologna, and the scene on the Pisa triptych by Francesco Traini; J. Berthier, *Le Tombeau de Saint Dominique* (Paris, 1895), pl. XII; Millard Meiss, *Francesco Traini* (Washington, 1983), fig. 16.

[32] One famous case occurred in 1099, when, on the First Crusade, the champion of the Holy Lance undertook to prove its authenticity–and the authenticity of his own divine commission–by passing through fire. He died. See the conflicting accounts in Raymond of Aguilers, *Historia Francorum qui ceperunt Jerusalem*, ed. John Hugh and Laurita L. Hill, *Le 'Liber' de Raymond d'Aguilers* (Paris, 1969), pp. 120-3; Fulcher of Chartres, *Historia Hierosolymitana*, 1.18, ed. H. Hagenmeyer (Heidelberg, 1913), pp. 235-41; Guibert of Nogent, *Gesta Dei per Francos*, 6.22, *Recueils des historiens des croisades, Historiens occidentaux*, 4 (Paris, 1879), p. 218. Four centuries later, in 1498, this still seemed to many the best way to discover if Savonarola had God's blessing; see Josef Schnitzer, *Savonarola* (2 vols., Munich, 1924), I, pp. 499-523, 'Die Feuerprobe'.

A decade later twelve men in Ypres underwent the ordeal of hot iron on charges of heresy. The reforming priest, Lambert le Bègue, who was accused of heretical beliefs, offered to rebut the charge by the ordeal of fire.[33]

In the eyes of frightened orthodox contemporaries, heresy was an insidious international conspiracy, all the more disturbing for being so invisible. It was hard for Catholics to know if their neighbours were harbouring heretical thoughts. The disease might even spread through contamination rather than through conviction: some heretics were supposed to 'entrap their guests by means of some one of the dishes they set before them, and those whom they dare not approach with the private discourses that they commonly make, thus become like themselves'.[34] This creeping, nightmarish quality of heresy, as apprehended by the orthodox, created a mood similar to that of the witch persecution of the sixteenth and seventeenth centuries or McCarthyism in the twentieth. Normal judicial procedures were inadequate; only extreme measures, in this case the ordeal, would do. Now, even though the hot iron was symbolically appropriate to try the charge, it had the disadvantage of not producing an immediate result. There was a three-day waiting period before the hand was unbound. For an angry orthodox crowd trial by cold water was much more satisfactory. It gave a verdict at once, for failure to sink into the water would be publicly visible there and then. Unlike the trials by hot iron, the swimming of heretics allowed no neutral period of waiting in which crowds would disperse and emotions calm, and the cold water trial of heretics was thus particularly susceptible to crowd influence and mob justice. At Soissons in 1114, for instance, the condemned heretics were lynched by the crowd while the bishop's court was still discussing the sentence.[35]

Some historians have argued that a kinship exists between some of the fearful attributes of the medieval heretic and the images that

[33] *Chronica regia Coloniensis*, ed. G. Waitz, MGH, *SRG* (Hanover, 1880), p. 122; *Continuatio Acquicinctina* to Sigebert of Gembloux, ed. L. C. Bethmann, MGH, *SS* 6 (Hanover, 1844), p. 421; P. Frédéricq, *Corpus documentorum inquisitionis haereticae pravitatis Neerlandicae* (5 vols., Ghent, 1889–1906), 2, pp. 10–11. For some general discussion of the trial of heretics by ordeal, see R. I. Moore, *The Origins of European Dissent* (rev. edn., Oxford, 1985), pp. 258–61.

[34] Walter Map, *De nugis curialium*, 1.30, ed. and tr. Montague R. James, rev. Christopher N. L. Brooke and R. A. B. Mynors (Oxford, 1983), p. 120; for an alternative translation see the review by A. G. Rigg, *Speculum*, 60 (1985), p. 180.

[35] Guibert of Nogent, *De vita sua*, 3.17, ed. R. Labande (Paris, 1982), pp. 428–34.

contemporaries attached to witches.[36] The same point can be made in connection with the mode of trial employed against them. It was, perhaps, natural to employ the ordeal against the inner, religious crime of heresy in the twelfth century, when it was already common practice in the trial of suspected witches and sorcerers. The use of the ordeal against magicians, and against the closely related category of those who maintained pagan practices, was widespread in time and place. A Carolingian capitulary reads

Since we have heard that sorcerers and witches are rising up in many parts of our kingdom, whose magic has killed and injured many men, and since, as the holy men of God have written, it is the king's duty to rid the land of the impious and not to permit witches and sorcerers to live, we command that the counts should take great pains in their counties to search out and seize such people . . . if the suspects cannot be proved guilty by trustworthy witnesses, let them be tried by the ordeal, and thus through that ordeal either freed or condemned.[37]

Similar provisions can be found in Anglo-Saxon England, in the towns of Spain, and the Norwegian countryside in the twelfth and thirteenth centuries.[38] As early as the eleventh century there is evidence for the swimming of witches,[39] a practice which did not die out in Europe and America until the eighteenth or even nineteenth centuries (see Chapter 7). Thus, when the truth of belief was at stake, when charges of heresy or witchcraft were raised, the ordeal was a favoured form of proof over many centuries.

Ordeal, Testimony, and Oath

The use of ordeals discussed so far may seem somewhat exotic: treason, adulterous queens, dramatic conversions. There were, of course, more regular and frequent applications, not only in the special cases, like heresy and sexual offences, but also in a wide range of crimes and disputes. The very earliest laws refer to the use of the ordeal in cases of theft and the ordinary criminal charges which required the employment of the ordeal were very varied. In what

[36] Norman Cohn, *Europe's Inner Demons* (London, 1975), *passim*; Edward Peters, *The Magician, the Witch and the Law* (Philadelphia, 1978), pp. 33-45.

[37] MGH, *Capit.* 2, ed. Alfred Boretius and Victor Krause (Hanover, 1897), p. 345.

[38] e.g II Athelstan 6, ed. Liebermann, *Gesetze*, 1, pp. 152-5; *Fuero de Cuenca* (as in n. 19), caps. 293-4 and 296, ed. cit., p. 328; Borgarthing Law, 1.16, ed. Rudolf Meissner, *Bruchstücke der Rechtsbücher des Borgarthings und des Eidsivathings* (Weimar, 1942), pp. 44-5.

[39] *Annales S. Stephani Frisingensis*, ed. George Waitz, MGH, *SS* 13 (Hanover, 1881), p. 52.

might, perhaps anachronistically, be called civil cases–those involving disputes over property or status–the ordeal was also frequently adopted. Such cases take us away from the stormy atmosphere of royal courts, riven with plots and pressures, or the unhealthy excitement of heresy trials, to regular judicial process.

The legal records of Europe are full of references to the ordeal. One good example is provided by the series of laws issued by English kings, from the laws of Edward the Elder, in the tenth century, to the Assizes of Henry II in the twelfth. In these laws the ordeals of hot iron and cold water are prescribed for a wide range of offences, including murder, fire-raising, witchcraft, and forgery, as well as simple theft. If we combine other types of evidence, such as rituals or accounts of cases, with that of the law codes, it is possible to construct a reasonably well-modelled picture of the ordeal in England in this period.[40] France and Germany did not have comparable royal legislation, but, nevertheless, there is a substantial body of material, legal, liturgical, and narrative, describing the use of the ordeals of fire and water in both criminal and civil cases in those countries. Charters often record the outcome of trials of this kind. This is how we learn, for instance, that around 1090 Gautier of Meigné claimed a piece of land from the monks of St Aubin of Angers. He appeared before the bishop's court and said 'that his lord, Alberic, the former tenant, had given him the land in return for a fine horse. The judges answered that he must prove this by the hot iron.'[41] A charter records a dispute in 1152 between the abbey of Siegburg on the Rhine and the local inhabitants over the right to use a nearby wood. It was resolved, in favour of the abbey, by the ordeal of cold water.[42] Such incidental references enable us to picture the workings of the ordeal at the local level of dispute settlement in its ancient French and German milieu. Beyond the confines of the former Carolingian empire, the law codes of Spain, Scandinavia, and eastern Europe all provide material useful in analysing trial by ordeal.

Between the ninth and the twelfth centuries the ordeals of fire and water were used throughout Latin Christendom against a whole range

---

[40] The provisions of English law regarding the ordeal are conveniently summarized in Liebermann, *Gesetze*, 2, pp. 601-4 (s.v. 'ordal'); see also the outline in Hyams, 'Trial by Ordeal', pp. 106-11.

[41] *Cartulaire de l'Abbaye de St-Aubin d'Angers*, ed. Arthur Bertrand de Brousillon (3 vols., Paris, 1903), 2, no. 406, p. 12.

[42] *UB für die Geschichte des Niederrheins*, ed. Theodor J. Lacomblet (4 vols., Dusseldorf, 1840-58, repr. Aalen, 1966), 1, p. 257.

of crimes and in a great variety of cases. Nevertheless, it is essential to stress that, while envisaged as a regular part of judicial activity, they were employed only in certain specified circumstances and only against certain kinds of criminal. The most significant limitation on the use of the ordeal was that it was only employed when other ways of discovering the truth were not available. This is a crucial point, and it negates the claims of those who would see 'a tendency to fly to the ordeal in all matters of doubt whatsoever',[43] or regard them as 'the main instrument of judicial proof'[44] in the early medieval period. It is clear that the ordeal was a last, not a first, resort. It was used only if there were no 'certain proof'.[45] Such an attitude was occasionally elevated to a general principle. As it was stated in twelfth-century England, 'the ordeal of hot iron is not to be permitted except where the naked truth cannot otherwise be explored'.[46] Or, in the words of the *Sachsenspiegel* of *c.* 1220,'It is not right to use the ordeal in any case, unless the truth may be known in no other way'.[47]

Another crucial point about the use of the ordeal, or perhaps another way of expressing the same point, is that it existed in a judicial framework which recognized many other forms of proof. The history of the ordeal is closely linked with these other forms of proof. These might include swearing an oath or compurgation, the examination of written evidence or witnesses, or some form of inquest. All were recognized forms of proof in the age of the ordeal and, in general, men went to them first. As Professor Bongert has observed, in her study of the French lay courts from the tenth to the thirteenth centuries, 'References to the ordeal are fairly rare, at least in comparison with the mass of documents relating to agreement, arbitration, witness or duel'.[48] It has also been pointed out that, in the Salic law, the ratio of mentions of the ordeal to mentions of witness is 1 : 6.[49]

The ordeal coexisted with many other forms of proof and it was often, indeed, the first task of the court to decide what manner or

---

[43] Richard W. Southern, *The Making of the Middle Ages* (London,1953), p. 96.
[44] Idem, in S. C.Neill and H. R. Weber (eds.), *The Layman in Christian History* (London,1963), p. 89.
[45] *Pactus legis Salicae*, 14.2 and 16.5, ed. Karl August Eckhardt, MGH, *LL nat. Germ.* 4, pt. 1 (Hanover, 1962), pp. 64-5, 74.
[46] Pseudo-Cnut de Foresta, 11.2, ed. Liebermann, *Gesetze*, 1, p. 622.
[47] *Lehnrecht*, 40.3, ed. Karl August Eckhardt, MGH, *Fontes iuris*, NS 1/2 (2nd edn., Göttingen, 1956), p. 62.
[48] Bongert, *Recherches*, p. 216.
[49] Colman, 'Reason and Unreason', p. 577.

mode of proof should be applied. Up to the twelfth century the main alternatives to ordeal were testimony and the swearing of oaths. Mapping the circumstances in which these two proofs might be absent or unacceptable will necessarily reveal the areas where the ordeal was most likely to be applied.

Testimony could be either written or oral–human witnesses. Written testimony was usually presented to the courts in the form of charters, or similar documents, supporting property claims. Such written instruments were more current in some parts of Europe than others, but even in areas where the forms of Roman law were less significant, such as northern France, parties might be asked whether they wished to defend their claim 'by witness, by [proof of] investiture or by charter'.[50] It has sometimes been asserted, and probably rightly, that the increase in the use of documents over the course of the Middle Ages resulted in a diminution of the number of cases involving the ordeal, since where written testimony was available, the ordeal was redundant.[51] But a simple evolutionary picture does not fit all the facts. There are examples of regions like Catalonia, where, in the tenth century the courts relied almost exclusively upon written evidence, but adopted the ordeal as a main form of proof in the eleventh.[52] In other areas, like England, resolution of civil cases by the ordeals of fire and water was always rare; with the exception of a few post-Conquest instances, the ordeal was a criminal proof only.[53] Again, it should be noted that, both in England and on the continent, property disputes were resolved by the duel–trial by battle–more often than by the hot iron or cold water.

A completely effective system of authenticated documentary record would, of course, make recourse to the ordeal unnecessary in civil disputes. Indeed, in areas like Italy, with high literacy and a public

[50] *Cartulaire de St-Aubin* (as in n. 41), 1, p. 120.

[51] e.g Southern, *Making of the Middle Ages* (as in n. 43), p. 97: 'with the greater abundance of written evidence . . . disputed facts about ownership, which had been one of the most fertile sources of appeal to the ordeal, became amenable to the test of human testimony'.

[52] P. Bonnassie, *La Catalogne du milieu du xe à la fin du xie siècle* (2 vols., Toulouse, 1975), 2, pp. 728-9.

[53] See the remarks of Hyams, 'Trial by Ordeal', pp. 107, 112-134, who oscillates between regarding the absence of unilateral ordeals in property disputes as an original feature of Anglo-Saxon law and speculating that this absence was the result of a period of 'natural attrition' in the later Anglo-Saxon period. The post-Conquest cases in which the ordeal was offered in property disputes are collected in Melville M. Bigelow, *Placita Anglo-Normannica* (Boston, 1879), pp. 36, 38, 40-3, 61, 304-6.

notariate, ordeals designed to resolve property issues were increasingly rare. But in most parts of Europe, for most of the Middle Ages, there was no approach to such a perfect system. Verbal agreements were always commoner than written. When a Spanish peasant and his lord disputed over the agreed level of rents and renders, for example, there would be no signed and sealed contract to turn to; if an oath could not settle the issue, they would turn naturally to the ordeal.[54] At a higher social level transfers of property and grants of rights and honours took place in public rituals, and, even when a written record of such transactions was made, it was often a memorandum rather than an authentic legal record. The legal validity of the transaction resided in the ceremonial act, not in the writing that recorded it. Documentary evidence was accepted only gradually and partially. The military aristocracy sometimes took the attitude of Count Berthold of Hamm, who, when presented with royal charters which backed the claims of the opposing party, the abbot of Prüm, 'laughed at the documents, saying that anyone's pen could write what they liked, he ought not to lose his rights because of it'.[55] The preference for witnesses over documents was also held in more respectable circles. 'We put greater faith in the oral testimony of living witnesses than in the written word', opined Pope Calixtus II in 1124.[56]

In the medieval period oral testimony was thus crucial in determining property disputes. This was even truer in the case of criminal charges. This is where men looked first for resolution of a charge and it seems to have been a universal principle that some deficiency in human testimony was necessary before recourse could be had to the ordeal. Thus, in the Salic law, one provision begins, 'If anyone is accused and truly has no witness to absolve him and it is necessary that he clear himself at the cauldron ...'.[57] 'A dispute should be

[54] *Fuero General de Navarra*, 3.5.11., ed. Pablo Ilarregui and Segundo Lapuerta (Pamplona, 1869, repr. 1964), p. 88.

[55] MGH, *DD Heinrici IV*, ed. D. von Gladiss and Alfred Gawlik (Berlin, Weimar and Hanover, 1941–78), no. 476 pp. 648-9.

[56] Ubaldo Pasqui (ed.), *Documenti per la storia della città di Arezzo nel medio evo*, 1, *Codice diplomatico (an. 650?–1180)*, Documenti di storia italiana, 11 (Florence, 1899), p. 433. This reference and the preceding one are discussed by Harry Bresslau, *Handbuch der Urkundenlehre für Deutschland und Italien* (2 vols. and index, 2nd/3rd edn., Berlin, 1958-60),1, p. 651; his whole surrounding discussion, 'Die rechtliche Beweiskraft der Urkunden des Mittelalters' (pp. 635-738), is important for this subject. See also, for England, Michael Clanchy, *From Memory to Written Record* (London, 1979), esp. pp. 202-57.

[57] *Pactus legis Salicae* (as in n. 45), 112, ed. cit., p. 262.

resolved by the mediation of a cauldron or the casting of lots where witnesses are lacking', rules a seventh-century Irish text.[58] In Russian law the ordeal of iron was employed in cases of homicide when the defendant was unable to produce witnesses.[59] The twelfth-century customs of Tournai specify the ordeal of cold water for accusations of night-time assault, if witnesses were lacking.[60] Even Ivo of Chartres, writing in the early twelfth century, who frequently criticized ordeals, admitted 'nevertheless, we do not deny that there should be recourse to divine witness [i.e. the ordeal] when the accusation is in order and human testimony is lacking.'[61] Sometimes the exact extent of the lack of human testimony was specified. The town law of Enns in Austria, granted in 1212, ruled that, in accusations of rape, when there were only two witnesses, the accused should have the option of the ordeal, but, when there were as many as seven witnesses, this option was not allowed.[62] Somewhere between two and seven, human testimony became sufficient.

The most characteristic situation in which the ordeal was employed as a result of the absence of witnesses was the charge which was only a matter of general suspicion, a charge in which not only witnesses but even a specific accuser would be lacking. Normal criminal procedure in the early Middle Ages hinged upon the appearance of an accuser, who brought the charge, offered to prove it and took the consequences for failure to do so. There were also, however, various common procedures for dealing with more amorphous charges or suspicions, when no individual accuser appeared. The Capitulary of Quierzy of 873 ordered that bondsmen suspected of crimes should be brought before the count 'and if no-one wishes to accuse them, let them nevertheless clear their ill fame through the ordeal'.[63] In the Assizes of Jerusalem there is detailed provision for one particular kind of charge without accuser. It explains what should happen

If two or three men come before the court, bringing a dead man and also leading along a living man and say to the justice, 'Sir, we found this man dead

[58] E. J. Gwynn (ed.), 'An Old-Irish Tract on the Privileges and Responsibilities of Poets', *Ériu*, 13 (1942), pp. 1-60, 220-36, at p. 22, lines 7-8.

[59] *Russkaia Pravda* (expanded version), cl. 21, tr. George Vernadsky, *Medieval Russian Laws* (New York, 1947), p. 38.

[60] Charter of Philip Augustus of 1188, cap. 4, ed. Mina Martens in *Elenchus fontium urbanae*, 1, ed. C. van de Kieft and J. F. Niermeijer (Leiden, 1967), p. 350.

[61] *Epistola* 252, *PL* 162, col. 258.

[62] *Urkundenbuch zur Geschichte der Babenberger in Österreich*, ed. Heinrich Fichtenau and Erich Zöllner (3 vols., Vienna, 1950-55), 1, pp. 251-2.

[63] Cap. 3, MGH, *Capit.* 2 (as in n. 37), p. 344.

in the street, all warm like one who has just been killed, and we found this man, whom we have brought here, near the corpse, going along the street; we went to him and asked him who had killed the man and he replied that the dead man attacked him in the street and that he had killed him in self-defence'.

If the man maintains his story and calls on God as his witness, then the judge must order 'since he calls on God as his witness, let him carry the hot iron'.[64] Other cases of procedure without accuser can be found in Norman and Magyar law. In the latter instance there existed not only a developed procedure for obtaining the names of suspected thieves, who then had to clear themselves at the ordeal, but even an inquiry as to 'whether any village had a bad reputation for thieving'. Every tenth man in the indicted village then had to bear the hot iron to refute the accusation if he could.[65]

In all these cases, the absence of evidence, or witnesses, or even of accusers has been a necessary precondition for the use of ordeal. But such situations need not lead to the ordeal if an oath were acceptable. The oath, the corner-stone of medieval judicial procedure, was, in some sense, an ordeal, but one which relied upon God's eventual rather than his immediate judgement. Where this kind of ordeal was employed, however, the others need not be. Exculpation by oath alone and exculpation by ordeal were mutually exclusive; hence, where oaths were unacceptable, the ordeal became a natural recourse.

The oath might be taken either alone or with oath-helpers, compurgators, and the choice between the two methods depended partly upon the nature of the offence but much more upon the status of the individual involved. The higher an individual's status, the more 'oath-worthy' he would be. Thus recourse to oath might be inappropriate in two situations: when the individual's own oath was no longer credible, or when the necessary number of compurgators could not be mustered. Both cases reflected the reputation of the accused and it is clear that the laws envisage a class or category of 'persons of ill-repute' or 'the outsworn'. Obviously a man who had once been convicted of perjury had irretrievably damaged his chances of ever again clearing himself by oath. One of the laws of Edward the Elder reads, 'We have further declared, with regard to men who have been accused of

---

[64] *Assises de la cour des bourgeois*, cap. 286, ed. A.-A. Beugnot, *Recueil des historiens des croisades, Lois*, 2 (Paris, 1843), p. 217.
[65] *Sancti Ladislai regis decretorum liber tertius*, I, in Györffy, 'Anhang', pp. 294-5.

perjury: if the charge has been proved, or if the oath on their behalf has collapsed, or has been overborne by more strongly supported testimony, never again shall they have the privilege of clearing themselves by oaths, but only by the ordeal'.[66] The laws of Canute make a distinction between 'trustworthy men of good repute, who have never failed in oath or ordeal', who are allowed to clear themselves by their own oath; 'untrustworthy men', who require compurgators; and untrustworthy men who cannot find compurgators–this last group go to the ordeal.[67] English law was finely attuned to this question of reputation, was composed of a mixture of status and previous record. The ordeal which itself was gradated to the different categories–a triple ordeal, in which the iron weighed three times the usual weight, was employed alongside the simple ordeal. One of the laws of Ethelred the Unready specified that a man of bad reputation should go to the triple ordeal, unless his lord and two other thegns swore that he had not been accused recently; then he could go to the simple ordeal.[68]

This sensitivity to reputation, as expressed in oath-worthiness, is found perhaps most elaborately in English law, but there are many examples from other areas. The capitulary and conciliar legislation of the continent in the ninth century reflects these principles too. In 895, for example, the Council of Tribur ruled that freemen suspected of a crime could clear themselves by oath, 'but if they are suspected of such a crime that they are deemed guilty by the people and they are outsworn, they should either confess or be examined by the hot iron'. The same council specified occasions on which compurgation might not be acceptable: 'if [the accused] has been caught in theft, perjury or false witness, let him not be admitted to an oath'.[69] This influential ruling eventually passed, via the canonical collections of Regino and Burchard of Worms, into Gratian's *Decretum*.[70] Burchard, in fact, not only recognized the principle, he also applied it in the rules he drew up for his own household and dependants around 1024–the so-called *Lex familiae Wormatiensis*. Here he listed certain offences–thefts of over five shillings, perjury, false witness, conspiracy–which would forfeit a

---

[66] I Edward 3, ed. Liebermann, *Gesetze*, 1, pp. 140-1.

[67] II Cnut 22 and 30, ed. Liebermann, *Gesetze*, 1, pp. 324-5, 330-3.

[68] I Ethelred 1.2; cf. III Ethelred 4 and II Cnut 30, ed. Liebermann, *Gesetze*, 1, pp. 216-17, 228-9, 330-3.

[69] Cap. 22a, MGH, *Capit.* 2 (as in n. 37), p. 225.

[70] Regino, *De ecclesiasticis disciplinis et religione christiana*, 2.302, *PL* 132, col. 342; Burchard of Worms, *Decretum*, 16.19, *PL* 140, col. 912; Gratian, *Decretum*, C.2, q.5, c.15, a *palea* according to Friedberg, *Corpus iuris canonici*, ed. Emil Friedberg (2 vols., Leipzig, 1879), 1, col. 459.

man's law, 'so that he lose the law to which he is born and if he is accused by anyone of any offence, he may not clear himself by oath but only by combat, the boiling water or the hot iron'.[71] Another example can be found in the late-twelfth-century customs of Bruges, which specify that a first accusation of theft could be settled by witnesses, but a second, when the reputation of the accused was no longer pristine, must be resolved by ordeal.[72]

All these cases concern men who had forfeited their oath-worthiness. Another class was composed of those who were unable to attain oath-worthiness through no fault of their own. Foreigners are an obvious example. When juristic standing depended upon one's position in a web of kindred ties, bonds of lordship and dependency, blood status, and ethnic-territorial identity, the stranger was adrift. He hardly had an identity in legal terms. The Ripuarian code orders that if a foreigner 'cannot find co-jurors in the Ripuarian province, then he must clear himself by cauldron or lot'.[73] In English law there are frequent references to the ordeal as the proof appropriate to 'the foreigner or friendless man'.[74] The situation was accentuated on borders, where men not only of different kindreds but also of different laws would have to resolve their disputes. In the tenth-century legal document *Dunsaettas*, which lays down arrangements to be observed in dealings between English and Welsh, the ordeal is specified as the only kind of proof.[75] Obviously, neither oaths nor witnesses would be trusted in a hostile march-land.

Parallel to the foreigner was the slave, the internal stranger. He, too, was not, in himself, oath-worthy, not because of bad reputation or lack of local kin, but because of low status. He could, of course, be vouched for by his lord, and this was a common practice. Nevertheless, accusations against slaves and the unfree must have been viewed as one of the main categories likely to result in the ordeal. The ordeal was not applied *only* to the unfree–there are numerous instances of the ordeal applied against free men–but a large body of legal material makes it clear that it was very commonly decided that compurgation

[71] Cap. 32, ed. Ludwig Weiland, MGH, *Const.* 1 (Hanover, 1893), p. 644.

[72] *Keure de la châtellenie de Bruges*, cap. 28, ed. Leopold A. Warnkönig, *Histoire constitutionelle et administrative de la ville de Bruges* (Brussels, 1856), p. 371 (printed as 471).

[73] *Lex Ribuaria*, cap. 31.5, ed. Karl August Eckhardt, *Lex Ribuaria II. Text und Lex Francorum Chamavorum* (Hanover, 1966), p. 40.

[74] VIII Ethelred 22; I Cnut 5.2a; II Cnut 35; pseudo-Cnut de Foresta, cap. 13, ed. Liebermann, *Gesetze*, 1, pp. 266, 286-7, 336-9, 622; *Leges Henrici primi*, 65.5, ed. L. J. Downer (Oxford, 1972), p. 208.

[75] Cap. 2.1, ed. Liebermann, *Gesetze*, 1, pp. 376-7.

(or, occasionally, the duel) was the proof of the free, the ordeal of the unfree:

[When someone is accused of killing a priest] if he is a free man, let him swear with twelve co-jurors, if unfree, let him clear himself through the twelve red-hot ploughshares.[76]

If anyone breaks this peace, let them clear themselves with a twelvefold oath if they are free or noble, with the ordeal of cold water if unfree.[77]

A man accused of poisoning, who denies the charge, must uphold his case by combat if he is free, or the ordeal if unfree.[78]

Such provisions, widespread in time and place, point to an important aspect of the ordeal, its use against the servile classes. Unless special arrangements were made for their lord to stand for them, the unfree were not allowed to enter fully the legal world of oath-swearing and compurgation.

The apparent diversity of the situations in which the ordeal was employed should not hide the fact that, beyond this variety, there was common ground. Sexual issues, such as adultery or disputed paternity, are, by their very nature, the cases least usually resolved by witnesses, there being no visible evidence on which to base a judgement. This also explains the frequent use of the ordeal in crimes of stealth—murder as distinct from homicide, theft by night, and so on. Heresy and the other cases in which trials of faith were used have a similar 'invisible' quality—what was at issue was belief, and belief is intangible. The ordeal was a way of getting at it. In the case of those who were not oath-worthy, the inaccessibility of the truth was produced in a slightly different way: the absence of evidence was compounded by the impossibility of believing a man's word. In all these situations a clear resolution of the issue by normal means was impossible; these cases all share a common tenacious opacity. Yet they were causes which had to be decided— there could be no suspension of judgement. The faithfulness of a wife, the falsity of a monk's doctrines, the unresolved theft where all suspicions pointed to one man: these had to go to trial, to judgement. This was the role of the ordeal. It was *lex paribilis*, or *apparens*, or *aperta*—the 'manifest proof'. It was a device for dealing with situations in which certain knowledge was impossible but uncertainty was intolerable.

[76] Council of Mainz (847), MGH, *Capit.* 2 (as in n. 37), p. 182.

[77] *Pax Dei incerta (saec. XI. ex.)*, cap. 5, MGH, *Const.* 1 (as in n. 71), p. 608.

[78] *Constitutio Langobardica de veneficiis, ibid.*, p. 101; *veneficia* could well be translated as 'sorcery'.

4

The End of the Ordeal and Social Change

FROM the ninth to the twelfth centuries, in every part of Latin Christendom and over a very wide range of cases and situations, the ordeal was in regular use. By 1300 it was everywhere vestigial. The demise of the ordeal demands explanation and there have been many attempts to meet the demand, in which explanations of very diverse kinds have been advanced. A useful starting point may be a consideration of one powerful body of arguments, developed by those who believe that the abandonment of the ordeal is best seen as a consequence of certain social changes which took place in the eleventh and twelfth centuries.

The Functionalist Case

The general perspective, that the history of the ordeal must be related to levels of social development, is not new. The classic works of Patetta and Lea in the late nineteenth century were informed by an evolutionary and comparative perspective partly inspired by Tylorian anthropology. For them the ordeal could be related to a specific 'social stage'. More recent writers share this view. For Professor Van Caenegem, the abandonment of the ordeal was part of 'the rationalization of proof in Europe', reflecting 'the modernization demanded by more advanced social structures and a higher intellectual level'.[1] Professor Bongert explains the wide dissemination of the ordeal by 'the socioeconomic environment'.[2]

The latest and most penetrating presentations of this case are those of Peter Brown, developed and modified by Paul Hyams. One distinctive feature of their arguments is that they attempt to specify the particular social features which encouraged or militated against the ordeal. They have attempted to explain its workings and its demise by the kinds of communities, the kinds of society, in which it operated. They have tried not to condescend to the apparent irrationality of the procedure and claim that, for early medieval society, the ordeal was 'a satis-

---

[1] *La Preuve*, p. 750.
[2] Bongert, *Recherches*, p. 295.

factory solution to some difficulties' and that 'in its context the ordeal is rational'.[3]

For our purposes, Professor Brown's subtle and sensitive argument must be briskly summarized: the ordeal was 'an instrument of consensus' in a world of 'small face-to-face groups'. It was slow, flexible, therapeutic–it 'applied a discreet massage to the ruffled feelings of the group' and was 'reassuring and peace-creating'. 'The withering of the ordeal in the course of the twelfth century' is to be explained by the fact that this consensus was no longer so central a concern, firstly because population growth and associated changes made society more impersonal, secondly because there was a 'shift from consensus to authority' as lay rulers developed their coercive power.[4]

This functionalist approach has been pursued by Paul Hyams, using more detailed legal evidence, especially the English material of the tenth to twelfth centuries. He, too, characterizes the ordeal as 'a device of small communities' and attempts to show how the device might work in a judicial context. In these communities there is a 'premium on consensus' and judicial activity is concerned to 're-establish a workable peace in the community'. This 'world of the ordeal' was transformed during the eleventh and twelfth centuries. In the twelfth century it 'atrophied', partly under the impact of faster communications and the extension of political units: 'the old ordeals were progressively less useful as communities' horizons became less restricted'. Because of his belief that the demise of the ordeal is basically attributable to social changes, Dr Hyams has to de-emphasize the role of the clerical criticism which culminated in the 1215 canon against ordeals and, as a logical corollary, must regard as the most important process 'a slow, silent revolution' by 'men of affairs' in the eleventh and twelfth centuries.[5]

One central objection to the approach of Peter Brown, and of others

[3] Brown, 'Society and the Supernatural', p. 137 (repr., p. 310), Hyams, 'Trial by Ordeal', p. 115.
[4] 'Society and the Supernatural', quotations at pp. 137, 138, 135, 142-3 (repr., pp. 310-11, 313, 307, 324). The wide influence of Professor Brown's views on the ordeal is shown by the way they have almost become a new orthodoxy; see, for example, Edward Peters, *The Magician, the Witch and the Law* (Philadelphia, 1978), p. 152, on 'the fundamental role of community consensus in determining guilt and punishment' in ordeal cases, or Angold, 'The Interaction of Latins and Byzantines', p. 8, or R. I. Moore, *The Origins of European Dissent* (rev. edn., Oxford, 1985), pp. 258-61, who disarmingly acknowledges (p. 310 n. 18) that his argument is 'entirely derived' from Professor Brown's.
[5] 'Trial by Ordeal', pp. 110-11, 106-7, 115-16, 121.

who have followed him, is that it over-emphasizes both the cohesiveness and the autonomy of the group. In this it is deeply influenced by the bias of social anthropology. A functionalist and depoliticizing tendency, which first emerged in the study of the peoples of Africa and the Pacific, has here coloured perceptions of medieval Europe. The crucial element which is missing from the picture is lordship–hard, intrusive, rule-making lordship. The ordeal may have been, in some sense, 'a device of small communities'; it was certainly also a device of lords.

As has already been shown, after an obscure protohistorical phase, the ordeal burst into history in the Carolingian period. It makes sense as an adjunct of the Christian kingship of the Carolingian dynasty. For kings who defined and reinforced their kingship by their Christianity and who prided themselves on inculcating that Christianity through their kingly power, the ordeal was an ideal judicial instrument. It could be enforced in an exercise of power, yet represented submission to that power as submission to the deity. Alongside their extensive use of the oath for freemen, the Carolingians spread and sanctioned the ordeal as the best means of dealing with hard cases, men of ill-repute, or the servile classes.

Kings in the Carolingian tradition maintained the close association of the ordeal with royal power. The English kings of the tenth and eleventh centuries used it extensively, devised particularly severe forms for those accused of false coining or plotting against the king, and ruled that ordeals should take place only at royal manors.[6] In a similar spirit William the Lion of Scotland ruled that barons could not judge cases involving ordeals in the absence of the royal sheriff.[7] When the Polish Duke Boleslaw specified the rights of the comital castellans in 1252, he laid down that 'the count has the power to judge all cases following the model of our court (*iuxta formam curiae nostrae*), namely, the

[6] IV Aethelred, 5 and 7, ed. Liebermann, *Gesetze*, 1, pp. 234-7; V Aethelred, 30 and VI Aethelred, 37, *ibid.*, pp. 244-5 and 256-7, ed. D. Whitelock, M. Brett and C. N. L. Brooke, *Councils and Synods*, 1.i (Oxford, 1982), pp. 359-60 and 372 (cf. II Aethelstan, 4, ed. Liebermann, *Gesetze*, 1, pp. 152-3); III Aethelred, 6, *ibid.*, pp. 230-1. In this last case, where the text reads *on thaes kyninges byrig*, the translation 'manor' is only one possibility for *byrig*. 'Town' is another. See A. J. Robertson, *The Laws of the Kings of England from Edmund to Henry I* (Cambridge, 1925), pp. 67 and 320. The *Quadripartitus* text has *in curia regis*.

[7] *Assise Willelmi regis*, cap. 12, *Acts of the Parliament of Scotland*, 1, ed. T. Thomson and C. Innes (Edinburgh, 1844), p. 375. This is one of the clauses accepted as 'probably genuine' by A. A. M. Duncan, *Scotland. The Making of the Kingdom* (Edinburgh, 1975), p. 200 n. 30.

water, the hot iron, and the duel.[8] The right to hold ordeals was regalian.

The cases that fit most obviously into this picture of the ordeal as an adjunct of royal power are the political ones. When the bishop of Lincoln had to clear himself of a charge of treason against William the Conqueror by sending a man to the hot iron,[9] when Duke Sobeslas of Bohemia, having crushed an aristocratic conspiracy in 1130, rounded up the relatives of the conspirators, sent them to the hot iron, and had them executed,[10] when Valdemar of Denmark threatened the rebel Magnus Erikson with the hot iron,[11] we are clearly not dealing with small face-to-face communities in search of consensus.

But the characterization of the ordeal as coercive and intrusive rather than therapeutic and popular can be extended beyond the dramatic state trials. It has already been argued that in criminal cases the ordeal was applied most commonly to the out-sworn, to foreigners, and the unfree. Defined in relation to a community of the law-worthy, these figures would be outsiders. Seen in this light, the ordeal was not so much a device for maintaining consensus when divisions arose within the community as a mechanism for dealing with trouble outside it, for cases beyond the reach of usual procedures such as compurgation. Any judicial process is, in a weak sense, a device for achieving consensus, since a result is obtained which is intended to be binding. What distinguished the ordeal was not so much the consensus it might produce, but the fact that it was a way of obtaining a result in peculiarly intractable cases. But the communities faced with these intractable cases were not autonomous, they could not make their own rules. They had lords, and the functioning of the ordeal reflects not only the needs of a community but also the demands of a lord.

Around 1024, as has already been mentioned, Bishop Burchard of Worms drew up 'laws' for his *familia*. He was a man of great legal learning but also one with vast practical responsibilities. He was the

---

[8] *Kodeks Dyplomatyczny Malopolski*, 1, ed. F. Piekosínski, Monumenta medii aevi historica res gestas Poloniae illustrantia, 9 (Cracow, 1886), no. 436, p. 86.

[9] Henry of Huntingdon, *Historia Anglorum*, 6.41, ed. T. Arnold, (RS, 1879), p. 212. While it may be argued that we should doubt such a story from the writer who gave us 'King Canute and the waves', it is worth noting that Henry was raised in the household of Robert Bloet, the immediate successor to the bishop of Lincoln supposedly involved in the treason case.

[10] *Canonici Wissegradensis continuatio Cosmae*, ed. R. Köpke, MGH, *SS* 9 (Hanover, 1851), p. 136.

[11] Saxo Grammaticus, *Gesta Danorum*, 14.54.19-20, ed. J. Olrik and H. Raeder (2 vols., Copenhagen, 1931-57), 1, p. 508.

head of a large, and sometimes violent, German household and retinue, with fighting-men, officials, and dependants throughout the
countryside. Burchard had been disturbed by the recent lawlessness
of the *familia* and this had prompted the drawing up of new laws. Naturally enough, he had done this in consultation—*cum consilio cleri et mili-
tum et totius familie*. No lord was isolated or absolute, and consultation
was an essential prerequisite for the effective exercise of authority.
Nevertheless, '*I, Burchard* ... have ordered these laws to be written
down'.

The rules discuss a range of matters, details of inheritance and marriage laws, as well as offences and penalties. There is an easy assumption of the rights of lordship: 'of the wergild of a dependant, five
pounds will go to the bishop's treasury, two and a half to the relatives'.
Burchard is known to have felt a particular unease about perjury and
this is reflected in several of the provisions. For him, the ordeal probably seemed preferable to the swearing of oaths. As to the specific case
of the use of the ordeals of fire and water, there are two clauses which
mention them.[12] One is the provision, already cited, for a man convicted of perjury 'to lose his law', that is to forfeit his right to clear himself by oath. The other clause specifies that, if a man accused of
culpable homicide offers duel, but the dead man's relatives decline the
offer, 'then let him clear himself before the bishop by the boiling water
and pay the wergild and make his peace with the relatives; and these
must accept. But if, through fear of this ruling, they go to another
household and stir them up against their own fellows, and if there is no
one to challenge them to a duel, they must each clear themselves
before the bishop by the boiling water.'

The situation envisaged here is one in which a member of the
bishop's retinue, or one of the dependants of the bishop, has killed
another. It is considered possible that combat may be refused. In this
intractable situation, the bishop was willing to force the issue by
accepting the verdict of an ordeal even against the wishes of the dead
man's kin. He was not interested in maintaining consensus or sooth-
ing ruffled feathers. He intended to force an agreement and ensure
peace. If the dead man's kin refused to accept the verdict of the ordeal
and pursued the vendetta, then, by a kind of poetic justice, their return
to favour must be through the ordeal. Certainly the ordeal, like any
judicial procedure, was intended to lead to decision, to close an argu-

[12] Ed. Ludwig Weiland, MGH, *Const*. 1 (Hanover, 1893), pp. 640-4 (caps. 30 and 32).

ment, but, as it appears in the laws of Bishop Burchard, it was not so much a form of local therapy as an instrument for disciplining an unruly following.

The presence of an insistent lord could sometimes, indeed, be essential, for though it might seem that remitting the verdict to God would ensure that the last word had been said on the matter, not everyone, even then, might accept the verdict. It is worth remembering that Charlemagne had to command 'let all believe in the ordeal without any doubting'[13] and, in Scotland, an assize attributed to William the Lion is directed against the kinsmen of a man condemned at the ordeal seeking revenge against the accuser.[14] There were clearly those who upheld a right of appeal even against the judgement of God.

The theory that trial by ordeal functioned in such a way as to produce group consensus requires the assumption that ordeal procedure, which was supposed to place the issue in God's hands, could, in reality, easily become the channel for group feelings. 'There was a built-in flexibility in the ordeal', suggests Professor Brown, 'that enabled the group, which had the main interest in reaching certainty, to maintain a degree of initiative quite contrary to the explicit ideology of the ordeal'.[15] In particular, he argues, such initiative was exercised in the interpretation of the outcome of an ordeal, when the decision had to be made whether a hand was clean or unclean, whether a body floated or sank. This is a crucial issue. If there were some latitude in the interpretation of the outcome, and if the local group could make its influence felt at that moment, then the consensus theory would be much strengthened.

The role of group feeling, and the limits upon it, are well illustrated by the events at Vézelay in 1167.[16] Two men accused of heresy were tried by cold water. One 'was judged by everybody to be saved by the water (though there were some who afterwards cast doubt on the verdict)'. The other was convicted, but 'at the request of many, including the priests, and by his own request, was brought out from prison and submitted to the judgement of water again', whereupon he was again convicted. Clearly these two ordeals involved strong feelings on the

[13] MGH, *Capit.* 1, ed. Alfred Boretius (Hanover, 1883), p. 150.

[14] *Assise Willelmi regis* (as in n. 7) cap. 15, ed. cit., p. 375. Duncan, *Scotland* (as in n. 7) does not accept the attribution.

[15] 'Society and the Supernatural', p. 139 (repr., p. 315).

[16] Hugh of Poitiers, *Historia Viziliacensis monasterii*, bk. 4, *PL* 194, cols. 1681-2, *Recueil des historiens des Gaules et de la France*, 12 (new edn., Paris, 1877), pp. 343-4. See also the comments of Moore, *Origins of European Dissent* (as in n. 4), pp. 259-60.

part of the people assembled at the scene. But the mechanisms of group consensus were not working very well. In the case of the first heretic tried, the apparent unanimity did not last and was soon replaced by recrimination and doubt. The inherent element of ambiguity in the ordeal allowed dissension as well as consensus. In the case of the second heretic, we see the opposite process at work. He was readily allowed a second chance at the ordeal, which presumably suggests that most people thought he was innocent. Yet, even so, the water would not let him sink. There were limits to the ambiguity of the ordeal. Even the best will in the world did not allow this man to escape the verdict of the ordeal pit. So, these trials at Vézelay, where group opinion clearly was important, show that the ordeal could produce division as well as consensus and that there was an irreducible, non-subjective element in the procedure. Oddly enough, these heresy trials of the twelfth and early thirteenth century, with their participating crowds whose sudden swings of mood against or, more rarely, in favour of the accused might decide the issue, fit most closely the model advanced by Peter Brown, but what he says of 'small face-to-face communities' applies really to lynch mobs in the towns.

Another instructive case study can be found in the Icelandic *Ljósvetninga saga*. Eyjolf and Thorkel were involved in a dispute about the paternity of the child carried by Fridgerd, the daughter of one of Eyjolf's dependants. They agreed to abide by the decision of the hot iron. Fridgerd fasted and prepared herself. 'The priest who had to make the decision' was called in:

Eyjolf volunteered to examine the ordeal. He said that it was obvious that their opponents still wished to interfere with the procedure 'and so one must be all the more careful to make an exact examination'. Thorkel came and now the bindings were unwound from her hands. The priest did not give his judgement immediately. Then Thorkel said, 'What sort of degenerate are you, that you don't say she is badly burned!' And he designated himself a witness for that fact. The priest said, 'This is a heavy-handed action, to appropriate the sentence for yourself and take it out of my hands, when I should make the decision! We must have another and clearer proof.' Eyjolf answered, 'The result cannot be clearer. But because of your hostility and the bribes you have taken, I will demand compensation worth as much as my patrimony!'

The proceedings then broke up amid mutual threats.[17]

---

[17] *Ljósvetninga saga*, cap. 23, tr. Wilhelm Ranisch, *Fünf Geschichten aus dem östlichen Nordland* (Jena, 1921, 1939), pp. 195-6.

This story demonstrates once again the ambiguity that might arise in the interpretation of ordeals. Thorkel claimed that Fridgerd was badly burned. Eyjolf thought that 'the result cannot be clearer', and believed that she was absolved. The priest, whose job was to decide, hesitated before his pronouncement and was suspected of taking bribes. As at Vézelay, the ambiguity of the ordeal permitted tensions and dissension to emerge. Such 'disputed ordeals' were not uncommon.[18]

But the saga illustrates another important point. The priest was expected to decide. He was worth bribing. In the end his power was not respected. But in cases where the contenders were less powerful than these particular Icelanders, or in societies where judges and courts had greater coercive power than they did in Iceland, the power to decide the outcome of the ordeal would be a vital instrument in the hands of court presidents, judges, and priests.

Ordeals were a regular part of official judicial procedure and they were presided over by formally constituted authorities. These were the men who had the power to decide. The courts were run by ecclesiastics, royal officials, and lords, not by the small face-to-face communities from which plaintiffs or accused might emerge. Men were often sent away from their localities to be tried, to the greater churches with the right to hold ordeals, to the king's manors, or the sessions of his justices. Kings made a point of trying to keep away crowds of interested supporters.[19] Thus a few figures in authority, judges, court presidents (often lords), and priests decided the outcome of ambiguous ordeals. Having the power to determine, they also had the power to defraud. Sigurth Thorlakson had observed, 'The king is crafty and deceitful. . . . It will be easy for him to falsify the ordeal.'[20] Priests had to be ordered not to 'mishandle ordeals'.[21] Clearly, the initiative which had the most influence on the outcome of the ordeal was that of priests and judges, not the local group. The judicial processes of the Middle Ages were far more formal and complex than most of those studied by modern anthropologists. Kingdoms of millions of inhabitants were subject to one law and authority. The small-scale community existed, but did not form a self-contained jural unit. It was part of a larger entity.

[18] See Wulfstan, 'Canons of Edgar', *Councils and Synods* (as in n. 6) 1.i., p. 334.
[19] e.g. II Aethelstan 23.2, ed. Liebermann, *Gesetze*, 1, pp. 162-5.
[20] *Olafs saga helga*, cap. 135, tr. Lee M. Hollander, *Heimskringla* (Austin, 1964), p. 412.
[21] *Northumbrian Priests' Law*, cap. 39, *Councils and Synods* (as in n. 6) 1.i, p. 460.

Thus over-emphasis on the autonomy of the group leads to neglect of the role of lords and over-emphasis on the cohesiveness of the group obscures the factions, tensions, and dissension within any medieval jural community. The ordeal got results, but it did not generate consensus.

Beyond the specific question, however, as to whether the pursuit of consensus was such a vital component of the functioning of the ordeal, there still lies the more general problem of the association between the history of trial by ordeal and that of the lay communities in which it functioned. The thesis of Brown and Hyams is but one variant of the many which would see the decline of the ordeal as the result of the social transformations of the eleventh and twelfth centuries. As the ordeal became dysfunctional in the new social world, so the argument runs, it withered away. 'A new world arose and in this world there was no longer any place for the archaic proofs, rooted in the closed and primitive world which Europe was leaving behind her.'[22]

Such theories postulate a crisis of the ordeal in the period 1050-1200 and seek to characterize this crisis by some variant of the concept 'the withering of the ordeal'.[23] Given their current orthodoxies, it is natural for historians to seek to explain any given development by referring to 'changes in society' at the time in question. It is a reflex with deep roots, going back to the pioneer thinkers of the Enlightenment, and, in many ways, it is a respectable urge. However, as well as the inherent vagueness of the entity 'society', which is supposed to be the matrix of these changes, there is another problem with such an approach: it takes too much for granted. It presumes that, if the ordeal disappeared from Europe in the thirteenth century, there must have been prior social changes which explain it, and that, if this is the case, then the ordeal must have been in decline in the twelfth century. These presumptions do not, however, match the facts.

The Persistence of the Ordeal

Not only is there no evidence for the withering of the ordeal in the eleventh or twelfth centuries, there is a great deal of evidence which would suggest that the practice, far from decaying, was flourishing and, in fact, spreading. No explanation of the demise of the ordeal based on the assumption that men had become dissatisfied with its

---

[22] R. C. van Caenegem in *La Preuve*, p. 753.
[23] Brown, 'Society and the Supernatural', p. 135 (repr., p. 307).

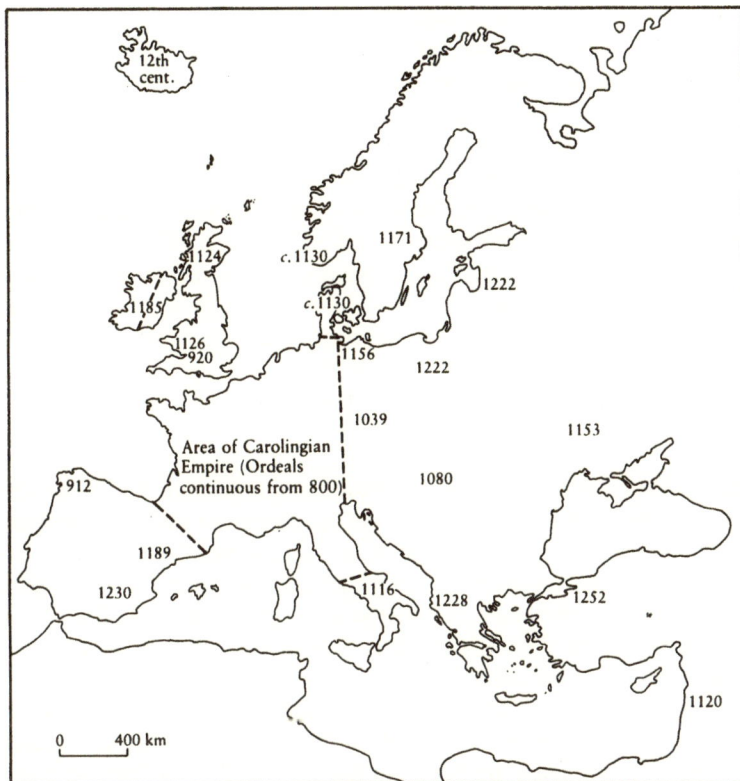

Map 2. References to Unilateral Ordeals after 800. The dates given are those of the first reference after 800. Some countries, such as England, have evidence prior to 800 as well. (For the date given for Ireland, see text.)

workings and hence gradually abandoned it over the period 1050-1200 can be reconciled with the evidence for the health of the ordeal in this period. This evidence falls naturally into two classes: evidence for the spread of trial by ordeal (for the following discussion, consult Map 2) and evidence for its flourishing state in areas of ancient use.

One important way that the ordeal spread in the eleventh, twelfth, and thirteenth centuries was in association with the spread of Christianity. This can partly be guessed at, from coincidences of timing and other hints, partly definitively demonstrated. Between the tenth and the thirteenth centuries a broad arc of Scandinavian and east European countries were Christianized, many of them, in the process, developing powerful Christian monarchies, and it seems to have been in association with these developments that trial by ordeal entered their judicial practice. In Denmark, for example, as mentioned above, men of the twelfth century associated trial by hot iron with the conversion, when it had been employed in a trial of faith: 'so it came about that the Danes abolished the custom of judicial duelling and decreed that various cases should be settled by this kind of ordeal; for they decided that differences would be resolved better by divine judgement than by human strife'.[24] In the lay of Gudrun in the *Edda*, when the ordeal is decided upon, Gudrun says:

> Send for Saxi the southern king!
> He can bless the boiling cauldron.[25]

Both these references suggest that the custom was introduced into the North, rather than indigenous, and associate it with the Christian, particularly the German, world. The chronology of references to the ordeals of fire and water in the Scandinavian countries also makes sense in this light: apart from the story of Poppo in Widukind, there are none before the twelfth century. References begin early in that century and are common thereafter.

The picture in eastern Europe is roughly comparable, though in Poland the first evidence for trial by ordeal is later (thirteenth century). In Hungary, on the other hand, the ordeals of fire and water were employed by the later eleventh century for charges of theft and false witness; they were supposed to take place only in the chief churches of the kingdom.[26] Bohemia provides a particularly illuminating example. Here the seeds of conversion went back as far as the ninth century, but the thorough Christianization of the country only began after the emergence of a dominant Christian dynasty, the Přemyslids. An event of great importance in the transformation of the Bohemians from a fragmented pagan people to a Christian nation

---

[24] Saxo Grammaticus, *Gesta Danorum*, 10.11.4, ed. J. Olrik and H. Raeder (2 vols., Copenhagen, 1931-57), 1, p. 282.

[25] 'The Third Lay of Gudrun', tr., Patricia Terry, *Poems of the Vikings. The Elder Edda* (Indianapolis and New York, 1969), p. 204.

[26] *Sancti Ladislai regis decretorum liber secundus*, 4; *Sancti Ladislai decretorum liber tertius*, 1, *Colomanni regis decretorum liber primus*, 22, 76, and 83, in Györffy, 'Anhang', pp. 289, 294-5, 308, 315, and 316.

under a single Christian dynasty took place in 1039.[27] Bretislav I, the Bohemian duke, led his army against their enemies, the Poles, and succeeded in capturing their ancient centre, the archiepiscopal see of Gniezno. In the cathedral church lay the bones of St Adalbert, not a Pole, but a Bohemian, a member of the Slavnik dynasty who had been the Přemyslids' chief rivals. He had been honourably interred in Gniezno cathedral by the Polish duke after his martyrdom by pagans in 999. The Bohemians determined to take the bones back with them, but, rushing into the business, they encountered miraculous obstacles, which prevented them disturbing the tomb.

The way forward was shown by their bishop, Severus of Prague, who, guided by a vision, gave them instructions. The Bohemian warriors fasted and did penance for three days, then assembled before St Adalbert's tomb: 'they shouted, in tears, "We are ready to make amends for any wrong that we or our fathers have done against the saint and to cease utterly from the works of wickedness". Then the duke stretched out his hand over the holy tomb and began to address the crowd of people: "Stretch out your right hands to God, my brothers, in one accord and listen to my words, which I want you to confirm with your oath . . .".' Then follows a long list of offences which the Bohemians are to swear to abandon. The duke and the bishop took turns at specifying the outlawed practices and the bishop added his anathema to the duke's prohibitions. The list of forbidden practices identifies the chief targets of a Christian prince and a bishop ruling a still half-pagan people. The Bohemians swore to give up polygamy, adultery, 'fratricide' and 'parricide', the killing of priests, frequenting taverns, holding markets and working on Sundays, and burial of the dead outside Christian cemeteries.

It was a programme for the conversion of a violent and semi-pagan people. In this reforming moment, when, in particularly solemn circumstances, the national identity of the Bohemians was symbolized by their new saint, in which a kind of covenant for a new Christian Bohemia was fashioned; in which, not least important, the power of the duke was emphasized and sanctified, the ordeals of fire and water emerge into Bohemian history for the first time:

If a woman declares that her husband does not love her but, rather, abuses and beats her, let the ordeal decide between them and let the guilty pay the

[27] Cosmas of Prague, *Chronica Boemorum*, 2.4, ed. B. Bretholz, MGH, *SRG*, NS. (Berlin, 1923), pp. 86-7.

penalty. Likewise, concerning those who are reputed to have committed homicide, let the archpriest give to the count of the castle their names in writing and let the count summon them. If they are intransigent let him put them in prison until either they perform a proper penance or, if they deny the charge, until their guilt is tested by the adjured iron or water.

The use of the ordeal in marital disputes, as it appears here in the oath-swearing at Gniezno, is quite in keeping with earlier Carolingian tradition. Its use to decide disputes between man and wife is first mentioned in a capitulary of Pippin, Charlemagne's father, and recurs throughout later capitulary and conciliar legislation. It was a standard canonical procedure in cases of dissolution on grounds of impotence.[28] In a more general sense, too, the link forged between ecclesiastical and princely power is also characteristic of Carolingian precedents. In these Bohemian provisions the bonds were very close. The Bohemian archpriests were actually to compile a list of suspects for submission to the 'counts of the castle', that is the castellans of the ducal strongholds on which Přemyslid power was based. Thus, as Bohemia was brought into the orbit of the Christian world, a new sacral and political order was created, in which trial by ordeal had an appropriate place.

The continued expansion of Latin Christendom in the twelfth and thirteenth centuries also involved the spread of the ordeal. In about 1156 the newly subjugated pagan Slavs of the diocese of Oldenburg-Lübeck experienced this change: 'the Slavs were forbidden to swear by trees, springs or stones any longer, but they offered those accused of crime to the priest to be tried by the iron or the ploughshares'.[29] The Crusaders brought the practice with them to the eastern Mediterranean. The ordeals of fire and water are mentioned as early as 1120, in the decrees of the Synod of Nablus,[30] they later appear in the Assizes of Jerusalem and probably spread via the Crusaders into Byzantium

---

[28] Pippin's *Decretum Vermeriense* of 758-68 specified ordeal of the cross 'if a woman claims that her husband has never lain with her', cap. 17, MGH, *Capit.* 1, ed. Alfred Boretius (Hanover, 1883), p. 41; the ruling was repeated by Regino, *De ecclesiasticis disciplinis et religione christiana*, 2.243, *PL* 132, col. 330; Burchard of Worms, *Decretum*, 9.41, *PL* 140, col. 821; and Ivo of Chartres, *Decretum*, 8.179 and *Panormia*, 6.118, *PL* 161, cols. 621 and 1276. Compare also the decrees of the Council of Salzburg, MGH, *Capit.* 1, p. 230, and MGH, *Conc.* 2, ed. Albert Werminghoff (Hanover, 1906-08), pp. 212-13; Haito of Basel, *Capitula* 21, MGH, *Capit.* 1, p. 365; Hincmar of Rheims, *epistola* 136, ed. Ernst Perels, MGH, *Epp.* 8 (Berlin, 1939), pp. 89-91.

[29] Helmold of Bosau, *Cronica Slavorum*, cap. 84, ed. Bernhard Schmiedler, MGH, *SRG* (Hanover, 1937), p. 164.

[30] Cap. 19, Mansi, 21, col. 264.

around the middle of the thirteenth century.[31] At the other end of the crusading world, the crusading orders carried trial by ordeal into the lands of the east Baltic, where, in 1222, the newly converted Livonians complained that they were being forced to submit to the hot iron.[32] In Spain, the Christian reconquest brought trial by ordeal to regions which had never known it. In 1177, for example, the Castilians captured Cuenca and shortly thereafter the ordeal of hot iron was in use in the town, as is shown by the local law code, the *Fuero de Cuenca*.[33] This code was the model for many other urban charters, as far south as Baeza and Iznatoraf in Andalusia, conquered by the Christians in the 1220s.[34] In this way, over the course of the twelfth and thirteenth centuries, the ordeal entered previously Islamic territory.

Thus trial by ordeal spread into Scandinavia, eastern Europe, and the Islamic world as part of the process of conversion and crusade which so greatly enlarged Latin Christendom between the eleventh century and the thirteenth. It seems also, however, to have diffused into new areas within western Christendom in the same period. In particular, it is probable that trial by hot iron and cold water was introduced (or reintroduced) into Wales, Ireland, and Scotland in the twelfth century by Anglo-Norman immigrants, assisted, in the case of Scotland, by native Normanizing kings.

The argument can be made with varying degrees of certainty. Wales is the clearest case of a twelfth-century importation of the ordeal, for the native Welsh laws contain no authentic reference to trial by ordeal (the solitary, apparent exception is actually the musing of a fifteenth-century legal antiquarian[35]). Outside of the special situation of the Anglo-Welsh border,[36] the ordeal was a judicial procedure unknown to the Welsh before the coming of the Normans. But early in the twelfth century the Norman Marcher lords introduced the practice. An agreement of 1126 between Urban, bishop of Llandaff, and Robert, earl of Gloucester, specifies 'ordeal of hot iron will take place at

---

[31] Angold, 'The Interaction of Latins and Byzantines'.

[32] X.5.35.3, Po. 6910 (Honorius III); repeated in 1232, Po. 8996b (the same, to the bishop of Oesel).

[33] Caps. 291-99, ed. R. Ureña y Smenjaud (Madrid, 1935), pp. 326-32.

[34] For a map showing the distribution of some of the daughter towns, see *Fuero de Baeza*, ed. J. Roudil (The Hague, 1962), p. 42.

[35] *Ancient Laws and Institutes of Wales*, ed. Aneurin Owen, 'Anomalous Laws', 14.13.4 (London, 1841), p. 707 in the one volume edition; 2, pp. 622-3 in the two-volume edition, from Peniarth MS 164, of the fifteenth century.

[36] Where the rules of *Dunsaettas* applied, Cap. 2.1, ed. Liebermann, *Gesetze*, 1, pp. 376-7.

Llandaff and the pit for the ordeal of water will be in the bishop's land next to the castle of Cardiff.[37] By the thirteenth century, although there is no mention of the ordeal in the Welsh law-books, it was familiar enough to Welshmen to be referred to in native bardic poetry.[38]

A somewhat similar situation developed in Ireland, though here the situation was more complicated and the evidence more ambiguous. As has been mentioned, early Irish law knew a variety of ordeals: the cauldron, casting of lots, passing the tongue over a red-hot axe, and others. Around the ninth century the ordeal of hot iron seems to have been introduced into Ireland,[39] but it was probably not widespread. The native Irish glossators of the twelfth century, commenting on the earlier laws, sometimes show perplexity or indecision about the details of the ordeal, suggesting, perhaps, that the ordeal was not frequent or current in the twelfth century. This is speculation, however. What is clear is that the ordeal of cold water was never mentioned in native Irish law, but was granted as a right, in the form of the franchise of 'ordeal of water and iron' or of 'pit and gallows', in the very earliest charters of the Anglo-French invaders.[40] It was obviously an importation. As we do not know if, or how often, trial by ordeal was undergone in pre-invasion Ireland, it would be rash to make the bald claim that the Normans reintroduced the ordeal; but it is clear that the ordeal pit of Anglo-Norman Ireland was a novelty, not a continuation of native Irish practice.

For Scotland, the evidence is less conclusive. Given the scarcity of sources, especially the absence of native laws, it is very hard to know much about pre-twelfth-century conditions and dangerous to argue from silence. Nevertheless, it is the case that the earliest references to trial by ordeal in Scotland, in charters of 1124, c. 1140 and c. 1163, are in

[37] *Liber Landavensis*, ed. J. G. Evans and J. Rhys (Oxford, 1893), pp. 27-9 (with facsimiles); *Cartae et alia munimenta quae ad dominium de Glamorgan pertinent*, ed. G. T. Clark (2nd edn., 6 vols., Cardiff, 1910), 1, pp. 54-6; *Episcopal Acts relating to Welsh Dioceses, 1066-1272*, ed. J. Conway Davies (2 vols., Cardiff, 1946-8), 2, L. 45, pp. 620-1; *Earldom of Gloucester Charters*, ed. Robert Patterson (Oxford, 1973), no. 109, pp. 106-8.
[38] *Llawysgrif Hendregadredd*, ed. John Morris-Jones and T. H. Parry-Williams (Cardiff, 1933), p. 291, 'Audyl yr haearn twymyn'. See also the story in Gerald of Wales, *Descriptio Kambriae*, 1.14, *Opera*, ed. J. S. Brewer, J. F. Dimock and G. F. Warner (8 vols., RS, 1861-91), 6, p. 191.
[39] Stokes, 'The Irish Ordeals', pp. 210-11.
[40] e.g. *The Red Book of the Earls of Kildare*, ed. G. MacNiocaill (Dublin, 1964), nos. 1 and 7, pp. 14, 19; *Calendar of Ormond Deeds*, 1, ed. Edmund Curtis (Dublin, 1932), no. 34, p. 18.

grants by Normanizing native kings to newly established religious houses of English canons.[41] This, of course, is suggestive rather than conclusive. After 1170 grants of jurisdiction 'with (ordeal) pit and gallows' are common in royal charters of enfeoffment.[42] It has been argued, by the leading Scottish medievalist, that a grant of 'pit and gallows' to a native Scottish aristocrat 'surely proves that this jurisdiction was not a foreign importation tied to tenure by military service',[43] but this is not a compelling argument. There is no reason why foreign importations cannot be sought by, or granted to, natives. After all, native Scots earls were holding fiefs by knight service as early as the 1130s.[44] Moreover, the unilateral ordeals were often granted along with the duel, which was indisputably an innovation introduced from outside in the twelfth century. The Scottish situation is thus not clear-cut. Given the possibility of prior traditions of the ordeal of either Anglian or Irish origin, one cannot be dogmatic. It remains the case, however, that the grants of 'pit and gallows' in the Scottish charters of the twelfth and thirteenth centuries are reminiscent, in both form and substance, of English and French documents rather than any other extant texts.

Thus, though it is not possible to be absolutely certain about the history of trial by ordeal in the Celtic countries, there is a reasonable likelihood that this form of proof entered those lands as part of a wider process of Anglo-French penetration and influence. This would make sense historically. The Anglo-French incomers who settled in Wales, Ireland, and Scotland in the twelfth century brought with them many of the assets of Carolingian and post-Carolingian kingship and lordship–military feudalism, the silver penny, charter forms–and trial by fire and water fits comfortably into this repertoire.

This evidence for the expansion of the world of the ordeal in the eleventh, twelfth, and thirteenth centuries is paralleled by material showing the continued vigour of the practice in its old heartland.

---

[41] Archibald C. Lawrie, *Early Scottish Charters* (Glasgow, 1905), no. 49, pp. 43-4, and no. 153, p. 116; *Regesta regum Scottorum*, 1, ed. G. W. S. Barrow (Edinburgh, 1960), no. 243, pp. 263-4, and no. 247, p. 267. The houses concerned were Scone and Holyrood. In his notes on the earliest of these documents, Lawrie commented that he 'was not sure that this is a genuine charter' (p. 297), but Professor Barrow sees no grounds for such scepticism (personal communication).

[42] *Regesta regum Scottorum*, 2, ed. G. W. S. Barrow (Edinburgh, 1971), nos. 136, 185, 200, 302, etc.

[43] Ibid., p. 49.

[44] G. W. S. Barrow, *The Kingdom of the Scots* (London, 1973), p. 283.

Nothing is harder to illustrate than the frequency of a custom in a society which recorded its activities in such a haphazard way as Latin Christendom did in the eleventh and twelfth centuries. Nevertheless, it is possible to point to certain developments and to certain facts which suggest that the ordeal was in no sense 'withering' in the period 1050–1200.

One thing working in favour of the survival of the ordeal was a continuing dissatisfaction with the uncorroborated oath as a means of proof. Bishop Burchard of Worms, for example, preferred ordeal to oath, in some circumstances, because he knew the frequency of perjury. He was not alone in this opinion, for there are many instances where an oath was seen as insufficient in itself and required the buttressing force of the ordeal. Catalan justice seems to have developed in this direction in the eleventh century; indeed, it has been argued that the 'appearance of ordeals in the peninsula has its *raison d'être* in the crisis of the oath'.[45] The impetus was also felt elsewhere. In a suit in Anjou in the 1070s a witness was ordered 'to swear on holy objects as to what he said he had seen and then confirm the oath by the ordeal of hot water, as is the custom of our region'.[46] At about the same time a dispute between a Lotharingian monastery and its advocate over labour services involved 'confirmation of the oath by the judicial ordeal by water'.[47] Many of the eleventh- and twelfth-century disputes about clerical immunity from the ordeal turned on the question of whether the oath of the accused was sufficient, or whether it needed confirmation by fire and water.[48]

The doubt about oaths expressed in these references emerged in a very distinctive way in the Peace and Truce of God movement, that remarkable attempt to impose some limits on the violence and lawlessness of the eleventh-century aristocracy. The ordeal was a natural tool for the Peace movement for several reasons. The spon-

---

[45] Iglesia Ferreirós, 'El processo del conde Bera', p. 208; cf. P. Bonnassie, *La Catalogne du milieu du x' à la fin du xi' siècle* (2 vols., Toulouse, 1975), 2, pp. 728–9.

[46] P. Marchegay, *Archives d'Anjou*, 1 (Angers, 1843), p.475.

[47] *Chronicon sancti Huberti Andaginensis*, cap. 41 (53), ed. L. Bethmann and W. Wattenbach, MGH, *SS* 8 (Hanover, 1848), p. 591, ed. K. Hanquet, *La Chronique de S. Hubert dite Cantatorium* (Brussels, 1906), p. 103.

[48] For example, see the case discussed in the letter of Pope Alexander II to Rainald, bishop of Como, in 1063, *PL* 146, col. 1406, JL 4505, which later found its way into Ivo of Chartres' *Decretum*, 10.15 and *Panormia*, 5.7-8, *PL* 161, cols. 695 and 1214-15 and, in a mutilated form, into Gratian's *Decretum*, C.2, q.5, c.7; or the ruling of Innocent II (1130-43) to the bishop of Worms, JL 8284, Browe, *De ordaliis*, 1, no. 21.

taneous origins of the movement were in great assemblies of bishops and nobles, swearing oaths on relics, reminiscent in many ways of the events at Gniezno in 1039, and thus their fusion of divine and secular sanctions found a logical expression in the ordeal. Moreover, a man accused of breaking the peace was also, inescapably, suspected of breaking the oath he had sworn to keep the peace. Hence some unwillingness might well arise as to whether he could clear himself by oath. An example is provided by the following clause from the Norman Peace of 1047: 'If anyone says he broke the peace unwittingly, let him first swear his oath and then carry the hot iron'.[49] Finally, there is no doubt that the ordeal was viewed as a brisker and more intimidating form of proof. In movements designed to meet the apparent danger of a breakdown of law and order, the ordeal had a deterrent effect.

In its Catalan and southern French homeland, the Peace movement seems to have been responsible for generalizing the use of ordeals. 'All proofs and expiations adjudged to those who disturb or break the Peace and Truce of God are to take place through the ordeal of cold water in the cathedral of San Pedro', prescribed the Council of Vich in 1068.[50] 'If anyone within the Truce of the Lord does any harm to anyone, let him pay double compensation and afterwards make good the Truce of the Lord through ordeal of cold water in the cathedral of St Eulalia', reads a similar canon from the diocese of Narbonne of about the same date.[51] These are eleventh-century references, but the Peace movement did not die out at the turn of the century. Twelfth-century practice was still influenced by the readiness with which Peace Councils had recourse to the ordeal. At Rheims in 1119, for example, Pope Calixtus II approved the local Truce of God, according to which the non-knightly had to clear themselves of charges of infractions of the Truce through the ordeal.[52] The Peace movement also had a deep impact on the legislation of secular princes. In Catalonia the *Usatges of Barcelona*, the core of which dates to the 1060s,

---

[49] Mansi, 19, cols. 597-600. On dating and texts see M. de Boüard, 'Sur les origines de la Trève de Dieu en Normandie', *Annales de Normandie*, 9 (1959), pp. 169-89, and H. Hoffmann, *Gottesfriede und Treuga Dei* (Stuttgart, 1964), pp. 166-7.

[50] Mansi, 19, cols. 1073-6; 1063 is a possible alternative date, Bonnassie, *La Catalogne* (as in n. 45), 2, pp. 656 ff.

[51] Mansi, 19, cols. 1041-4 and *PL* 151, col. 741; see Hoffmann, *Gottesfriede* (as in n. 49), pp. 98-101; it is printed by Browe, *De ordaliis*, 1, no. 71, with the date '*c.* 1047'. The probable root of this legislation of the 1060s is a council held in Catalonia in 1033, the decrees of which are edited by Hoffmann, p. 262 (with comments on pp. 78-9).

[52] Mansi, 21, col. 237.

'laid the foundations of an entirely new judicial regime', centred on
the ordeal.[53] These customs were deeply influenced by the Peace
legislation of the preceding half-century. Germany is the country
where the Peace legislation of the eleventh century leads most directly
to the secular legislation of the following period. The move from
Gottesfriede to *Landfriede* altered the form of the legislation more than
its substance. When we find the ordeal as a means of proof for a
peasant accused of wilful breach of the peace, in a *Landfriede* of
Frederick Barbarossa,[54] this is quite in the spirit of the Peace legislation of the previous century, which envisaged the ordeal of cold water
as a normal proof for the unfree accused of peace-breaking. The urge
to enforce the Peace through the deterrent effect of the ordeal was
clear in this eleventh-century legislation: the accused was commanded
to undergo the ordeal in person, not through a representative or
champion.[55]

The Peace of God shows how the ordeal could respond very well to
new needs and new institutions. Similarly, the new demands created
by the emergence of widespread heresy in the twelfth century could
also be met by the ordeal. Especially in the towns of northern France
and the Rhineland, trial by ordeal was commonly employed against
those accused of heresy. An early example was the trial in 1114 of two
brothers from Soissons, who were accused of being 'Manichees'.[56]
The years after 1140 saw trials of heretics by the ordeal in cities such as
Cologne, Arras, Ypres, Cambrai, and Strassburg. Both hot iron and
cold water were in use, the latter, as has been pointed out, being particularly well-suited to the needs of an orthodox crowd bent on a
lynching.

These trials were countenanced by some of the highest dignitaries
of the Church. 'The accusation against the heretics was made in St
Peter's cathedral', reports a German annalist of a trial in Cologne in
1143, 'and archbishop Arnold was present; many were captured and
chained and cleared themselves by the ordeal of water, others took to
guilty flight'.[57] Many other prelates participated in such trials. St Bernard was also willing to accept the verdict of the ordeal in heresy

[53] Bonnassie, *La Catalogne* (as in n. 45), pp. 728–9.
[54] MGH, *Const.* 1 (as in n. 12), no. 140 (1152).
[55] Ibid., no. 424 (Cologne, 1083); Browe, *De ordaliis*, 1, no. 77 n. (Bamberg, 1085).
[56] Guibert of Nogent, *De vita sua*, 3.17, ed. R. Labande (Paris, 1982), pp. 428–34.
[57] *Annales Brunwilarenses*, ed. G. H. Pertz, MGH, *SS* 16 (Hanover, 1859), p. 727.

cases.[58] At the Council of Rheims, assembled in 1157, at a time when clerical criticism of trial by ordeal was increasing in strength, it was nevertheless this form of proof that was prescribed for accusations of Catharism: 'If anyone is suspected of belonging to this filthy sect and wishes to prove his innocence, let him clear himself by the ordeal of hot iron. If he is proven guilty, let him be branded with hot iron, if innocent, he is to be regarded as Catholic'.[59] The prelates at the Council here approved a particularly ingenious procedure, in which the instrument of condemnation became also the instrument of punishment. Incidentally, this provision fits rather ill with Peter the Chanter's claim that Samson, archbishop of Rheims at this time, 'completely prohibited the employment of the ordeal of fire in his diocese'.[60] Perhaps heresy was so heinous and intractable an offence that Samson was willing to make an exception, or perhaps, more likely, Peter the Chanter was mythologizing.

At any rate, trial of heretics by the ordeal continued into the early decades of the thirteenth century. Innocent III wrote to the bishop of Strassburg in 1212, rebuking him for allowing suspected heretics to be tried in this way.[61] Up to the very eve of the condemnation of trial by ordeal at the Lateran Council of 1215, therefore, ecclesiastics of high position felt that the ordeal was a useful and appropriate process for dealing with heresy.

Exemptions

In general, then, the laws and legal prescriptions of the later eleventh and twelfth centuries indicate that trial by ordeal continued to be an important and frequent mode of proof in most regions, and for a wide variety of legal actions. There is, however, one apparent exception: the exemptions from trial by ordeal granted to certain privileged groups. Urban exemptions, in particular, have been seen as evidence that the ordeal was already in decline in the twelfth century, when the privileges were granted, before clerical opposition to the ordeal could have had much effect. The exact significance of these exemptions is therefore very important for the argument advanced here.

Exemptions were granted to three groups, clerics, Jews, and

---

[58] *Sermones super Cantica Canticorum*, serm. 66, cap. 12, in *Opera*, ed. J. Leclercq, C. H. Talbot and H. M. Rochais (8 vols., Rome, 1957-78), 2, p. 186.

[59] Mansi, 21, col. 843 (cap. 1).

[60] *Verbum abbreviatum*, 78, *PL* 205, col. 230.

[61] *Epistola*, 14. 138, *PL* 216, col. 502; Po. 4358.

townsmen, and the grounds for the exemption varied according to the group concerned. Clerical exemption, reflecting the clergy's post-Gregorian assertiveness, will be discussed in the next chapter. The exemption of the Jews had a fairly straightforward rationale. They were exempt from trial by ordeal for the very obvious reason that such a sacral proof, so deeply hedged about with Christian liturgy and ritual, a proof which normally required a vigil in church and prior communion, was so indelibly Christian that it would be not only unfair but also, more important in Christian eyes, virtually meaningless to apply it to non-Christians. This was recognized as early as the Carolingian period. Lewis the Pious ordered, 'We have received certain Jews under our protection . . . we do not wish them to be tried by the ordeal of fire or of hot water'.[62] The Jews of the Rhineland were likewise exempted from the ordeal by the German kings of the eleventh and twelfth centuries.[63] Jews were as keen to obtain exemption as kings were ready to grant it. The Jewish opinion of trial by ordeal was summed up by Ephraim ben Jacob, writing in the late twelfth century: 'such are the laws of the Christians who judge by ordeals–bad laws and customs by which one cannot live!'[64] There were occasions when Jews were forced to participate in trial by battle, as at Limoges in 994,[65] but such happenings occurred only when a local situation got out of hand. Generally, trial by ordeal was not applied to Jews. Thus there is no special significance to be attached to exemptions granted to Jews in the twelfth century.

Urban exemptions are a different matter. It has often been assumed that townsmen were universally hostile to the ordeal and that the rise of towns in the twelfth and thirteenth centuries was an important cause of the supposed decline of trial by ordeal in that period. In some ways this belief is simply a reflection of the common a priori assumption that the bourgeoisie is invariably progressive and rational. Hence it follows axiomatically that townsmen and traders would oppose a practice so patently primitive and irrational as the ordeal. 'The towns-

---

[62] Zeumer, *Formulae*, p. 310.

[63] MGH, *DD Heinrici IV*, ed. D. von Gladiss and Alfred Gawlik (Berlin, Weimar and Hanover, 1941-78), no. 411, pp. 543-7 (1090 for the Jews of Speyer); MGH, *DD Friderici I*, pt. 1, ed. Heinrich Appelt (Hanover, 1975), no. 166, pp. 284-6 (1157 for the Jews of Worms).

[64] *A Book of Historical Records*, tr. Jacob R. Marcus, *The Jew in the Medieval World* (Cincinnati, 1938, repr., New York, 1969), p. 128, from A. Neubauer and M. Stern, *Hebräische Berichte über die Judenverfolgungen während der Kreuzzüge* (Berlin, 1892), pp. 66-8.

[65] Eidelberg, 'Trial by Ordeal', p. 113.

man', wrote Hermann Nottarp, 'quickly loses his connection with Nature, which is the true foundation of the ordeal, and, from the thirteenth century, the money economy promoted rationalism'.[66] The same equation of the town, commercialism, rationalism, and hostility to the ordeal can be found, less quaintly expressed, in many other writers.

There is no question that several urban communities obtained exemption from the ordeal in the twelfth century. An early example is provided by the rights granted by Baldwin VII, count of Flanders, to the men of Ypres in 1116:

I have given this privilege to all the burgesses of Ypres, that they shall be exempt from the duel, ordeal of hot iron and of water within the jurisdiction of Ypres. If a charge is brought against any of them which used to be decided by duel or ordeal of hot iron or of water, he may clear himself by a fivefold oath with four selected relatives. . . . If he cannot make the oath . . . the count will have three pounds. . . .'[67]

Here compurgation replaced the ordeal. The main sufferer, presumably, would be the man of ill-repute, who could not raise compurgators. Prior to the change in the law he could have taken his chance in the lottery of the ordeal, but now this option was closed.

In considering these exemptions, we must try to form an idea of the number of such privileges granted in the period before the papal condemnation of the ordeal in 1215, and to assess their significance and meaning. Although there is always the chance that new documents will turn up, existing available evidence suggests that twelfth-century exemptions were not very numerous. Outside the Iberian peninsula, only a dozen or so were granted in the period 1050-1200 (see Map 3). The Ypres grant of 1116, cited above, was among the earliest. In 1159 the bishop of Passau granted exemption from the ordeal to the burgesses of his town of St Pölten.[68] By the later twelfth century, London, Oxford, and some other towns in England had the same privilege.[69] At

---

[66] *Gottesurteilstudien*, p. 192.

[67] Ed. Mina Martens in *Elenchus fontium urbanae*, 1, ed. C. van de Kieft and J. F. Niermeijer (Leiden, 1967), pp. 309-10. This document is to be distinguished from a much-disputed *Pax* supposedly sworn at Ypres in 1114; see Hoffmann, *Gottesfriede* (as in n. 49), pp. 152-3.

[68] Monumenta Boica 28 (Munich, 1829), pt. 2, n. 14, pp. 114-15; for discussion, see K. Helleiner, 'Österreichs ältestes Stadtrechtsprivileg', in *Beiträge zur Stadtgeschichtsforschung*, ed. Karl Gutkas (St Pölten, 1959), pp. 49-57.

[69] *Materials for the History of Thomas Becket*, ed. J. C. Robertson (7 vols., RS, 1875-85) 4, p. 148.

the founding of Riga in Livonia in 1200 four of the most valued rights were 'exemption from duel, toll, hot iron and wreck'.[70]

The grant to burgesses of exemption from trial by ordeal did not mean that ordeals ceased to take place in the town concerned. This was for two reasons. Firstly, the usual form of the privilege specified that burgesses could not be forced to undergo the ordeal. It remained, however, a form of proof to which they were permitted to appeal. In London, 'if a citizen is accused . . . he can make answer in his own city and be judged by his own laws; he need not clear himself by duel or by the ordeal of water or iron unless he freely chooses to do so'.[71] In Montpellier, a clause of the statutes of 1204 (from its phrasing possibly influenced by clerical opinion) reads, 'Duel and ordeal of hot iron or hot water, or other proofs condemned by the canons and the laws, are not to be allowed in the court of Montpellier, unless both parties agree'.[72] Such provisions obviously varied slightly according to local ordeal usage, the English case reflecting the situation in which a man was appealed or indicted on a criminal charge, the French case referring to disputes between parties, but, in both instances, trial by ordeal continued to be a valid form of proof in certain circumstances.

Secondly, the privilege was not granted to all inhabitants, or to anyone who might come before the local court, but to the citizens or burgesses alone. This explains why, despite the exemption of the citizens of London, trial by ordeal was a commonplace occurrence in London throughout the later twelfth and early thirteenth century. In 1214, for example, it was recorded that 'Ralf fitzHugh, imprisoned at Newgate and suspected of robbery, should clear himself by the water. He has cleared himself and abjured the realm. . . . Hereward of Shoreditch, imprisoned for the death of S. de L. . . . asserts his innocence. Therefore let him clear himself by the water. He has cleared himself and abjured the realm.'[73] Exemptions from the ordeal do not, therefore, either mean that ordeals stopped completely in the privileged community or even that no privileged citizen would ever undergo trial by ordeal. There are cases, too, where the ordeal was abolished in gen-

---

[70] Ed. B. Diestelkamp in *Elenchus* (as in n. 67), pp. 205–6: an admission by the bishop of Riga in 1225 that these rights had been conceded *a constitutione civitatis.*

[71] As in n. 69.

[72] A. Germain, *Histoire de la commune de Montpellier* (3 vols., 1851), I, p. 317, art. 63.

[73] *Curia Regis Rolls*, 7 (HMSO, 1935), p. 241.

eral, but restored for special cases. In Ypres, granted exemption in 1116, heretics were tried by the ordeal of hot iron in 1183.[74]

If we turn now to the question of the significance of these exemptions, the first thing that becomes clear is that the case for a correlation between commercial rationalism and the privilege of exemption is very implausible. A glance at the map is enough to raise doubts. It is true that a few exemptions were granted in great centres of commercialization, like Flanders, but many of the major cities continued to employ trial by fire and water. The customs of Milan of 1216, for example, specify the ordeal of cold water for those unable to undergo the duel.[75] On the other hand, a town like the Austrian St Pölten was not a major commercial centre. Most striking of all is the very large number of exemptions granted to urban and quasi-urban communities in Spain: around twenty are recorded for the period 1050-1200, twice the number for the rest of Europe.

Another important fact is that the number of exemptions granted from trial by fire and water, the unilateral ordeals, was tiny in comparison with the number of exemptions from the duel. While the evidence for a specific association between towns and hostility to the unilateral ordeal is weak or ambiguous, the desire of townsmen to have done with trial by battle is plain to see. It begs the question to presume that hostility to the duel necessarily implied hostility to trial by fire and water. There are cases, such as St Omer, where the duel was abolished in 1127, but the unilateral ordeals continued in use for such crimes as rustling and theft.[76] A community of self-governing merchants, officials, and artisans would be quite happy to continue applying trial by fire and water to suspected law-breakers in their own town, but would be less happy about becoming involved in the dangers of a duel or the expense of hiring a champion every time they made an accusation or raised a claim. In particular, they wished to ensure that outsiders could not challenge them to battle. This is the motive behind provisions such as the following, granted to Freiburg im Breisgau in 1120:

[74] *Continuatio Aquicinctina* to Sigebert of Gembloux, ed. L. C. Bethmann, MGH, *SS* 6 (Hanover, 1844), p. 421.

[75] *Liber consuetudinum Mediolani anni 1216*, caps. 31-3, ed. E. Besta and G. L. Barni (Milan, 1949).

[76] *Actes des comtes de Flandre, 1071-1128*, ed. Fernand Vercauteren (Brussels, 1938), no. 127, p. 296, for the abolition of 1127; G. Espinas (ed.), *Recueil des documents relatifs à l'histoire du droit municipal. Artois*, 3 (Paris, 1934), pp. 312 (cl. 23) and 315 (cl. 43), cf. p. 319, for a charter of 1164 prescribing unilateral ordeal.

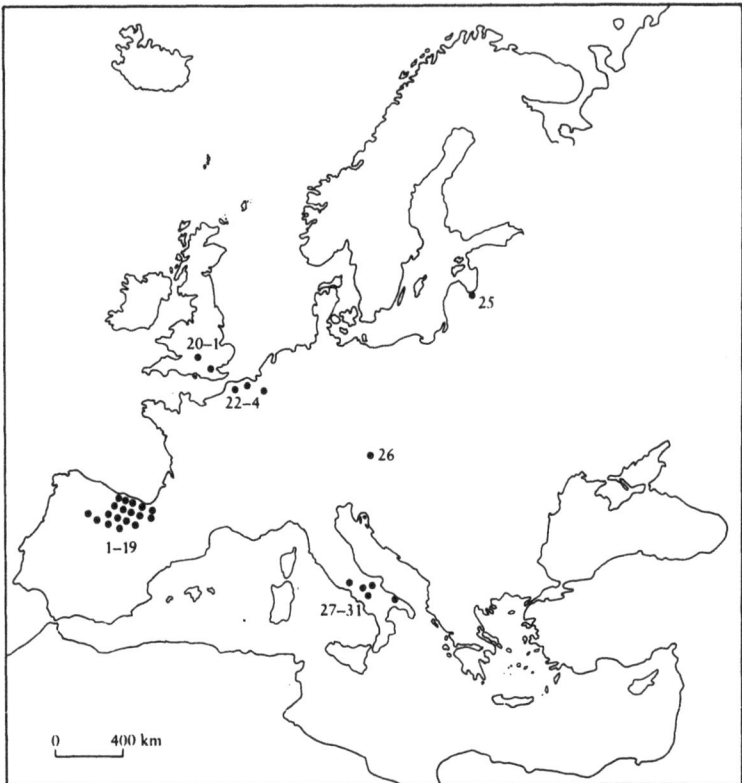

Map 3. Exemptions from Unilateral Ordeals granted to Lay Communities, 1050-12.

Key to Map 3

It would be impossible for a map of this kind to be complete. It is hoped, however, that further additions to it will not so alter the pattern that the argument advanced in the text becomes untenable.

1. Antoñana, 1182. G. Martínez Díez, *Alava medieval* (2 vols., Vitoria, 1974), 1, p. 220.
2. Asín,1132. J. M. Lacarra de Miguel and A. J. Martín Duque, *Fueros de Navarra* (Pamplona, 1969), 1.2.6, p. 124.
3. Bernedo, 1182. Martínez Díez, *Alava*, 1, p. 233.
4. Caparroso, 1102. A. Ubieto Arteta, *Colección diplomática de Pedro I de Aragon y Navarra* (Saragossa, 1951), no. 114, p. 370.

Key to Map 3 (*cont.*)

5. Frias, 1190-1214, J. Gonzalez, *El reino de Castilla en la epoca de Alfonso VIII* (3 vols., Madrid, 1960), 3, no. 950, pp. 641-2.
6. Labraza, 1196. Martínez Díez, *Alava*, 1, p. 240.
7. Laguardia, 1164. Martínez Díez, *Alava*, 1, p. 220.
8. Lapuebla de Arganzon, 1191. Martínez Díez, *Alava*, 1, p. 237.
9. Lerida, 1196. F. Valls-Taberner, 'Les fonts documentals de les "Consuetudines Ilerdenses" ', *Estudis Universitaris Catalans*, 11 (1926), p. 150.
10. Lerma, 1148. Alfonso Andrés, 'Apuntes para la historia de Lerma', *Boletín de la Real Academia de la Historia*, 67 (1915), p. 288.
11. Logroño, 1095. *Fuero de Logroño*, ed. T. Moreno Garbaya, *Apuntes históricos de Logroño* (Logroño, 1943), pp. 42-9, at p. 44.
12. Medina de Pomar, 1181. Gonzalez, *Alfonso VIII*, 3, no. 951, p. 646.
13. Miranda de Ebro, 1099.* *Fuero de Miranda de Ebro*, ed. F. Cantera (Madrid, 1945), p. 47.
14. Palenzuela, 1074.* L. Serrano (ed.), *Colección diplomática de San Salvador de El Moral* (Valladolid, 1906), no. 2, p. 26.
15. S. Domingo de Silos, 1135. M. Ferotin, *Recueil des chartes de l'abbaye de Silos* (Paris, 1897), no. 44, p. 64.
16. Sahagún, pre-1135. Ibid.
17. Santacara, 1102. Ubieto Arteta, *Pedro I*, no. 115, p. 373.
18. Tafalla, 1157.* *Fuero de Tafalla*, ed. Jose M. Lacarra, *Anuario de historia del derecho español*, 10 (1933), pp. 262-4.
19. Vitoria, 1181. Martínez Díez, *Alava*, 1, p. 225.
20. London, pre-*c*.1175. *Materials for the History of Thomas Becket*, ed. J. C. Robertson (7 vols., RS, 1875-85), 4, p. 148.
21. Oxford, pre-*c*.1175. Ibid.
22. Grammont, attrib. 1070, prob. *c*. 1190. *Elenchus fontium urbanae*, 1, ed. C. van de Kieft and J.F. Niermeijer (Leiden, 1967), p. 302.
23. Liège, 1198. J. J. Raikem and M. L. Polain, *Coutumes du pays de Liège*, 1 (Brussels, 1870), pp. 362-6.
24. Ypres, 1116. *Elenchus*, 1, pp. 309-10.
25. Riga, 1200. *Elenchus*, 1, pp. 205-6.
26. St Pölten, 1159. *Monumenta Boica* 28 (Munich, 1829), pt. 2, n. 14, pp. 114-15
27. Sant'Angelo in Theodice, 1188-1215. Luigi Tosti, *Storia della Badia di Monte-Cassino* (3 vols., Naples, 1842-3), 2, pp. 201-3.
28. Mercato San Severino, 1116. *Regii Neapolitani archivi monumenta edita ac illustrata* (6 vols., Naples, 1845-61), 6, no. 564, pp. 17-19.
29. Montecalvo, 1190. G. Tria, *Memorie storiche . . . di Larino* (Rome, 1744), p. 475.
30. Bari, 1132. *Codice diplomatico Barese*, 5, ed. F. Nitti di Vito (Bari, 1902), p. 138.
31. Troia, 1127. L. Zdekauer, 'Le franchigie concesse da Onorio II alla città di Troia (1127)', *Rivista Italiana per le Scienze Giuridiche*, 25 (1898), pp. 254-6.

* Known only in later confirmations.

'No outsider will be able to fight a duel with a burgess without the burgesses' consent'.[77]

Exemptions from trial by ordeal are, therefore, neither very numerous nor closely tied to commercialism. The real significance of the scattered urban exemptions must be looked for elsewhere.

One of the earliest Spanish charters granting exemption is that issued by Alfonso VI of Castile and León for the *populatores* (the new settlers) of Logroño in 1095, which stated, 'They shall be judicially exempt from the duel, the hot iron, hot water and inquest (*pesquisa*)'.[78] If we look at the other provisions of the charter to see the context of this exemption, several points stand out. The community is clearly not highly urbanized. The inhabitants have the right to graze animals and cultivate wasteland within the town boundaries, they have their gardens and vineyards, and the king keeps an oven in the town where all bread must be baked. This is a privileged agricultural community rather than an urban commune. Again, the main purpose of most of the provisions is the protection of the inhabitants against force and injustice from above: 'no bailiff may enter their houses to take anything by force . . . they shall remain free in perpetuity'. The restrictions on the exactions and powers of the local lord and judges are in a similar spirit. This *fuero*, or charter of liberties, like the hundreds of other urban and rural charters of liberties that were granted in this period, represents the outcome of bargaining between a lord and a new, or nascent, community. The members of such communities sought simple and important rights: personal freedom; if they were traders, commercial privileges and monopolies; guarantees about inheritance; fixed and low rent; and the easing of some onerous seigneurial taxes and powers. Exemption from the ordeal is best seen as an instance of this last category. The right to hold ordeals was a right appurtenant to lordship and, like other such rights, could be given away or relaxed for favoured recipients.[79] The ordeal was an unpleas-

---

[77] Ed. B. Diestelkamp, in *Elenchus* (as in n. 67), pp. 91-2.

[78] *Fuero de Logroño*, ed. T. Moreno Garbaya, *Apuntes históricos de Logroño* (Logroño, 1943), pp. 42-9.

[79] Compare the remarks of G. Martínez Díez, *Alava medieval* (2 vols., Vitoria, 1974), 1, pp. 137-8, summarizing the detailed study of Ramos Loscertales, 'El derecho de los francos de Logroño en 1095', *Berceo*, 2 (1947), pp. 347-77: 'This Frankish law was not a complete judicial ordinance, but a series of fundamental privileges whose essence consisted in the freeing of the persons and goods of the settlers from all seigniorial superiority.'

ant and frightening form of proof which privileged groups would evade if they could. The settlers of Logroño, coming from France and Spain to a newly-conquered border town, had something to offer Alfonso VI. He was willing to concede some of his rights in return. From Logroño, this particular charter of liberties was to diffuse widely to many of the military settlements of twelfth- and thirteenth-century Spain.[80] We do not have here a wave of rationalizing urbanism, but a specific privilege for new settlers in an empty land.

The *fuero* of Logroño became the model for many town privileges in the surrounding area. The upper Ebro valley had, as a result, more numerous exemptions from the ordeal than all the rest of Europe. The explanation lies in the history of the legal privileges of the region, not in the level of its urbanization. Other towns in Spain, those, for example, that were granted the *fuero* of Cuenca-Teruel rather than that of Logroño, continued to employ the ordeal. Other, more urbanized, centres in other parts of Europe also did so. In the first decade of the thirteenth century the ordeal was in use in Milan but not in the privileged community of Santo Domingo de la Calzada in the Rioja. The difference cannot be explained by relative levels of urbanization.

It is also significant that the exemptions granted to lay communities in the twelfth century often specified not only freedom from the ordeal but also freedom from inquest. The Spanish *fueros*, like that of Logroño, frequently granted immunity from 'duel, hot iron, hot water and inquest'. The inquest to which they refer is the *pesquisa*, a form of inquisitorial prosecution of crime initiated by the king or his representative.[81] Clearly, the common motive for townsmen seeking exemption from the ordeal and from *pesquisa* was that both exemptions enhanced the burgesses' juridical autonomy and made their customary proof less onerous. The fact that one form of proof might be classified as 'irrational' and the other as 'rational' was completely irrelevant. The townsmen of Spain, like their contemporaries in precociously urbanized Ghent and Bruges,[82] sought to escape the pressure of externally organized inquests because they aimed at corporate privilege. Sometimes, though not very often, they sought exemption from the ordeal for the same reason.

[80] Narcisco Hergueta, 'El Fuero de Logroño. Su extensión á otras poplaciones', *Boletín de la Real Academia de la Historia*, 50 (1907), pp. 321-2.
[81] Evelyn Procter, 'The Judicial use of *Pesquisa* in Leon and Castille 1157-1369', *English Historical Review*, suppl. 2 (1966).
[82] R. C. van Caenegem, in *La Preuve*, pp. 396-7.

The existence of some exemptions from the ordeal in the twelfth century does not, therefore, suggest that townsmen experienced 'a general crisis of faith in its efficiency',[83] but rather that, where they could, and when they did not think the dangers of abandoning the ordeal outweighed the advantages, they sought to avoid this particularly rigorous form of trial and undergo, in its place, the lesser demands of compurgation. Twelfth-century exemptions testify to the fact that it was a privilege not to be subject to the ordeal; they do not testify to a growing disillusion with the results of the ordeal. The urban privileges of this period are no more evidence for a particularly critical and rational spirit on the part of twelfth-century townsmen than the fourteenth-century chrysobulls granting exemption to the dependants of remote Balkan monasteries argue that Serbian monks and peasants were especially critical and rational.[84] Both point rather to a demand for exemptions from heavy burdens and a willingness of lords to concede them. We are in the world of negotiated favours, not that of critical disillusion. A few exemptions from the ordeal in the twelfth century no more signify a general decline in the practice or an efflorescence of scepticism than the numerous fiscal exemptions granted to townsmen in this same period imply a general crisis of faith in taxation.

A survey of twelfth-century legal material does not, therefore, suggest a decline in the practice of the ordeal. As long as we bear in mind the limitations that had always existed on the employment of the ordeal, then the twelfth century does not show any conclusive evidence for a 'withering'. Jews were exempt, but Jews had always been exempt. Some town laws excluded ordeals, but, in general, the growth of towns in the twelfth century does not seem at all significant in the abandonment of the ordeal. With this one proviso, the ordeals of fire and water seem to have had as much life as ever in the laws of the twelfth century.

The Case of England

It is an extremely difficult matter to explore beyond the laws into actual judicial practice. There are numerous references to the ordeal being used in cases, but there is no sure way of judging the complex relationship between the number of cases recorded in, say, the ele-

---

[83] Idem. *The Birth of the English Common Law* (Cambridge, 1973), p. 68.

[84] D. Stojcevič in *La Preuve*, pp. 656-61, citing privileges for St George, Skoplje (1300), Chilander (1328), and St Michael Archangel (1348).

venth century and the number recorded in the twelfth, given the absolute impossibility of knowing how much more likely accounts of the
twelfth century are to survive. The only statistical evidence on the
subject of the ordeal is the famous register of Varad in Hungary (modern Oradea in Rumania).[85] Here a record was kept of ordeals administered. Over the period 1208 to 1235 a total of 348 ordeals are recorded;
many other cases were abandoned or reached agreement before the
iron was carried.[86] Although it extends from 1208 to 1235, the register
only has information for fourteen of the years in that period–and is not
complete even for those years. 348 ordeals over 14 years averages 25 or
so a year. This is for one Hungarian church. We know that at least half
a dozen other Hungarian churches had the right to hold ordeals. It is
impossible to know whether this is a high figure or a low figure; without any comparative statistics, the Varad register is virtually worthless
as a tool for deciding the trend in ordeals (although see below). It can
be interpreted as a sign of the flourishing of the ordeal, the decline of
the ordeal, or even relegated to irrelevance because it comes from the
peculiar environment of Hungary.[87]

In the absence of reliable, statistical evidence, one can only proceed
on the basis of careful interpretation and examination of non-statisti-
cal evidence. This consideration of the social explanation of the
demise of the ordeal will conclude by analysing such evidence in
England in the twelfth and thirteenth centuries. England is distinctive
in relation to the ordeals of fire and water, since it appears that they
were almost never employed in disputes concerning property, or 'civil
cases' as they might be called. Before the Conquest testimony and the
oath, after the Conquest testimony, the oath, and the duel must have
determined such cases. The exceptions to this rule, occasions when
the ordeal was offered in a property dispute, are rare in the extreme.[88]

If we compare the place of the ordeals of fire and water in England

[85] *Regestrum Varadinense*; discussed by Zajtay, 'Le Registre de Varad'.

[86] 348 is the number of individuals who bore the iron. Sometimes several individuals
bore the iron on the same charge and sometimes the ordeal was ordered but did not take
place. This explains the discrepancy between the figures cited here and those given by
Zajtay, 'Le Registre de Varad', p. 541, followed by Brown, 'Society and the Supernatural', pp. 137 and 139 (repr. pp. 310 and 314), or those used by van Caenegem, *La
Preuve*, pp. 699-700. Hyams, 'Trial by Ordeal', p. 105 n. 66, is doubtful about the useful-
ness of such statistics.

[87] e.g. Brown, 'Society and the Supernatural' (repr. only), p. 324 n.: 'the crimes tested
by the ordeal at Varad do seem to reveal a more "sleepy" economy than that of those
areas of Europe where the ordeal came to be abandoned.'

[88] Most are in Domesday Book and are collected by Melville M. Bigelow, *Placita
Anglo-Normannica* (Boston, 1879), pp. 36, 38, 40-3, 61, 304-6.

in the tenth century with their place in the twelfth, the strongest impression is continuity. The treatise called Glanvill, written around 1188, has a succinct discussion of criminal cases which the king's justices might encounter: treason, concealment of treasure trove, homicide, arson, robbery, rape, and falsifying. Two procedures are envisaged: the first in which no specific accuser appears, but the case rests upon public notoriety; the second in which a specific accuser appeals the accused. In the latter case the issue is normally decided by battle. The former case, accusation by public notoriety, is dealt with in the following way: the accused is either imprisoned or finds sureties, 'then the truth of the matter shall be investigated by many and varied inquests and interrogations before the justices, and arrived at by considering the probable facts and possible conjectures both for and against the accused, who must as a result be either absolved or made to purge himself by the ordeal'.[89] The most striking contrast with the tenth or eleventh century is the disappearance of the oath from criminal process.[90] Its only role, as described in Glanvill, is to ensure that the accuser pursues his charge. Proof is entirely through inquisition, ordeal, or battle.

This change probably did not, however, result in any comparable change in the role of the ordeal. The ordeal is still only used in the absence of a specific accuser against men who are ill-famed, when clear evidence is lacking. These are exactly the circumstances in which we would anticipate the employment of the ordeal. We are not witnessing a shrinkage in the area where the ordeal would be applied. It is possible that, on the contrary, the eclipse of the exculpatory oath might have made the ordeal more common in the England of Henry II than in the England of Edgar or Canute. The basic circumstances in which recourse was had to the ordeal, however, were the same. Lack of evidence and bad reputation combined to lead a man to the ordeal. In cases of concealment of treasure trove, for example, the ordeal was employed only if, although a specific accuser was lacking, 'it has previously been proved against, or admitted by, him in court that metal of some other kind was found and recovered in the place in question'.[91] The ordeal existed in that narrow place where suspicion was considerable but guilt was not unquestionable.

[89] Bk. 14, *The Treatise on the Laws and Customs of England commonly called Glanvill*, ed. G. D. Hall (London, etc., 1965), pp. 171-7, quotation at p. 171.
[90] Though it continued into the thirteenth century in petty criminal jurisdictions.
[91] *Glanvill* (as in n. 89), p. 173.

The use of the ordeal in twelfth-century England is reflected in the law books, from the *Leges Henrici primi*[92] of the first decades, to Glanvill in the last, in occasional narratives of cases, in grants of the right to hold ordeals, and in the liturgical rituals for the ordeal which were copied throughout this period. In the reign of Henry II a new type of source becomes important: the official records of the royal government, both financial and legal. In the half-century or so between the Assize of Clarendon in 1166 and Magna Carta, the Pipe Rolls and plea rolls of the royal government give some information, at last, on the regular application of the ordeal.

1166 is a good starting point, for that year saw, in the Assize of Clarendon, the initiation of a major royal campaign against crime. Those who were suspected of criminal offences were to be brought to the ordeal. The results are clearly visible in the Pipe Roll for 12 Henry II (1165-6).[93] Here the accounts for each shire include an entry for the chattels of 'fugitives and those who failed in the judgement of water'. There is, of course, no way of knowing how many fled and how many failed. It is possible to assert, however, that in 1166 around 600 men either went to the ordeal and were convicted, or were so unnerved by the prospect that they went into hiding or on the run. This does not show the ordeal in a therapeutic role, unless a purgative is therapeutic, but it does suggest that the ordeal was, still in the 1160s, a forceful instrument in active use. The Pipe Roll for 22 Henry II (1175-6) shows a similar burst of activity after the Assize of Northampton.[94]

The records of other years do not portray activity on such a grand scale. They do, however, give plenty of evidence of the routine employment of the ordeal. The Pipe Roll for 13 Henry II (1166-7), for example, contains references to the cost of holding five ordeals in London or Middlesex and a fine of ten marks imposed on a man who had conducted an ordeal without a royal officer being present.[95] Such items are scattered throughout the Pipe Rolls–payments for digging the ordeal pit, payment for the officiating priest, continuing renders of account of 'the chattels of those who failed at the water', and occasional payments 'to be quit of the ordeal'.[96]

[92] 9.6, 18.1, 45.1a, 49.6, 62.1, 64.1, 65.3-5, 67.1b, 87.6, 89.1a, ed. L. J. Downer (Oxford, 1972), pp. 107, 120, 154, 164, 200, 202-4, 208, 212, 266, 278.
[93] (Pipe Roll Soc. 9, 1888), *passim*.
[94] (Pipe Roll Soc. 25, 1904), *passim*. Around 500 names are listed.
[95] (Pipe Roll Soc. 11, 1889), pp. 1 and 91.
[96] e.g. *Pipe Roll 12 Henry II* (Pipe Roll Soc. 9, 1888), pp. 18 and 72; *Pipe Roll 14 Henry II*

These casual references can be supplemented by those in the judicial records. These start to be useful rather later than the Exchequer accounts, but they do illuminate the reigns of Richard I and John. Between 1194, the date of the earliest surviving plea roll, and 1214, the last ones relevant for the ordeal, some 110 cases involving the ordeal are mentioned in the fragmentary extant evidence.[97] The procedures applied seem to be, in their general outlines, those described by Glanvill. A variety of criminal charges might lead to the ordeal. In the Pleas of the Crown heard at Launceston in 1201, for example, 15 cases (involving 27 individuals) went to the ordeal–5 of homicide, 3 each of assault, burglary, and receiving an outlaw, and one of arson. Both water and iron were used, water being much more common.[98] This is interesting in the light of Glanvill's remark that iron is the ordeal appropriate for the free man, water for the villein.[99] There also seems to have been a tendency for women to be sent to the iron.

Compared with the overall total of cases heard at Launceston, the number that involved the ordeal is small–15 out of 170. But this simple arithmetical fact is misleading. The number of cases that went to the ordeal is more impressive when we compare it, not with the total of cases recorded but with the total of those that went to trial. Many charges, of course, would not have led to the ordeal in any case–selling wine 'contrary to the assize', irregular presentments, and other minor affairs. Many of the entries, too, are inconclusive, leaving us no idea how things turned out. The vast majority of serious cases, however, result not in judgement, but in flight. The biggest problem of criminal law enforcement in the Middle Ages was not which mode of proof to use, but how to get the accused to court.

A case that occurred in Lincolnshire in 1202 may illustrate the

---

(Pipe Roll Soc. 12, 1890), pp. 2, 48, 90, 188, 198; *Pipe Roll 15 Henry II* (Pipe Roll Soc. 13, 1890), p. 24; *Pipe Roll 18 Henry II* (Pipe Roll Soc. 18, 1894), p. 10; *Pipe Roll 23 Henry II* (Pipe Roll Soc. 26, 1905), p. 114.

[97] Virtually all these rolls are in print, in *Rotuli curiae regis*, ed. F. Palgrave (2 vols., Record Commission, 1835), the *Curia Regis Rolls* 1–7 (HMSO, 1922-35) or in the publications of the Pipe Roll Society, the Selden Society or local record societies. Convenient lists can be found in the *Memoranda Roll 10 John*, ed. R. Allen Brown (Pipe Roll Soc., NS 31, 1955), pp. 95-6, and *The 1235 Surrey Eyre*, 1, ed. C. A. F. Meekings (Surrey Record Soc. 31, 1979), pp. 156-61.

[98] D. M. Stenton (ed.), *Pleas before the King or his Justices 1198-1202* (4 vols., Selden Soc. 67-8, 83-4 for 1948-9 and 1966-7), 2 (= 68), pp. 51-83 *passim*, 177-8.

[99] *Glanvill* (as in n. 89), bk. 14.1, ed. cit., p. 173.

point.[100] Eight men were accused of a burglary. One of them sought sanctuary and eventually abjured the realm. One of them fled. Three managed to obtain pledges, thus enjoying a form of bail, but they did not turn up at court for the hearing. One turned up and was not suspected by the jury, and so simply had to find pledges for his good behaviour. The two last turned up and were suspected by the jury. One of these was a clerk and went to Court Christian. This process of elimination thus left one man who turned up, was suspected, and had to go to the ordeal of water. His accomplices may have been wiser in their flight; he failed at the ordeal. Here within the confines of a single offence, we see the forces at work that limited the sphere of the ordeal: flight, satisfactory reputation, special status. These forces were not new and such a circumscription of the ordeal was part of its very nature. The custom had never been intended as anything but a last resort.

It would be capricious to leave the subject of the role of the ordeal in English justice in the twelfth and early thirteenth century without giving some consideration to an argument often raised about the Assizes of Henry II. The Assizes of Clarendon and Northampton,[101] whose criminal provisions created such a flurry of judicial activity in 1166 and 1176, enact as follows: anyone accused of murder, robbery, or other serious crimes by a jury of twelve lawful men of the hundred, and by the oath of four men from each vill in the hundred, should go to the ordeal of cold water; if they failed, they would be mutilated; if they were cleared, they could find pledges 'unless they are accused of murder or some other foul felony by the commune of the county and the law-worthy knights of the country; if they are accused in this way, even if they are cleared by the ordeal of water, nevertheless they must quit the realm within forty days, taking their chattels with them'.[102]

This provision has universally been interpreted as a sign of Henry II's lack of faith in the ordeal. If being cleared at the ordeal could not free a man from some punishment, then, it is argued, the

---

[100] D. M. Stenton (ed.), *The Earliest Lincolnshire Assize Rolls* (Lincolnshire Record Soc. 22, 1926), p. 104.

[101] Roger of Howden, *Chronica*, ed. W. Stubbs (4 vols., RS, 1868-71), 2, pp. cii-cv, 89-91, 248-52; *Gesta regis Henrici secundi Benedicti abbatis*, ed. W. Stubbs (2 vols., RS, 1867), 1, pp. 108-11; W. Stubbs (ed.), *Select Charters* (9th edn., rev. H. W. C. Davis, Oxford, 1913), pp. 170-3 and 179-81. For a discussion of the texts, see J. C. Holt, 'The Assizes of Henry II: The Texts', *The Study of Medieval Records*, ed. D. A. Bullough and R. L. Storey (Oxford, 1971), pp. 85-106.

[102] Assize of Northampton, cap. 1.

legislator clearly did not take the verdict of the ordeal seriously. The preliminary accusation by the jury of presentment mattered more.[103] This interpretation rests on a misconception about the ordeal. The fact that the ordeal was a judgement of God and the liturgical solemnity around it have encouraged modern commentators to see in the practice something more monolithic and absolute than in fact it was. The tendency has been to argue that either the ordeal was God's incontrovertible declaration on a man's guilt or innocence, or it was nothing. Any doubts about individual verdicts are then ascribed to a growing scepticism about the ordeal. This is simplistic. The ordeal, as has been stressed, was one of a range of judicial procedures, and it formed part of an interlocking system. These other procedures influenced the way the ordeal itself was regarded.

The so-called Franco-Chamavian law, the law of those Franks whose lands bordered Frisia and Saxony, was probably put into writing in 802. In it we read, 'If a thief is proved guilty of seven thefts, let him go to the ordeal. If he is burnt, let them deliver him for execution. If he is not burned after he has gone to the ordeal, then his lord may go surety for him and make amends on his behalf and free him from death.'[104] The similarities with the Assize of Clarendon are clear. A man whose reputation is completely besmirched and who has been accused on very powerful grounds, must go to the ordeal. Failure means mutilation or death. But success at the ordeal does not enable him to leave the court without a stain on his character. His character is already stained. Careful provision has to be made for him–sureties and the restitution of stolen property. This only makes sense. Other factors–the nature of the accusation, the man's status–would be weighed alongside the verdict of the ordeal. This may not be very pleasing to those who would see the ordeal as a dramatic transfer of events on to a completely different level, the level of the supernatural, but it seems to have been how the system worked.

A final example from Anglo-Saxon law will illustrate the point. In Athelstan's second code the penalty for killing a man through witch-craft was death. However, if the accused made a formal denial, he was

---

[103] The following remark can stand for many: 'Clearly, however, little faith was put in these ancient modes of proof, for it was enacted . . . that if the accused were men of very bad reputation, even if they succeeded in the ordeal, they must leave the country and be accounted outlaws', A. L. Poole, *From Domesday Book to Magna Carta* (2nd edn., Oxford, 1955), p. 402.

[104] *Lex Francorum Chamavorum*, c. 48, ed. Karl August Eckhardt, *Lex Ribuaria II. Text und Lex Francorum Chamavorum* (Hanover, 1966), p. 94.

sent to the triple ordeal; if he failed at the ordeal, he was imprisoned for 120 days; then his kinsman could bail him out, if he paid a large fine to the king and the wergild to the victim's family.[105] The difference between death, on the one hand, and a short imprisonment and financial penalties, on the other, was made by the formal denial. This weighed heavily. Failure at the ordeal was clearly not deemed equivalent to a confession. This law shows, just as clearly as the Franco-Chamavian and the Assize of Clarendon, though in a rather different way, that the verdict of the ordeal need not be absolute. If a careful consideration of other factors is a sign of scepticism about the ordeal, then that scepticism was at work in the ninth and tenth centuries as well as the twelfth.

It seems, then, that, in the English royal justice of the Angevin period, ordeals continued to play the role they had always played in English law. Rather than there being an innate antagonism between the effective exercise of royal power and the use of ordeals, ordeals could be a means of exercising that power. It is an error to associate the ordeal with weak central authority. Like feudalism, the ordeal was compatible both with political decentralization and with strong kingship. No less an authority than Maitland was willing to describe the ordeal as 'flourishing' in John's reign.[106]

The balance of the evidence is thus overwhelmingly against any interpretation of the decline of the ordeal based on a decline in its use in the twelfth century. The impetus given to it by the expansion of Christendom, the Peace movement, and the campaign against heresy has been described. Evidence that has been interpreted as showing the decline of the ordeal in the twelfth century simply shows time-honoured limitations on its use. In judicially precocious England, with its powerful royal dynasty, the ordeal flourished. From Jerusalem to Scotland, from Portugal to Novgorod, in the wastes of Livonia, and in the great cities of Italy, the twelfth century was fully part of the age of the ordeal.

---

[105] II Aethelstan 6.1, ed. Liebermann, *Gesetze*, 1, pp. 152-5.

[106] Frederick Pollock and Frederic W. Maitland, *The History of Engish Law before the time of Edward I* (2 vols., 2nd edn., reissued with an intro. by S. C. Milsom, Cambridge, 1968), 2, p. 599.

5

The End of the Ordeal: Explanations in Terms of Belief

THERE is, then, no good evidence for a crisis in the social function of the ordeal. There was, however, a crisis of the ordeal in the twelfth century. But it did not consist in the dissatisfaction of lay communities, who were prepared to abandon the ordeal; it consisted in a growing unease, in some ecclesiastical circles, about whether it was right to use the ordeal. Belief in 'a withering of the ordeal' in the twelfth century is a presupposition not based on the evidence; a crisis in clerical confidence, however, needs no argument—the evidence is everywhere. Naturally, our convictions about the nature of the decline of the ordeal shape, and are shaped, by our judgements on its chronology. For Paul Hyams and others who see the ruling of 1215 as a belated rubber-stamping by ineffective intellectuals, then the ordeal must have already declined over the course of the twelfth century. If we see the ordeal as flourishng in 1200, then the date of 1215 becomes more significant. The emphasis is thrown off the general social changes which Europe underwent in the high Middle Ages and onto the doubts and debates of an intellectual élite. These issues must become our central focus.

Critics of the Ordeal

A serious consideration of the role of doubt and criticism in the abandonment of the ordeal must grapple with two questions. We must ask, firstly, what kinds of criticism were voiced but also, secondly, why these criticisms become more compelling over the period, say, 1050–1215. For, as we shall see, doubts about the ordeal were expressed from a very early stage in its history, but with little effect. If we wish to argue that clerical opinions were decisive in the abandonment of the ordeal, we must try to show why clerical opinion mattered so much in the twelfth and thirteenth centuries.

It is clear that criticism of, and doubts about, the ordeal boil down to two central concerns: whether ordeals give a just result, and whether they are licit. These issues are related, of course—one strand, doubt about the legitimacy of ordeals, interweaving with the other, scepticism about their results, in a complex way—but for purposes of analysis they can be disentangled. Naturally, a thinker who did not believe that ordeals were licit could not maintain that God was revealing just judgements by their means. But there is, in practice, a distinction between those critics who thought the ordeal failed to meet certain general and theoretical standards which all licit practices should attain, and those who baulked at the outcome of specific trials.

Even in the protohistorical period, 500–800, there is evidence of doubt and wariness. In the first ever recorded case of the ordeal of the cauldron, for example, the clash between the Arian and the Catholic recorded by Gregory of Tours, the Catholic whose zeal had cooled while awaiting the trial 'spread his arm with oil and covered it with ointment' as a preparation for the test. When the Arian saw this he cried, 'You have thought to protect yourself by magic and by using ointment—the trial is invalid'.[1] Concern that the results of the ordeal could be interfered with through magic was recurrent. Laws directed against the abuse of chrism for this purpose,[2] the stripping of the proband of amulets, the repeated exorcisms in the rituals, all point to elementary precautions against magical or diabolical interference. The belief had a long life. In the fifteenth-century witch-hunting guide, the *Malleus Maleficiarum*, the authors suggested that witches should be offered the chance of ordeal; since they believe that the devil will help them in it, they will agree—and this will prove their guilt.[3] However, despite its recurrence, concern over such interference in the results of the ordeal was never a central objection, and certainly did not contribute significantly to the twelfth-century crisis in confidence.

The case recorded by Gregory of Tours is not the only early example of doubts about the absolute dependability of the results of

---

[1] *De gloria martyrum*, cap. 80, ed. Bruno Kisch, MGH, *Scriptores rerum Merovingicarum*, 1 (Hanover, 1885), pp. 542-3.

[2] e.g. MGH, *Capit.* 1. ed. Alfred Boretius (Hanover, 1883), p. 149; Benedictus Levita, *Capitularum collectio*, 1.104, *PL* 97, col. 714; *Liber Papiensis*, ed. A. Boretius, MGH, *LL* 4 (Hanover, 1868), p. 498; Regino of Prüm, *De ecclesiasticis disciplinis et religione christiana*, 1.72-3, *PL* 132, col. 206; Burchard of Worms, *Decretum*, 4.80, 19.5, *PL* 140, cols. 741, 973; Ivo of Chartres, *Decretum*, 1.274, *PL* 161, col. 123.

[3] Henricus Institoris and Jakob Sprenger, *Malleus Maleficiarum*, 3.17. The work went through dozens of editions between 1486 and 1669.

the ordeal. Early in the eighth century, in the context not of the ordeals of fire and water but of the duel, the Lombard King Liudprand observed 'we are uncertain about the ordeal (*incerti sumus de iudicio dei*) and we have heard of many men who have lost their case through the duel unjustly'.[4] Such early indications of scepticism are an important warning against constructing too uniform and homogeneous a picture of the mental world of the early Middle Ages. There was always doubt and dispute.

The beginnings of serious and developed argumentation against ordeals belongs, however, to the ninth century, the same period that saw their first efflorescence. The coincidence is not surprising; criticism will address itself to matters of central and increasing importance. In the eleventh century, for example, King Robert of France expressed opposition to the eucharistic ordeal which he described as 'daily growing in favour'.[5] Just so, in the ninth century, contemporary critics were moved to express their opinions by the efflorescence of the ordeals of fire and water.

The earliest and fullest Carolingian critic was Agobard, archbishop of Lyons (816-40), who had a decisive position on the subject: 'The faithful should not believe that almighty God wishes to reveal men's secrets in the present life through hot water or iron'.[6] Agobard's arguments were developed in his *Liber contra iudicium dei*. The heart of this work is an attack on the duel, and many of the arguments are relevant only to this variant of the ordeal, but there are objections to the ordeals of fire and water too. His basic premiss was that, although Christians should avoid litigiousness, judges and instruments of justice are necessary and that wise judgement, testimony, and the oath are sufficient for reaching judicial verdicts. Ordeals are not, therefore, necessary; but neither are they right. The attack on the legitimacy of the ordeal in the *Liber contra iudicium dei* involves two arguments.

The first is that the ordeal was not authoritatively instituted. It is 'an invention of men' a 'proof which God never ordered and never wished and which, as can be demonstrated, was not introduced through the example of the saints or any of the faithful'.[7] The illicit nature of the

---

[4] *Leges Langobardorum, Liutprandi leges, Anni XIX*, cap. 118 (II), ed. Franz Beyerle (2nd edn., Witzenhausen, 1962), pp. 155-6.

[5] Helgaud, *Epitoma vitae Roberti regis, PL* 141, cols. 911-12, *Recueils des historiens des Gaules et de la France*, 10 (Paris, 1760), p. 100.

[6] *Liber adversus legem Gundobadi*, 9, ed. cit., p. 25. For general discussion of Agobard's critique, see Grelewski, *La Réaction*, Leitmaier, *Die Kirche und die Gottesurteile*.

[7] *Liber contra iudicium dei*, cap. 2, ed. cit., p. 32.

ordeal is, in Agobard's view, connected with its superfluousness. If God had ordained the ordeal 'then he would not have ordered judges and magistrates to be established in every city, those who deny a charge to be convicted by witnesses or, in the absence of witnesses, the case to be brought to an end by an oath . . .'[8] The ordeal was thus a superfluous invention.

The second main argument Agobard advanced against the legitimacy of the ordeal was based on the inscrutability of God's judgement. He believed, of course, that God intervenes in human affairs, but he did not think this could be harnessed to predictable judicial process. 'God's judgements are secret and impenetrable', he wrote. Again his main target is the duel: 'If all future events are uncertain, what astonishing fatuousness it is to try to make uncertain things certain through detestable combats'.[9] The point, although directed against the duel, could equally well be raised against any kind of ordeal. To seek certainty on uncertain events, even if they are past events, is deemed equivalent to seeking certainty on future events–the divination which secular and ecclesiastical authorities so frequently condemned.[10] In the twelfth century, too, Peter the Chanter cited the Mosaic injunctions against soothsaying and divination against the ordeal.[11]

Some of Agobard's arguments are echoed in other criticisms raised in the period. A contemporary of Agobard's, from Freising in Bavaria, wrote that 'true reason (*vera ratio*) proves that [the ordeal] is totally futile . . . There would be no need for reason or wisdom' if uncertain things could be revealed in this way. The Freising poet inflates his argument until the ordeals of fire and water appear as threats to speech, the works of the Fathers, even the faith itself. The convoluted thought and language of this poet make his exact meaning unclear; what is certain is that he saw the vigorous pursuit of mutilatory criminal justice, which he praises, as more rational than the ordeals which he saw as the alternative.[12]

---

[8] Ibid., cap. 1, ed. cit., p. 31.   [9] Ibid., cap. 6, ed. cit., pp. 43 and 47.

[10] For explicit equation of duel and sortilege see Henry of Ghent, writing in the thirteenth century, who condemned duels not only for the mutual killing intended by the participants, but also because 'anticipating a divine judgement from the outcome of combat . . . is a crime similar to sortilege', *Quodlibeta*, 5.32, (2 vols., 1518), 1, fols. 210-11.

[11] *Verbum abbreviatum*, 78, *PL* 205, col. 226.

[12] *Carmen de Timone comite*, ed. Ernst Dümmler, MGH, *Antiquitates, Poetae Latini aevi Carolini*, 2/1 (Berlin, 1884), pp. 122-3, lines 65-86; for the possibility of connections between Agobard and the Freising poet see van Acker's comments in his edition of Agobard, p. XL.

A much more straightforward picture emerges from the writings of Hincmar of Rheims. He was writing in defence of the ordeal, but, as he did so, he necessarily gave the arguments of those opposed to the practice. The sixth section of Hincmar's *De divortio Lotharii* contains his most sustained reflections on the subject. 'Some say', he wrote, 'that proof through hot water or cold water or hot iron has no authority or credibility, but that these are wilful inventions of men; in them very often falsehood takes the place of truth through sorcery and thus they should not be believed'.[13] The ordeal is an invention; it can be fixed by magic–these are two arguments we have already encountered.

Later in the section Hincmar discusses a more ingenious point. Some people, he says, object that while the hot water is supposed to burn the guilty and spare the innocent, in the ordeal of cold water the innocent sink and the guilty float. The miraculous security of the first instance is not paralleled in the second. The Bible had instances of God saving people from the waters, notably the Flood and the Parting of the Red Sea, but in this ordeal the result seems to be curiously inverted. The guilty float, the innocent go under.[14] This argument is more involved than the others. It was, however, of some importance. The ordeals of hot water, hot iron, and hot ploughshares all worked on the same principle: God had to intervene to protect the innocent from the natural results of contact with something very hot. The ordeal of cold water did not share this characteristic. If it were assumed that the human body, being heavy, would naturally sink, then God's intervention is here required to point out the guilty. This discordance between the cold water ordeals and the others was taken up again in the clerical debates of the twelfth century.[15]

A final ninth-century critic, Pope Stephen V, is important not only in providing evidence for the nature of criticism at this period, but also for his influence on later canon law. His letter *Consuluisti* of 886-9 eventually entered the canonical collections of the twelfth century. It is the first explicit papal condemnation of the ordeals of fire and water. In the letter, the pope wrote 'the holy canons do not consider that a confession should be forced from anyone by the examination of hot iron or hot water and what is not sanctioned by the teaching of the holy fathers is a superstitious invention and no one should dare practice it. Public crimes are to be judged by spontaneous confession or by the

---

[13] *De divortio Lotharii*, 6, *PL* 125, col. 659.
[14] Ibid.
[15] Peter the Chanter, *Verbum abbreviatum*, 78, *PL* 205, cols. 227-8.

proof of witnesses; hidden and unknown things are to be left to the judgement of Him who alone knows the hearts of the sons of men'.[16]

The ninth-century criticism, considered as a whole, is remarkably extensive. It contains, or prefigures, virtually all the arguments of later centuries. The lack of authoritative institution, internal inconsistencies in the practice, the existence of other means of proof, the inaccessibility of God's judgements were all advanced as arguments against the legitimacy of the practice. Nevertheless, although there is a wide and often forceful range of argument in the material, it had little influence. Agobard's criticisms survive in one manuscript alone (and that very nearly served a sixteenth-century bookbinder as useful spare parchment).[17] The Freising poet is more useful as evidence of a possible ninth-century position than as part of a trend. Hincmar, of course, recorded the objections against the ordeal in the course of what is probably the most important theological defence the practice ever received. Even the papal letter of Stephen V was less effective than might be imagined. It was premissed on the erroneous belief that the ordeal was a form of torture rather than proof; its manuscript tradition begins only in the early twelfth century, when it appears in the collections of Ivo of Chartres; and, although it contained a prohibition, this referred explicitly only to the hot water and hot iron. Gratian himself was unsure about this ruling: 'there is justifiable doubt about whether this canon refers to all forms of ordeal or to these two alone'.[18]

The existence of this ninth-century material demonstrates that it was possible, even in the Carolingian period, to be hostile to the ordeal; it shows us that objections were raised against the practice early in its history and it reveals the grounds for those objections. The critics were, however, a minority: most laymen, most clerics, and most popes in the period up to 1050 would not have shared their views.

In the period 1050-1215, however, criticism of the ordeal grew in importance. It is vital, naturally, to analyse which particular objections grew stronger and who raised them. Let us turn first to objections based on mistrust of the results of ordeals. There are, from lay rather than clerical mouths, a few famous expressions of hard-line scepticism.

[16] JL 3443; Ivo of Chartres, *Decretum*, 10.27, *PL* 161, col. 699, ep. 74, *PL* 162, cols. 95-6; Gratian, *Decretum*, C.2, q.5, c.20.

[17] Egon Boshof, *Erzbischof Agobard von Lyon* (Cologne and Vienna, 1969), p. 1. Grelewski's considered opinion was that, 'en somme, la voix d'Agobard n'eut pratiquement presque aucune influence', *La Réaction*, p. 54.

[18] *Decretum*, C.2, q.5, c.20.

Some of these sceptical individuals were quite exceptional and emerge in the monastic chronicles as monstrous free-thinkers. William Rufus is a prime example. Eadmer describes him as so proud that he refused to admit his dependence upon God, denied any intercessory role to the saints and 'maintaining this faith in himself, he erred also in this, that he ceased to believe in the judgement of God, claiming that it was unjust; he said that either God did not know the deeds of men or He did not wish to weigh them in the scales of justice.'[19] Eadmer's coupling of the second point, that God did not wish to weigh men's deeds in this way, with the first, and blasphemous, point, shows how scepticism about the ordeal could strike someone, in the early twelfth century, as sheer irreligion.

A somewhat similar statement came, later in the century, from the lips of the Danish noble Magnus, when he was offered the chance of clearing himself of a charge of treason by the hot iron. 'He replied that this kind of proof was very doubtful and did not always produce a miracle; it often condemned the innocent and cleared the wicked; the outcome of the test was largely a matter of chance. For the divine power is not so concerned with human beings that it compels the natural order to change according to their wishes.'[20]

Radical scepticism of the kind advanced by William Rufus or the Dane Magnus is isolated and rare. We cannot look here for an explanation of the abandonment of the practice. This secular scepticism, a real denial of God's involvement with human concerns, does, however, seem to have been a continuing strand, and it is not implausible to see its culmination in Frederick II's prohibition of ordeals in the *Constitutions of Melfi* or *Liber Augustalis* of 1231:

We, who study the true science of laws and reject errors, abolish from our courts those proofs, called by some simple-minded people 'apparent' (*paribiles*), which neither consider physical nature nor attend to the truth ... We hold that their opinions should be nullified, rather than corrected, since they believe that the natural heat of hot iron grows cooler or, what is more foolish, becomes cold without any good cause, or that the element of cold water will not receive a guilty man on account of his bad conscience, when, in fact, it is the retention of sufficient air that does not allow him to sink.[21]

---

[19] *Historia novorum*, 2, s.a. 1098, ed. Martin Rule (RS, 1884), pp. 101-2.
[20] Saxo Grammaticus, *Gesta Danorum*, 14.54.19-20, ed. J. Olrik and H. Raeder (2 vols., Copenhagen, 1931-57), 1, p. 508.
[21] 2.31, ed. J. L. A. Huillard-Bréholles, *Historia diplomatica Friderici secundi* (6 vols., Paris, 1852-61), 4/1, p. 102; *Die Konstitutionen Friedrichs II. für sein Königreich Sizilien*, ed.

His thoroughgoing naturalism, as expressed in this law, is unusual, but not without precursors.

Nevertheless, the cases of William Rufus and Magnus must be placed in context. The description of William Rufus' unbelief is part of an attempt to show what a monster he was–he *even* went so far as to disbelieve in the ordeal. Nor did his scepticism prevent his employing the ordeal in judicial proceedings. Magnus was an exile at the court of Henry the Lion and in a very difficult situation; his offer of duel had been declined and he feared the ordeal was going to be used to crush him. The response of those around him is also recorded: 'many people thought his answer very suspicious.' The story of scepticism must be placed in its setting, for it is the monastic reaction to Rufus and the response of Henry the Lion's courtiers to Magnus that illustrate the majority feeling about the ordeal.

Scepticism about the ordeal did, therefore, exist and there are examples of doubts about the results of the ordeal from the earliest days onward. But, for the most part, people found ways of retaining a belief in the value of the ordeal as an institution even when they doubted its verdict in a given case. Naturally, such mistrust implies that observers had made an independent assessment of the guilt or innocence of the accused before the ordeal took place and, moreover, that they stood by this assessment in the face of the result of the ordeal. This need not, however, necessarily imply complete scepticism about the practice. There was more than one kind of answer to the problem of why the result was wrong and many of these answers did not require the total abandonment of belief in the ordeal.

The most obvious case of unjust results, for example, is one in which the outcome had been fixed. As has been discussed above, it was believed that this could be done by magic. In this situation, the answer was not to abandon the ordeal, but to take precautions against magic. In the case of merely human interference, similar precautions might be necessary. When Hincmar gave the reasons for tying the proband with rope in the ordeal of cold water, he explained that this was not only so that the innocent could be pulled out in time, but also to prevent fraud.[22] In the case of both magical or human trickery, the possibility of a cooked result could be faced and guarded against without the practice of the ordeal itself being jeopardized.

and tr. (into German), Hermann Conrad *et al.* (Cologne, 1973), pp. 216-18. The reading *deridendum* ('mocked') has been suggested instead of *delendum* ('nullified').

[22] *De divortio Lotharii*, 6, *PL* 125, col. 668.

There were other ways of dealing with the dilemma of seeing the guilty saved and the innocent condemned at the ordeal. One response, which seems to have been increasingly prevalent in the eleventh and twelfth centuries, was to claim that the guilty had been cleared because they had confessed or because God wished to give them one more chance, and that the innocent, though not guilty of the specific charge brought against them, were condemned on some other count.

A remarkable story from the mid-eleventh century that illustrates the point is the case of the man accused of horse-stealing who failed at the ordeal, even though he was innocent, because he had shaved like a cleric rather than letting his beard grow as a layman should. After he had promised to stop shaving, he succeeded in a second attempt at the ordeal.[23] The opposite situation, the escape of the guilty, is found in the pages of Galbert of Bruges, describing the events of 1127-8. Lambert of Aardenburg had been charged with complicity in the murder of the count of Flanders. He had cleared himself through the ordeal of hot iron. Shortly afterwards, however, he fell in battle. These are Galbert's reflections:

It should be noted that in this battle Lambert, who had recently cleared himself by hot iron of the charge of having betrayed Count Charles, was now killed. For as long as he acted humbly towards God, God forgave him for having taken part in the murder of his lord. But, after being cleared by the ordeal, Lambert and his men had arrogantly, without any sense of mercy, used a force of 3,000 men to besiege a handful . . . he had refused to put off the fight . . . and so he deserved to be killed since he disregarded the mercy of God and the dispensation by which God had saved his life . . . So it happens that while in battle the guilty one is slain, in the judgement of water or iron the guilty one, if he is penitent, does not succumb.[24]

These comments reveal the tortuous arguments of a man trying to reconcile a deep belief in God's immanent justice with a most intractable sequence of events. Incidentally, in the light of some recent interpretations which see the decline of the ordeal as part of the process of the decline of belief in immanent justice, it is worth stressing here that Galbert combined a willingness to recognize the judicial vagaries of ordeal verdicts with a deep commitment to a picture of the world in which God punished the wicked and rewarded

---

[23] Othlo of St Emmeran, *Narratio de miraculo, PL* 146, cols. 241-4.

[24] Galbert of Bruges, *De multro . . . Karoli comitis Flandriarum,* caps. 105 and 108, ed. Henri Pirenne, *Histoire du Meurtre de Charles le Bon* (Paris, 1891), pp. 150, 154-6, tr. James Bruce Ross, *The Murder of Charles the Good* (rev. edn., New York, 1967), pp. 282, 287-9.

the good. It was a central concern of his to answer the question, 'How can God's dispensation be explained?'[25] In the end, one must say that Galbert's explanatory strategies succeed. He preserved both the status of the ordeal as a manifestation of divine will and also security in his own knowledge that Lambert was guilty. There was a price to pay, however. If the ordeal could no longer be seen as a valid test of the point at issue, then its judicial utility was at an end. For the ordeal was intended to reveal a specific fact;[26] it was designed to deal with specific allegations when other evidence or proof was lacking. This judicial function was diluted by the belief that God might be using the ordeal to show mercy, justify the good at heart, or punish the sinner regardless of whether he happened to be guilty in the case at issue.

In particular, the reinvigoration of the practice of lay confession in the twelfth century had repercussions for the ordeal. The twelfth century was a formative period in sacramental theology, in which the sacraments were analysed with a precision never known before, and this theoretical elaboration was matched by a new effort to make the sacraments the real centre of the religious life of laymen. Communion and confession were to be the statutory duty of the pious layman. As part of this growing appreciation of, and concentration on, the sacraments, there arose a campaign to impress upon laymen the need for, and the efficacy of, confession. The theological debate on this issue was lively, some seeing contrition, the internal sorrow of the heart, as sufficient in itself for the remission of sin, others arguing that recourse to a priest was, in most circumstances, indispensable. But, whatever the theoretical debates, the drift of pastoral theology was clear: the duty of confession was inculcated in ever more effective ways.

The history of confession and that of the ordeal intersect in the twelfth century because the question arose: if a guilty man were truly contrite and had confessed, was he not then absolved of the guilt, and, if he then went to the ordeal, surely God would have to reveal his innocence? Several pieces of evidence from the twelfth and early thirteenth centuries suggest that it was increasingly difficult to give full weight both to confession and to the ordeal. One chronicler, for example, writing of events in the year 1183, reported that 'in the town of Ypres twelve men were submitted to the ordeal of hot iron, but, by

---

[25] Ibid., cap. 121, tr. Ross, p. 310.

[26] *Pace* Brown, 'Society and the Supernatural': 'God is revealing "truth", not any specific fact', p. 137 (repr., p. 311); Gaudemet in *La Preuve*, p. 100; cf. Hyams, 'Trial by Ordeal', p. 111 and n. 108.

the virtue of confession, all were delivered safely'.[27] Forty years later the Cistercian author Caesarius of Heisterbach, in the section of his *Dialogus miraculorum* dedicated to confession, entitled one chapter 'The heretics of Cambrai tried by the hot iron and burned, of whom one was saved by the benefit of confession'. This lucky heretic saw the burn mark on his hand slowly disappear as he proceeded with his confession.[28]

Another tale told by Caesarius recounts how a fisherman in the diocese of Utrecht, who was notorious for fornication, was faced with the prospect of formal accusation at the next synod. 'What will you do, you wretch?' he said to himself. 'If you are accused of fornication at this synod and plead guilty, you will have to marry the woman. If you deny it, you will be a in worse situation when you are found guilty by the hot iron.' In this dilemma the fisherman went to his priest, 'more through fear of punishment than love of righteousness', and confessed. The priest then advised him, 'if you have a firm intention of sinning with her no more, you can carry the hot iron in safety and deny the sin, for I trust that the power of confession will free you.' This is exactly what happened, 'to everybody's astonishment'.[29]

Stories such as these served to highlight the efficacy of confession, but also, incidentally, cast doubt on the trustworthiness of ordeal verdicts. In the case of the lecherous fisherman, we even have the prospect of priests sending their guilty charges to undergo the ordeal and assuring them that they would be cleared. The issue was general enough to require explicit treatment in the handbooks for confessors that were beginning to be written in this period. Thomas of Chobham, the author of a popular *Summa confessorum* of the early thirteenth century, discussing the analogous problem of the oath, wrote, 'The question can also be raised if the counsel should be approved of those who say that, if a guilty person is accused and fully repents and promises true emendation to God, he can licitly swear that he is not guilty of that crime.' Thomas reports that 'some prudent and pious priests' do allow such men to swear a form of oath asserting their innocence.[30] He makes it clear that, sometimes at any rate, the priests, with their newly enhanced sacramental powers, and the repentant

[27] *Continuatio Aquicinctina* of Sigebert of Gembloux, ed. L. C. Bethmann, MGH, *SS* 6 (Hanover, 1844), p. 421.

[28] p. 3. 16, ed. J. Strange (2 vols. and index, Cologne, etc., 1851-7), 1, p. 132.

[29] Ibid. 10. 35-6, ed. cit., 2, p. 243.

[30] *Summa confessorum*, 7.4.6.8, ed. F. Broomfield (Analecta mediaevalia Namurcensia, 25, Louvain and Paris, 1968), pp. 429-30.

layman could form a tacit alliance against secular rulers and their machinery of justice.

The crux of the issue was how much of a distinction, if any, there should be between a sin and a crime. For the priests who advised their penitents to swear an oath to their innocence, the category 'crime' was obviously unimportant. What mattered was to resolve the offence with God. For the ministers of the secular power, however, there must have been an important working distinction, for crime was their business while sin was not–'man is not competent to judge of interior movements, that are hidden, but only of exterior acts which are observable'.[31] The disappearance of trial by ordeal from the courts in the thirteenth century was part of a process whereby an increasingly sharp distinction was drawn between sin and crime. If God was interested in an offence only as a sin, then priestly rituals should suffice to cleanse a man from guilt. Rulers and judges, of course, had to work with a less spiritual sense of guilt. So, the development of the sacramental theology and pastoral practice of penance and confession in the twelfth and early thirteenth centuries produced a frame of mind among many clerics which made it difficult to countenance the continuation of the ordeal. God's verdict was heard in confession and absolution, supervised by the priest, alone with the sinner in the church, not in the secular publicity of the courts. One form of priestly power, the management of the ordeal, would have to be sacrificed to another form, the authority of the confessional.

Doubts about the outcome of individual trials did not, however, form the crucial motor of change. The major thrust in the intellectual attack on the ordeal was that the practice was wrong: it was wrong because it was uncanonical and because it tempted God. These are the arguments that eventually drove the ordeal from most of the law courts of Christendom. They were arguments adumbrated in the ninth century, but advanced more frequently and more forcefully by reformers and canonists from around 1050 onwards. The process of the development of clerical opinion has been studied in some detail[32] and its main outlines are clear.

In the tenth and early eleventh century clerical opinion seems to have accepted the ordeal quite comfortably. The canon law collections

---

[31] Thomas Aquinas, *Summa theologica*, 1.2.91.4, Blackfriars edn., ed. T. Gilby *et al.* (60 vols., London, 1963-76), 28, p. 30.

[32] Esp. Baldwin, 'Intellectual Preparation'.

of Regino and Burhard envisage its use[33] and there are frequent
cases in which clerics were prepared to recognize it as a proof. This
applies to the ordeals of fire and water as well as the more specifically
clerical ordeal of the eucharist. From around the mid-eleventh
century, there is the beginning of a change. In 1063 Pope Alexander II
ruled that a priest accused of murder could clear himself by compurgation if specific accusers were lacking. He added, 'By apostolic
authority, we strictly forbid you to use on him that popular proof,
which has no canonical sanction, namely hot water, cold water, hot
iron or any other popular invention, since these are the fabrications of
malice.'[34] The ruling thus launched was of great importance. It was a
definite papal ban. Alexander II's letter found its way into the
canonical collections and exercised considerable influence on the
canonists of the twelfth century. Nevertheless, it took time for this
opposition to become overwhelming. The attitudes of Ivo of Chartres,
the greatest canonist of the early twelfth century, have been carefully
analysed on this issue. In general, he was hostile to the ordeal, but
admitted it against laymen when other proofs were lacking.[35] Gratian's
collection of around 1140 showed a similar uncertainty. He included
in his *Decretum* several condemnations of the duel and of the unilateral
ordeal which popes of earlier centuries had issued, but also found a
place for the passage from the Book of Numbers prescribing the
'ordeal of bitter waters' (discussed below) and several canons which
ordered either the eucharistic ordeal or some unspecified 'judgement
of God'. Moreover, he was unsure whether the papal provisions
'applied to all kinds of ordeal'.[36] Between 1140 and 1215, however, the
tide began to flow all one way. The reign of Pope Alexander III
witnessed an active papal policy against the use of ordeals, to a back-
ground of increasingly unanimous scholastic opinion; the papacy of
Innocent III decided the issue as far as church law was concerned.

If we examine the arguments advanced in the period 1050–1215,
there is not much novelty. Many of the points that were made had

[33] Regino of Prüm, *De ecclesiasticis disciplinis et religione christiana*, 1.72-3; 2.31, 43, 234,
243, 302, 381, *PL* 132, cols. 206, 291-2, 294, 329-30, 342, 355; Burchard of Worms,
Decretum, 3.22; 4.80; 6.7, 38; 9.41, 79; 10.25; 16.19; 19.5, *PL* 140, cols. 677, 741, 768, 773,
821, 829, 836, 912, 973.

[34] *PL* 146, col. 1406, JL 4505, Ivo of Chartres, *Decretum*, 10.15, and *Panormia*, 5.7-8,
PL 161, cols. 695 and 1214-15, Gratian's *Decretum*, C.2, q.5, c.7.

[35] Grelewski, *La Réaction*, pp. 70-83; see also Baldwin, 'Intellectual Preparation',
pp. 617-18.

[36] Gratian's passages on forms of proof are in C.2, q.5. See Baldwin's admirable
summary, 'Intellectual Preparation', pp. 618-19.

been raised in the ninth century. Yet now they were able, eventually, to change the actual practice in the world. Clearly the circumstances in which the debate took place had changed. Firstly, the uncanonical nature of the practice was of much greater importance in an age when canon law was, on the one hand, codified and studied more intently than ever, and, on the other enforced more effectively. The issue, of what was canonical and what was not, was now highlighted. The twelfth century was the great age of sifting, and the credentials of the ordeal were among the things sifted. By around 1150 both theology and canon law had become academic disciplines. As a result, questions which had remained unresolved or disputed for centuries were subjected to intense intellectual winnowing and crystallized or polarized. New dogmatic definitions were advanced on such topics as the number and nature of the sacraments, the rules of marriage, and the process of transubstantiation. The ordeal, too, was placed under this new and rigorous scrutiny.

The result was not a foregone conclusion. The texts assembled by Gratian on the subject show what a varied and conflicting body of ecclesiastical opinion had developed over the course of time. These materials, in themselves, did not give an answer to the question of the legitimacy of ordeals. They had to be interpreted, certain texts explained away, others emphasized and developed. The process of clarification could have led to a vindication of the ordeal rather than a condemnation–after all, many other customary practices were embraced by the Church. But, if we compare Gratian's *Decretum* of 1140 with the *Decretals* issued by the authority of Gregory IX in 1234, the transition from equivocation to forthright prohibition is clear: 'Proof of this kind is completely forbidden according to legitimate and canonical decrees'.[37] The emergence of a clear papal voice on this subject in the later twelfth and early thirteenth century was deeply shaped by theological and legal discussion.

The uncanonical nature of ordeals was determined fairly early. Here, the most fundamental fact was their almost complete absence from the Bible. Both canon law and theology built on a foundation of Scripture and when the scholastic theologians and canonists of the twelfth century asked what the Bible had to say on the subject of ordeals, they found very little. There was no clear directive.

There was, however, one exception. In the Book of Numbers a

---

[37] X.5.35.3, Po. 6910 (Honorius III, 1222); repeated in 1232, Po. 8996b.

procedure is described in which a wife suspected of infidelity is subjected to the ordeal of bitter waters.[38] There were even legendary and
iconographic offshoots of this passage, since the Apocryphal Gospels
record that the Virgin Mary was subjected to this ordeal, and it was a
theme occasionally represented in fresco and mosaic.[39] The passage
was, apparently, the most authoritative statement on the ordeal
available—and it sanctioned the practice. Serious biblical commentary
on the passage did not really take up its implications for contemporary
judicial practice. The passage is invariably approached symbolically
in the exegesis of the ninth to twelfth centuries; the wronged husband
is Christ or the Church, the adulterous woman the human soul,
heretics, or the synagogue, the waters Scripture.[40] But, though the
implications of the passage were ignored by monastic exegetes, they
were taken up by the ninth-century polemicists, the canonists, and
scholastic thinkers. Agobard grappled with it boldly, Hincmar quoted
it triumphantly.[41] In the mid-twelfth century it caused Gratian some
perplexity.[42] The critics of the ordeal eventually dealt with the
Numbers passage by arguing that it was an exceptional concession. In
the words of Peter Comestor, author of the standard text, the *Historia
Scholastica*, 'this law was introduced because of the hardness of their
hearts, just as the petition for divorce was allowed'.[43] Peter the
Chanter shared this view.[44] It had always been known that Christians
were not bound by the whole law of the Old Testament; now this
belief was reinforced by the contextualist scholarship of the twelfth
century, which taught that due consideration should be given to circumstances and exceptions when studying the authorities of the past.

---

[38] Numbers 5: 11-31; for some discussion, with reference to further secondary literature, see Eidelberg, 'Trial by Ordeal', pp. 110-11 and notes, W. McKane, 'Poison, Trial
by Ordeal and the Cup of Wrath', *Vetus Testamentum*, 30 (1980), pp. 474-92.

[39] Protoevangelium of St James and 'Pseudo Matthew', tr. M. R.James, *The Apocry-
phal New Testament* (Oxford, 1924); K. Weitzmann, *The Fresco Cycle of S. Maria di
Castelseprio* (Princeton, 1951); C. R. Morey, in *Art Bulletin*, 34 (1952), p. 154; Priester
Werner, *Maria*, ed. Karl Wesle (2nd edn., Tübingen, 1969), pp. 165-73.

[40] e.g. Hrabanus Maurus, *Enarrationes in librum Numerorum*, 1.9, *PL* 108, cols. 619-21;
Bruno of Segni, *Exposito in Numeros*, 5, *PL* 164, cols. 467-70; Rupert of Deutz, *De sancta
trinitate et operibus eius 16. In Numeros*, 1.10, ed. Hrabanus Haacke (4 vols., Corpus
Christianorum, Continuatio Mediaevalis, Turnhout, 1971-2), 2, pp. 924-7; *Glossa
ordinaria, PL* 113 (attrib. Walafrid Strabo), cols. 390-1.

[41] Agobard, *Liber adversus iudicium dei*, cap. 1, ed. cit., p. 31; Hincmar, *De divortio
Lotharii*, 6 *PL* 125, cols. 660, 664.

[42] *Decretum*, C.2, q.5, c.21.

[43] *PL* 198, col. 1220.

[44] *Verbum abbreviatum*, 78, *PL* 205, cols. 226-7.

By corralling off the passage in Numbers in this way, the full force of the biblical silence on the practice could be felt. Scripture is, of course, liable to multiple interpretation. But the lack of good biblical precedent for the ordeal was a weakness when the issue came to be debated. In the ninth century Hincmar's convolutions show both the need felt for biblical authority and the difficulty in squeezing it out of the text: 'Purge out the old leaven that ye may be a new lump, as ye are unleavened,' he writes, quoting I Corinthians, 5:7, 'As if the Apostle clearly said: Anyone accused of a crime who denies it must, in the absence of suitable witnesses, be cleared by oath or ordeal.'[45]

The absence of strong biblical sanction was compounded by the absence of the ordeal from Roman law. Here was a major system of law, in the young vigour of its glamour and prestige, studied intensively alongside the canon law, which seemed to condemn the duel (see below) and certainly had no place for the ordeals of fire and water. In these circumstances, it was not impossible to explain away also the embarrassing earlier canons sanctioning the ordeal. The canonists of the later twelfth century went to work on this project. The canons of the ninth-century Council of Tribur, it was argued, were passed during a schism and were less than authoritative. The passages in Burchard were 'outdated' or referred only to the unfree.[46]

The controversy over the legitimacy of the ordeal must be seen in the overall context of ecclesiastical attitudes to custom in this period. It is commonplace–and true–to characterize the Gregorians as championing law against custom. This dichotomy is reflected in the debate on the ordeal. Some defended it as a custom; others attacked it as nothing but a custom. There was a presumption in favour of custom in certain circumstances; but the circumstances had to be defined. 'The authority of ancient custom', specified Gregory IX in the *Decretals*, 'is not slight but it can only prevail against positive law if it is rational and has legal prescription'.[47] Hostiensis, in his commentary, agreed: 'Custom is a rational usage ratified by time.' The crucial question, then, was whether a custom was rational. Hostiensis again: 'Whether a given custom is rational or not, I leave to the judge, since there is no rule on this.'[48]

---

[45] *De divortio Lotharii*, 6 PL 125, col. 670.
[46] See the texts cited by Browe, *De ordaliis*, 2, nos. 98-100, 103, and Baldwin, 'Intellectual Preparation', pp. 617-23.
[47] X.1.4.11.
[48] *Lectura in quinque decretalium gregorianarum libros* (2 vols. in 1, Paris, 1512), 1, f. 26ᵛ.

In the course of the twelfth century the ordeal became one of the targets in the campaign which high churchmen launched against custom in the name of law. They did not attack all customs, however, and, as Hostiensis observes, the decision as to what was irrational rested with the judge. Put another way, the decision of the canonists and popes of the twelfth and early thirteenth century determined that the ordeal would be 'irrational'. They did not abandon it because it was irrational, it became irrational because they abandoned it.

The ordeal was thus categorized as a superstitious and vulgar custom. In a period when 'reformers ... tended to dismiss as "popular" all that could not be legitimized by textual means',[49] it was vulnerable because it lacked good written authority. But it was not only wrong because it was uncanonical; it was also wrong because it 'tempted God'. It is hard to say which is the more frequent objection in the clerical criticism of the period 1050-1215. Both objections are common and both have a long history. Some canonists, naturally enough, saw the one as a consequence of the other: 'These proofs are nowadays completely forbidden in the canons since those who perform them seem to be tempting God'.[50]

The objection to ordeals because they tempted God breaks down into two points: human reason should be used to its utmost; miracles are not guaranteed. As expressed by Peter the Chanter, one of the most vociferous critics of the ordeal, 'no one ought to tempt God when he has rational courses of action' and 'if the miracles the Lord promised in the Gospel ... are not guaranteed (*nec sunt in necessitate*) how can these ordeal miracles be guaranteed to happen or have their result?'[51]

Confidence in the ordeal rested upon the conviction that its results were guaranteed to manifest God's judgement. Growing doubts about the ordeal in the twelfth century were not primarily due to an increasing uncertainty about the fact of such manifestations of God's judgement. Rather it was the guaranteed nature of the result which was in question. It was increasingly viewed as impious to believe that a constructed human test–the ordeal–could 'force' God to show his hand. That was testing God.

---

[49] Brian Stock, *The Implications of Literacy, Written Language and Models of Interpretation in the 11th and 12th centuries* (Princeton, 1983), p. 523.
[50] *Summa monacensis*, cited by Browe, *De ordaliis*, 2, no. 100 and Baldwin, 'Intellectual Preparation', p. 620.
[51] *Verbum abbreviatum*, 78, *PL* 205, cols. 226 and 228.

There is a curious convergence between this argument and the belief discussed earlier, that the verdict of the ordeal might not reflect guilt or innocence in the case at issue, but God's punishment or forgiveness on quite other grounds. This belief, as expressed, for example, by Galbert of Bruges, postulates a God who can do what He will, who can use the ordeal as He wishes. In this picture of an untrammelled deity there is something reminiscent of Peter the Chanter's insistence that miracles cannot be guaranteed. Both recognized God's power and transcendence. The mechanical and manipulative concept of ritual which lay behind the ordeal did not fit in very well with such a deity. Around 1130 the steward of the bishop of Münster wanted to undergo the ordeal in order to convert a Jew. The bishop forbade this: 'God should not be tempted by such tests, but rather prayed to that he should deign to dissolve the knots of infidelity when and how he wishes'.[52] The shift from a manipulative ritual to supplication (which anthropologists used to see as the distinction between magic and religion) is clear. As Aquinas put it, succinctly, 'ordeal by hot iron or water is illicit because a miraculous effect is required of God'.[53]

Scholastic criticism of trial by ordeal did not reflect sceptical naturalism or rationalism but rather a new and more rigorous metaphysics. Over the course of the period 1050-1215, the years of early scholasticism, refined abstract speculation created or intensified the divisions that were held to exist between different categories of event. A harder line was drawn between the natural and the supernatural, but also, within the supernatural, between the miraculous and the sacramental. Thus three orders or categories of event came into being: natural, miraculous, and sacramental.

The ordeal fell between these three stools. It was clearly not natural: if it was anything, it was 'God's power' working 'contrary to nature'.[54] Indeed, the claim that its results were simply natural, that the horny-handed did better in the ordeal of hot iron or that the outcome of the trial of cold water could be explained by specific gravity, was one of the arguments advanced by sceptics and opponents. But if it was not natural, neither was it clear how it fitted into the new distinction between the miraculous and the sacramental.

---

[52] Hermann quondam Iudaeus, *Opusculum de conversione sua*, 5, ed. Gerlinde Niemeyer, MGH, *Quellen zur Geistesgeschichte des Mittelalters* (Weimar, 1963), pp. 83-7.
[53] *Summa theologica*, 2.2.95.8.
[54] Caesarius, *Dialogus* (as in n. 28), 10.35, ed. cit., 2, p. 243.

A miracle was a free act of God. There was no regularly ordained procedure to procure it. If the ordeal were regarded as a miracle, then it was a very improper one, since it involved a ritual which 'demanded a miraculous effect'. To be judicially useful, the ordeal had to work every time. It could thus not be an unguaranteed, undemanded act of God, that is, it could not be a miracle as defined by scholastic thinkers. However, if one wished to argue that the ordeal was more like a sacrament, in that God guaranteed a result if proper ritual rules were followed (*ex opere operato*), as in the case of the Mass, one came up against the objection that a sacrament had to be canonically instituted, and that the ordeal was not. Peter the Chanter was careful to distinguish between sacraments which 'always have their effect' and the treacherous 'incantations' of the ordeal.[55]

In fact, to speculate hypothetically for a moment, it is probable that the ordeal could only have survived the critical scrutiny it received in the twelfth century if it had been sacramentalized. There were some indications that this would not have been impossible. Hincmar of Rheims, for example, in his defence of the ordeal, repeatedly stressed the similarities between ordeal and the sacrament of baptism. He wrote, for instance, 'The same authority which ordained that the Holy Spirit should be breathed into the water of baptism by the priestly breath also, it is believed, granted to the Church that there should be the hot water . . . in which the righteous are saved unharmed and those who are adjudged wicked are punished.' In the ordeal ritual, he claimed, 'the Lord is invoked according to the model of baptism'. The guilty party 'is unable to sink into the waters over which the voice of the majesty of the Lord has thundered, because the pure nature of water does not receive a human nature which has been cleansed of all deceit by the water of baptism but has subsequently been reinfected by lies'.[56] The parallel between ordeal and baptism is also demonstrated in some of the liturgies or rituals for the ordeal. One prescribed that a stick should be placed between the proband's arms to lower him into the water and on it should be written 'Saint John the Baptist bless this water'. Another invocation reads, 'O God, who has ordained baptism in water, reveal true judgement in this water.'[57] A church at Canterbury was designated as the proper spot for two specific functions:

---

[55] *Verbum abbreviatum*, 78, *PL* 205, col. 543.
[56] *De divortio Lotharii*, 6, *PL* 125, cols. 664, 668, 669.
[57] Zeumer, *Formulae*, pp. 689, 701 (n. 15), 702-5.

baptism and ordeal.[58] Curiously, the Old Norse words for 'ordeal' and 'baptism' were the same.[59] These hints show the way that trial by ordeal could have become a sacrament. Other non-scriptural institutions did, after all, become sacraments in the twelfth century. In the event, however, the weight of argument against the ordeal was too great for this to happen.

Hence, new and refined theories about the supernatural developed by the early scholastic thinkers excluded the ordeal. The only guaranteed supernatural events were the sacraments and these had to be canonical. No other supernatural events could be guaranteed. The two main thrusts of ecclesiastical objection to the ordeal–'it is uncanonical' and 'it demands a miracle' thus effectively deprived the ordeal of a licit status as a supernatural process.

It is often assumed that the twelfth and thirteenth centuries were a period of increasing 'naturalism', and that the scholasticism of the universities had an important part to play in the development of this naturalism. One recent historian of the universities has written that in the twelfth and thirteenth centuries 'the momentum of inquiry into natural phenomena was sustained and accelerated by an intellectual élite in the universities, and the frontiers of the supernatural were progressively moved back'.[60] Given such assumptions, it is worth stressing how unimportant, overall, was a rejection of the ordeal on the grounds that it involved a change in the natural properties of the physical elements, an objection that would bulk very large in the mind of most modern commentators. Naturalistic arguments against the ordeal were extremely rare. The ecclesiastics who protested against the ordeal were also, of course, the men responsible for giving definitive form to the doctrine of transubstantiation. The decrees of the Fourth Lateran Council (Lateran IV) of 1215 enshrine the latter, just as they prohibit the former. But the eucharist can be formally defined in such a way as to emphasize its kinship with, rather than its difference from, the ordeal. Both are priestly rituals, performed in prescribed conditions, wherein God transforms the nature of the physical elements. There was obviously no objection to the possibility

---

[58] Eadmer, *Vita Bregwini, PL* 159, col. 755. 'It could be converted from its sacramental to its judicial function with the minimum of disturbance', R. W. Southern, *Saint Anselm and his Biographer* (Cambridge, 1963), p. 263.

[59] Konrad Maurer, *Vorlesungen über altnordischen Rechtsgeschichte* (5 vols., Kristiana, 1907-38), 2, pp. 377-8.

[60] A. B. Cobban, *The Medieval Universities* (London, 1975), p. 14.

of such a transformative ritual. If the reformers and schoolmen of the twelfth century had decided that canonical authority for the ordeal was sufficient, its supernatural characteristics could have been accommodated with ease.

The point can be well illustrated by the case of Peter the Chanter, the most vocal and notorious critic of trial by ordeal in the twelfth century. Consideration of his polemics against the ordeal in isolation might give the impression that he wished to elevate human reason and diminish the scope of the supernatural. 'No one should tempt God when the resources of human reason are not yet exhausted,' he wrote. 'After human reason fails, let a man commend himself to God . . . Now is not the age of miracles but the age of faith and fulfillment of the commandments.' But the Chanter sometimes sang another tune. When discussing theological mysteries such as the Trinity or transubstantiation, he wrote 'a bold and audacious faith reaches further than the intellect . . . it does not understand, but only believes, stripping off all human, causal reasoning (*omnem humanam rationem quae est ex causis*). The faith for which human reason gives proof has no merit.' The last phrase is a quotation from Gregory the Great and it is a neat irony that this very same phrase had been used, three centuries earlier, by Hincmar of Rheims in his defence of the ordeal.[61] The recognition that human reason was circumscribed and a ready acceptance of the supernatural were universal preconditions of Christian intellectual activity in the Middle Ages, in the schools of Paris as well as the cathedrals of Carolingian Gaul.

Clerical Interests

There were, therefore, strong arguments against the ordeal, openly and skilfully advanced and debated in the twelfth century. Persuasion, however, is not always free from wishful thinking and it is worth asking if the twelfth-century reformers not only had good reasons for their opinions but also if they might have had a predisposition to those opinions, which was not based on argument. The ordeal, as a judicial practice, involved interests as well as opinions.

At first glance, it might seem that ecclesiastical opponents of the ordeal were acting contrary to both the political and the economic interests of the clergy. When clerics were urged to abandon the ordeal,

---

[61] *Verbum abbreviatum*, 78 and 92, *PL* 205, cols. 226-7 and 267; Gregory the Great, *Homiliae XL in Evangelia*, 26, *PL* 76, col. 1197; Hincmar, *De divortio Lotharii*, 6, *PL* 125, col. 665.

they were being asked to surrender an important right, for the privilege of conducting ordeals enhanced the dignity of their jurisdiction and, in many cases, placed in their hands the power to decide guilt or innocence. Ecclesiastical lords with their ordeal pits and consecrated irons, and priests accustomed to unwrap the proband's hand and pronounce the judgement of God would thus suffer a real diminution of power and authority if trial by ordeal disappeared. The high value which prelates placed on the right to hold ordeals is shown by the tenacity with which they defended that right. In the reign of William the Conqueror, for example, the abbey of Fontanelle was in danger of losing its right to hold ordeals because a simple-minded monk had used their ordeal iron for secular purposes and, when the abbot went to the archbishop of Rouen to have him bless another one, 'the archbishop doubted whether they had the ordeal iron by ancient custom'. The case eventually went to the king before the abbey's right was vindicated.[62] When the abbot of Elsenbach moved his convent to a new site in 1171, he was careful to obtain a charter from the archbishop of Salzburg stating, 'we have granted and confirmed to you ... the rights of burial, baptism and ordeal of fire and water in St Mary's Mount and in St John's church, just as we know you were granted there of old'.[63] The change of site was not to involve the sacrifice of any lucrative rights at their former location.

The mere fact that a given court had such a right gave it a jurisdictional authority that set it apart from other, lesser courts. Sometimes this took the form of a local monopoly. In the middle of the twelfth century the church of St Peter's, Northampton, acquired a charter from the bishop confirming that 'no one who is to be examined by any form of ordeal should undergo trial in the town or its banlieu except under the aegis of this church, and they shall undergo the preparatory vigil in that church'.[64] As late as 1227, the knights of Kent were still mindful of the careful way that the archbishop of Canterbury had maintained his rights in this area: 'asked about the liberties which the archbishop claims, they said that when ordeals of fire and water took place they saw that pleas of the crown were conducted in the court of the lord king and that then the ordeals took place in the court of the lord archbishop and they

---

[62] G. Bessin (ed.), *Concilia Rotomagensis provinciae* (2 vols., Rouen, 1717), 1, p. 76.

[63] *Die Urkunden des Klosters St. Veit/Rott*, ed. H. Hor and L. Morenz (Munich, 1960), no. 6, pp. 5-7.

[64] Ed. F. M. Stenton, 'Acta episcoporum', *Cambridge Historical Journal*, 3 (1929), p. 12, repr. in *Preparatory to Anglo-Saxon England*, ed. D. M. Stenton (Oxford, 1970), p. 177.

underwent there the ordeal of fire and water according to the opinion of the archbishop's court'.[65] The ordeal was thus a *libertas*, or privilege, defended by all the usual tools in the ecclesiastical armoury.

The right to hold ordeals was a form of property appurtenant to a church, similar, in this respect, to tithes, and was granted along with the church, as, in the early twelfth century, the church of Westfield in Sussex was transferred 'with the ordeal of water pertaining to it'.[66] In the description of the episcopal estates centred on Taunton given in the Domesday Book, we read, 'From all these lands those who have to swear an oath or undergo ordeal (*judicium portaturi*) come to Taunton. When the lords of these lands die, they are buried in Taunton'.[67] When new churches were founded in the lands of the pagan Wends of eastern Europe, they too were endowed with rights 'of burial, of oaths, of subjecting the accused to ordeal'.[68]

Sometimes the right to conduct ordeals was limited to certain categories of church. In Hungary, for example, a decree of King Coloman of 1100 reads, 'We forbid the ordeal of iron and water in any church except an episcopal see or the great collegiate churches like Bratislava and Nitra'.[69] In twelfth-century Norway ordeals took place in the 'shire church' in the country and an assigned church in the boroughs.[70] The Peace legislation of the eleventh century specified which churches should conduct ordeals arising from breaches of the peace. The Synod of Lillebonne in 1080, for example, ruled that ordeal by hot iron should take place 'at the mother church'.[71] When a chapel near Freisach in Carinthia was granted 'all parochial rights except ordeal by fire and water' (*omne ius plebis preter ignitum ferrum et iudicium aque*)',[72] the implication is clearly that the privilege of holding ordeals

[65] Naomi D. Hurnard, 'The Anglo-Norman Franchises', *English Historical Review*, 64 (1949), pp. 289-327 and 433-60, quotation at p. 457.

[66] *The Chronicle of Battle Abbey*, ed. and tr. E. Searle (Oxford, 1980), p. 120.

[67] *Domesday Book*, ed. Abraham Farley (2 vols., London, 1783), 1, f. 87'; cf. the 'Record of Dues Pertaining to Taunton', ed. A. J. Robertson, *Anglo-Saxon Charters* (Cambridge, 1939), pp. 236-9.

[68] *Pommersches UB* 1 (2nd edn., Cologne and Vienna, 1970), ed. Klaus Conrad, no. 120, pp. 159-60.

[69] *Colomanni regis decretorum liber primus*, 22, in Györffy, 'Anhang', p. 308; cf. cap. 46 of the Synod of Gran (1114), 'Ut qui ferrum accipit, in designato loco ponat', ibid., p. 324.

[70] *Frostathing Law*, 2, 'Church Law', cap. 45, tr. Laurence M. Larson, *The Earliest Norwegian Laws* (New York, 1935), p. 244.

[71] Orderic Vitalis, *Ecclesiastical History*, 5.5, ed. Marjorie Chibnall (6 vols., Oxford, 1969-80), 3, p. 34.

[72] Browe, *De ordaliis*, 1, no. 87, citing from *Monumenta historica ducatus Carinthiae*, ed. A. von Jaksch (2 vols, Klagenfurt, 1896-8), 1, no. 392.

pertained to parochial churches and should not be exercised by lesser institutions.

The churches of medieval Europe were great corporate bodies dedicated to the protection and extension of their rights and so, along-side the growing clerical criticism of the twelfth century, we should not be surprised to find those who asserted their vested interests boldly. The tone was that of an English jury of 1201: 'if anyone from that manor must clear himself through the law of England, he will clear himself at St Alban's and in the St Alban's pit; if he has to be hanged, he will be hanged on the St Alban's gallows.'[73]

Concrete financial interests were involved as well as jurisdictional authority, for ordeals produced revenue, not only in the shape of fines and confiscations, the usual perquisites of any judicial lordship, but also in the fees paid to the priest or the church for conducting the ordeal. Some law codes of the period specify the scale of payments to be made. In Hungary in 1092 it was decreed that 'the priest shall receive two *pensas* from the ordeal of iron and one from the ordeal of water'.[74] In the twelfth-century version of the *Russkaia Pravda* there are similar provisions on the subject, pithily concluded in the code by the words 'Those are the ordeal by water payments–who gets what.'[75] In Bohemia a law of Ottokar I reads, 'When anyone has to undergo the ordeal, no one except the priest and his assistant shall put him in the water; if God aids him, he shall pay two pence to the judge and fourteen pence to the priest; if he strips himself and then is unwilling to undergo the ordeal, he shall pay seven pence to the chaplain and twopence to the little old lady.'[76] The mention of the mysterious 'little old lady' (*vetula*) is a reminder that the priests and clerics who were the most obvious beneficiaries of the system of trial by ordeal were surrounded by a penumbra of assistants and hangers-on whose interests were also involved. At Sens cathedral, for example, four lay sacristans received sixpence for tending the vat used for the ordeal of water.[77] Specified payments in law codes seem to occur mainly in

[73] *Curia Regis Rolls*, 2 (HMSO, 1925), p. 56.

[74] *Sancti Ladislai regis decretorum liber primus*, 28, in Györrfy, 'Anhang', p. 284; cf. *Sancti Ladislai regis decretorum liber secundus*, 4, ibid., p. 289. A *pensa* was money of account, worth 30 to 40 deniers.

[75] *Russkaia Pravda* (expanded version), ch. 86, tr. George Vernadsky *Medieval Russian Laws* (New York, 1947), pp. 50-1.

[76] *Statuta ducis Ottonis*, 8, ed. Hermengild Jiriček, *Codex Juris Bohemici* (13 vols., Prague, 1867-90), I, no. 29, p. 55.

[77] *Cartulaire général de l'Yonne*, ed. M. Quantin (2 vols., Auxerre and Paris, 1854-60), 2, p. 285, no. 267 (1176).

eastern Europe, but the payment of priests for officiating was a general feature of trial by ordeal. The English Pipe Rolls record such payments as the following: 'Five shillings and four pence to the priest for the ordeal of two men',[78] and Peter the Chanter paints a typically derisive picture of the priest, hovering at the edge of the ordeal pit for his 'five *sous* for blessing the water'.[79]

The practice of paying the priest for conducting ordeals was open to abuse. In the early eleventh century criticism had been raised against 'priests who peer eagerly with shameless eyes at the women who have been stripped before they enter the water or who force them to ransom themselves at a great price'.[80] In the following century Popes Alexander III and Lucius III sent several injunctions to the English clergy attempting to repress the habit of 'extorting money from men and women in the ordeal of fire and water'.[81] The archdeacon of Coventry was supposed to be taking thirty pence a time, a sum which would, at this period (1174-81), have bought seven or eight sheep, or a cow.

The power and revenue which clerics obtained from trial by ordeal help to explain why, even after a century and a half of papal condemnation and learned criticism, many priests and prelates continued to countenance the practice and, indeed, did so well into the thirteenth century. In this instance, as in many others, there is a danger that the voice of the reforming party, being more insistent and, in the long run, successful, may drown out the numerous but less ideological ecclesiastics who took a more conservative attitude to the ordeal. Clerical inertia was as important as clerical reform.

The policy of abandoning priestly involvement in the ordeal completely, as it was enshrined in the canons of the Lateran IV, was an extreme one. A more moderate position, which must have been supported by many conservative clerics as well as by the reformers, was that ecclesiastics, by virtue of their status, should be exempt from the ordeal. In some ways, this simply represented the logical development of certain, already existing, immunities, as the number of clerics

---

[78] *Pipe Roll 14 Henry II* (Pipe Roll Soc. 12, 1890), p. 48; examples could be multiplied.
[79] *Verbum abbreviatum*, 24, PL 205, cols. 92-3.
[80] Ekkehard IV, *Casus sancti Galli*, cap. 124, ed. H. F. Haefele (Darmstadt, 1980), pp. 240-2.
[81] JL 13857, X.1.23.6 (Alexander III to the bishop of Coventry, 1159-81); JL 14315, X.5.37.3, Mansi, 22, col. 274 (the same to the archbishop of Canterbury,1174-81); W. Holtzmann, *Papsturkunden in England* (3 vols., Berlin and Göttingen, 1930-52), 1/2, no. 226, p. 508 (Lucius III to the abbot of Welbeck, 1181-5).

who went to the ordeal was limited by various restrictions from very early times. For example, in some places the ordeal was only applied to the unfree, which gave effective immunity to clerks. A less painful form of ordeal, the eucharistic ordeal, existed and this was the form usually applied to ecclesiastics rather than trial by fire or water. Moreover, when fire or water were employed, churchmen often underwent the trial by proxy, sending their unfree dependants to undergo the actual test. All these things limited the extent to which the ordeal was applied to clerics.

Nevertheless, there were cases in which men in orders underwent trial by fire and water in person. A clerk accused of heresy at Arras in 1172; another, from the diocese of Worms, facing a charge of homicide in the 1130s; a priest accused of homicide in the diocese of Chur in the early 1180s–all these underwent the ordeal themselves, despite their status.[82] To some minds, indeed, unilateral ordeal seemed peculiarly appropriate for ecclesiastics. In eleventh-century Angers, for example, the hot iron (albeit undergone by proxy) was 'the monks' proof', as contrasted with 'the secular proof' of battle.[83]

These instances make comprehensible the existence, from the later eleventh century, of clerical exemptions from trial by ordeal, either bestowed as a favour or asserted as a right. In 1087, for example, Alfonso VI of León-Castile granted to the clerics of the cathedral of Astorga exemption from a long list of impositions, including the *poena calda*–trial by cauldron.[84] A decade later the attempt by William Rufus to try the charge of treason against Hildebert, bishop of Le Mans, by ordeal elicited a vigorous protest from Hildebert's neighbour and fellow bishop, the canonist Ivo of Chartres. Writing to Hildebert, Ivo said

> He will only believe that you are not guilty of this charge of treason if you demonstrate your innocence by the ordeal of hot iron. You ask me, therefore, whether you may agree in good conscience or whether, whatever happens, you should not abandon your order (*ut non recedas ab ordine*) . . . the duel and the ordeal of hot iron are not accepted by ecclesiastical custom in determining ecclesiastical cases, nor were they instituted by canonical authority . . .[85]

---

[82] *Chronica regia Colonensis*, ed. G. Waitz, MGH, *SRG*, (Hanover, 1880), p. 122; JL 8284, Browe, *De ordaliis*, 1, no. 21; JL 15169, X.5.34.8.

[83] *Cartulaire de L'Abbaye de St-Aubin d'Angers*, ed. Arthur Bertrand de Brousillon (3 vols., Paris, 1903), 1, no. 29, pp. 49-50 (1056).

[84] Tomas Muñoz y Romero, *Colección de Fueros Municipales*, 1 (Madrid, 1847), p. 322; H. Florez *et al.*, *La España sagrada* (51 vols., Madrid, 1747-1879), 16, ap. doc. 21, pp. 470-3.

[85] *Epistola* 74, *PL* 162, cols. 95-6.

Thus, according to Ivo, it would be a denial of Hildebert's *ordo*, or status, to undergo trial by ordeal. The year after Ivo wrote this letter Robert of Arbrissel founded the monastery of Fontevrault in the Loire valley. The monks and nuns of Fontevrault, it was reported, 'were unwilling to defend their property by hot iron or by duel, since this is uncanonical and was prohibited by the blessed Robert, their master and the founder of the place'.[86] It had not been very long before that, in this very same region, trial by ordeal had been known as 'the monks' proof'. Clearly, the advocates of clerical immunity were asserting new norms and defining harder positions.

It is possible to imagine a new emphasis on clerical immunity from the ordeal developing in this period, without a corresponding campaign to abolish the procedure itself altogether. Indeed, there are occasional pieces of evidence from the twelfth century which show how this might have come about. In 1107 the emperor Henry V granted a privilege to the church of Liège. Its seventh clause rules,

'If anyone wounds or kills a servant of ours, he and all his property shall be adjudged to be in the bishop's power and amends fitting the person and the offence shall be paid to the servant. If anyone wounds or strikes the canons themselves, he shall be judged by an ecclesiastical sentence. But if anyone wishes to deny that they are guilty of such an offence, they must clear themselves not by oath but by ordeal, for breach of clerical immunity requires this form of proof' (*dei judicio se expurgabit quam hujusmodi contra clericos injuriae emunitatis legem obtinebit*).[87]

In a case such as this the stress on clerical privilege resulted not in a restriction but in an extension of the ordeal, since those accused of assaults on the canons of Liège no longer had the option of clearing themselves by oath. Similar cases can be cited. In Aragon, for example, the kings protected the favoured church of San Pedro de Jaca by insisting that anyone who advanced a claim against the church's property must support his oath with the hot iron.[88] It is clear, then, that the recognition of a special judicial position for the clergy need not involve the end of the ordeal. If simple clerical trade union-ism were the only force at work, then exemption for the clergy and

---

[86] *Epistola* 78, *PL* 179, cols. 118-19, JL 7528 (Innocent II to the bishops of France, 1132).
[87] Ed. Mina Martens in *Elenchus fontium urbanae*, 1, ed. C. van de Kieft and J. F. Niermeijer (Leiden, 1967), p. 309.
[88] *Colección diplomática de la catedral de Huesca*, ed. A. Durán Gudiol (2 vols., Zaragoza, 1965-9), no. 41, pp. 57-8.

continued use of the ordeal for laymen would have been the most likely outcome of events.

This did not, in fact, happen. In the late twelfth and early thirteenth centuries, alongside the continued vigorous pursuit of clerical exemption, notably by such popes as Alexander III, there was a parallel campaign aimed at unequivocal withdrawal of the priesthood from involvement in the ordeal, regardless of whether the accused were clerical or lay, the charge spiritual or secular, the court ecclesiastical or lay. This uncompromising position found expression in the words of that ardent reformer, Peter the Chanter: 'Even if the universal Church, under penalty of anathema, commanded me as a priest to bewitch the iron or bless the water, I would quicker undergo the perpetual penalty than perform such a thing.'[89] The two positions—complete abolitionism, on the one hand, simple disengagement of ordeal from ecclesiastical law, on the other—were being debated in the later twelfth century. The anonymous canonist who wrote the *Summa Monacensis* in the 1160s or 1170s, pondering the legitimacy of the ordeal, wrote, 'To some it seems that it is illicit, since it seems to tempt God. Others, who do not wish to speak against a custom prevalent in many regions, say that the only prohibition is that it should have no place in ecclesiastical jurisdiction, but is licit in secular courts. Hence the priest may licitly procede to the exorcism of the water or iron.'[90] The issue could hardly be put more sharply: abolition of the ordeal for ecclesiastics and in ecclesiastical courts did not necessarily imply that priests should refuse to participate in ordeal rituals in secular courts.

The men of principle who doubted or challenged the legitimacy of trial by ordeal not only disturbed vested ecclesiastical interests, they also upset the judicial arrangements of lay society. The twelfth century produced many instances of priests troubled in conscience over the issue of trial by ordeal and the secular powers were rarely sympathetic. Already, before the middle of the century, the English theologian, Robert Pullan, was discussing the case of whether a priest opposed to the ordeal must allow a man whom he knows to be guilty to undergo the trial. He believed he should.[91] Peter the Chanter had a harder position. A man who had been accused of murder and offered the

[89] *Verbum abbreviatum*, 78, *PL* 205, col. 543, as translated by Baldwin, 'Intellectual Preparation', p. 632; note also his comments on the question of the authenticity of this passage, p. 632 n. 117.

[90] Browe, *De ordaliis*, 2, no. 100, Baldwin, 'Intellectual Preparation', p. 622 n. 63 (gloss on *Monomachiam*).

[91] *Sentences*, 4.53-4, *PL* 186, cols. 903-5.

chance of clearing himself by the ordeal consulted the Chanter on the matter: 'Peter advised him not to submit to the test and was rewarded by seeing the unhappy defendant carted off to the gibbet'.[92]

There is evidence that priests were sometimes compelled to officiate at ordeals. A letter of Innocent III to a Sardinian magnate complains, 'Although canon law does not admit ordeal by hot iron, cold water and the like, unhappy priests are being compelled to pronounce the blessing and become involved in such proofs and are being fined by the secular officials if they refuse.'[93] A very similar protest was raised by the archbishop of Hamburg-Bremen around the same time. In Hamburg the secular judges forced priests to officiate at ordeals. The priests tried to insist that they would only conduct ordeals if the accused were granted immunity from corporal or capital punishment, but were unsuccessful in imposing these conditions.[94] Clearly, reservations about becoming involved in the shedding of blood were here mingled with doubts about the ordeal. This was an important contributory factor in the campaign against ordeals. It has been rightly pointed out that the prohibition of 1215 occurs 'in the general context of prohibiting clerics from involving themselves in judicial decisions which resulted in the shedding of blood'.[95] Canon 18 of the council, which condemns clerical involvement in the ordeal, also rules that clerics should not be involved in 'sentences of blood', command mercenaries, or practice surgery. This insistence that clerics should have no blood on their hands occurred at a time when secular justice was becoming increasingly bloody. As execution and mutilation grew in importance, edging out earlier systems based on compensation, the priest and the clerk found that the rules of their order and the practices of the secular courts were increasingly discordant.

The decree of 1215 found its widest dissemination as the universal law of the church in Gregory IX's *Decretals*. It was placed there in Book 3, 'On the Life and Honour of Clerks', under *titulus* 50: 'Clerks

---

[92] Baldwin, 'Intellectual Preparation', p. 627; the text is in Peter the Chanter, *Summa de sacramentis*, ed. J.-A. Dugauquier (3 vols. in 5, Analecta mediaevalia Namurcensia, 4, 7, 11, 16, 21, Louvain and Lille, 1954-67), 3/1 (= 11), pp. 363-4.

[93] *PL* 215, col. 394; Po. 2268 (1204).

[94] Browe, *De ordaliis*, 1, no. 86, citing *Hamburgisches UB*, ed. I. M. Lappenberg, 1 (Hamburg, 1842), no. 363 (1184-1207); according to Peter the Chanter, Samson, archbishop of Rheims (1140-61), had been successful in imposing such a condition, *Verbum abbreviatum*, 78, *PL* 205, col. 230.

[95] Baldwin, 'Intellectual Preparation', p. 613. On the rubrics of Canon 18 see A. García y García (ed.), *Constitutiones Concilii quarti Lateranensis una cum Commentariis glossatorum* (Vatican City, 1981), p. 147.

and monks should not be involved in secular affairs'. As this context makes clear, the end of priestly involvement in the ordeal was part of that attempt to draw sharper lines between the clerical and the lay which is traditionally associated with the name of Gregory VII. The resulting change, over the period 1050-1215, can be illustrated by a pair of contrasts. In England, in William the Conqueror's reign, it was laid down that, in ecclesiastical cases, no layman should make a man undergo trial by ordeal without the authority of the bishop and that the ordeal should take place only at the bishop's see or a place appointed by the bishop.[96] A century and a half later a legatine council at Paris ruled, 'Duels and ordeals should not take place in holy sites or churchyards or in the presence of bishops.'[97] The rules had been turned upside down. The close involvement of the bishop was an essential prerequisite in the eleventh century, an unseemly and unholy impropriety in the thirteenth. Similarly, in Holstein in the 1150s, trial by ordeal was forced on the pagan Wends as part of the process of Christianization. Within sixty years, however, Cistercians in Holstein were being given penances as a punishment for their involvement with trial by ordeal.[98] Church discipline was thus attempting to repress what the missionaries of an earlier generation had introduced as an essential adjunct of the new faith.

The doubts of the twelfth century were clearly, in part, doubts about the priestly role in the administration of secular justice. The mutual accommodation typical of Carolingian and post-Carolingian times had been fundamentally disturbed by Gregorianism. The result, over the course of a century and a half, was a new division between the regal and the priestly, involving a disentanglement of the priestly office from many aspects of secular justice. As a result, secular justice was now more clearly defined as such.

The issue of the ordeal was decided definitively in the twelfth and thirteenth centuries not only because of the growth of a body of

[96] W. Stubbs (ed.), *Select Charters* (9th edn., rev. H. W. C. Davis, Oxford, 1913), pp. 99-100; the phrase *judicium . . . portetur* means 'ordeal should be undergone [i.e. carried]', not the more general 'judgement shall be given', as translated in D. C. Douglas and G. W. Greenaway, *English Historical Documents*, 2 (2nd edn., London, 1981), no. 79, p. 648.

[97] Mansi, 22, col. 842 (Paris, 1213, here dated 1212), repeated at Rouen in 1214, ibid., col. 920, K. J. Hefele and H. Leclerq, *Histoire des Conciles* (20 vols., Paris, 1907-52), 5/2, pp. 1315-16.

[98] Helmold of Bosau, *Cronica Slavorum* cap. 84, ed. Bernhard Schmiedler, MGH, *SRG* (Hanover, 1937), p. 164; J.-M. Canivez, *Statuta capitulorum generalium ordinis Cisterciensium*, 1 (Louvain, 1933), pp. 410-11 (1213).

clerical opinion opposed to the practice but also because, by this period, there existed a real monarchical power in the Church, and this power, the papacy, became convinced that the practice should be suppressed. Popes of the ninth century had denounced ordeals and they had flourished nevertheless. Innocent III spoke out and they perished. The difference reflects a change in the structure of the Church as well as a shift of opinion on the substantive issue.

There were three preconditions that had to be fulfilled before the ordeal could be abolished. Firstly, a party within the Church had to be convinced that the practice was wrong. Secondly, this reforming group had to be in a commanding position within the Church–a reforming élite, in fact. Thirdly, the administrative machinery of the Church had to be of such a kind that it would respond to direction from the top. The centralization and systemization of the hierarchy, and the growth of effective bureaucracy and delegation in the twelfth and thirteenth centuries were as much conditions for the end of the ordeal as the change of mind of the clerical élite. As an alliance formed between the Roman Church, the reformers, and the leading school-men, an alliance reinforced by a common training in Romano-canonical law and common high church or Gregorian attitudes, so this curial-scholastic élite forged and exploited new legal and administrative forms to implement its decisions.

In the light of this argument, 1215 re-emerges as decisive. There was no decline of the ordeal; it was abandoned. The papal decision was not a belated recognition of a long process of withering away. It was a policy decision which resulted in the abandonment of the ordeal. The secular legal sources of the thirteenth century show this: the year after the prohibition the ordeal was banned by King Valdemar in Denmark 'because the lord pope has prohibited the ordeal of hot iron';[99] in 1219 it was abandoned in England 'since the ordeal of fire and water is prohibited by the Roman church';[100] in 1247 the *Fueros de Aragon* prohibited ordeals 'to the honour of him who said, "Thou shalt not tempt the Lord thy God"'.[101] The echoes go on into the late medieval law-books: 'Holy Christianity would not suffer God to be tempted thus';[102] the ordeal 'ist verbotten von der Christenheit'.[103]

---

[99] *Diplomatarium Danicum*, ed. N. Skylum-Nielsen, 1st ser., 5 (Copenhagen, 1957), no. 96, pp. 137-43.

[100] *Patent Rolls of the Reign of Henry III (1216–32)* (2 vols., HMSO, 1901-3), 1, p. 186.

[101] Cap. 330, ed. G. Tilander (Lund, 1937), pp. 192-3.

[102] *The Mirror of Justices*, 3.23, ed. W. J. Whittaker (Selden Soc. 7, 1893), p. 110.

[103] *Der richterlich Clagspiegel*, ed. Sebastian Brandt (Strassburg, 1533), fo. 116ᵛ (the

The non-ecclesiastical legislation of the thirteenth to fifteenth century thus recognized the origin and nature of the prohibition–it was a papal policy decision taken on general religious and political grounds. Wherever papal authority was strong, or where a powerful secular ruler chose to enforce the papal ruling, the ordeal could be virtually abolished at a stroke. In more decentralized regions, or places where papal power was weak, the practice survived longer. But the battle was won. The unanimity of clerical opinion in the thirteenth century contrasts decisively with the 'hesitancy' of the twelfth. Everywhere secular authorities had to devise new methods to replace the ordeal. The inquest and torture came into their own.

The ease with which this transformation was accomplished may seem surprising. But the ground had been well prepared institutionally and intellectually within the Church. And the nature of the ordeal was such that a unilateral decision by the Church to abandon the practice left the secular authorities no option. With trifling exceptions,[104] the ordeal could not continue without priests. It belonged to a world where priests and secular rulers had a close symbiosis. When that was destroyed, the practice died.

The ordeal was not primitive, popular, or pagan. It first flourished under a highly ideological Christian kingship. The involvement of the priesthood in the exercise of secular justice was part of that environment. When, over the course of the twelfth century, new views developed about that involvement, what resulted was a desacralizing of secular justice. It was decided, by an important body of Church opinion, that recourse to the ordeal was no longer an appropriate solution to the problem of obtaining proof in doubtful cases. These clerical thinkers and authorities insisted on drawing new lines. Kings and lords would have been quite happy to continue with the ordeal. None of the many changes that had taken place in the eleventh and twelfth centuries had made the ordeal a less appropriate proof–perhaps a few more civil cases could be decided by written evidence, but that is all. The purpose for which the ordeal was intended was the securing of a verdict in circumstances where no other mode of proof

work dates to the first half of the fifteenth century).

[104] e.g. the *Fuero General de Navarra*, a private compilation of between 1234 and 1253, records, 'But in Rome there was a prohibition on any cleric in orders blessing these pebbles [i.e. those used in the ordeal of the cauldron] or the hot iron. If they cannot have a cleric, let the judges bless them', cap. 5.3.18, ed. Pablo Ilarregui and Segundo Lapuerta (Pamplona, 1869, repr., 1964), pp. 184-5.

offered the chance of one. Alternative ways of achieving this goal had to be invented in the aftermath of the abandonment of the ordeal.

The Christian, regalian ordeals of fire and water had been spread throughout Christendom under the influence of Christian kings; they had a narrow but important role in the justice of the period 800-1200; in 1215 they were abandoned on the most ideological grounds.

6

Trial by Battle

TRIAL by battle[1] was a practice akin to the other ordeals and, as the relationship of kindred implies, it exhibited both a family resemblance and unique features. As an ordeal in the most fundamental sense of the word, it was supposed to reveal the judgement of God. On the other hand, its distinctive mode–a fight between individuals–meant that it was in a class of its own. Because of this, its operation, and hence its history, were distinctive. A study of judicial combat must, therefore, note both the differences and the similarities.

Trial by Battle: A Sketch

The early history of trial by battle is very different from that of trial by fire and water. The latter seems to have had its source in the customs of one Germanic people, the Franks.[2] In contrast, trial by battle is found in the early law codes of many Germanic peoples–the Burgundians, Lombards, Alamanni, Bavarians, Thuringians, Frisians, and Saxons. Moreover, although not mentioned in the most ancient version of the Salic law, battle was certainly employed as a proof by the Franks in the sixth century and it has been claimed that its emergence into the written record in the latter part of that century[3] was 'not an innovation but the revival of a practice that had been temporarily repressed'.[4] Thus there is no doubt that trial by battle was a

---

[1] For general discussion of this topic see George Neilson, *Trial by Combat* (Glasgow, 1890); Lea, *Superstition and Force*, pp. 101-247, reissued separately in *The Duel and the Oath*, ed. Edward Peters (Philadelphia, 1974), with the same pagination; G. E. Levi (ed.), *Il duello giudiziario. Encicliopedia e bibliografia* (Florence,1932); Nottarp, *Gottesurteil-studien*, esp. pp. 269-313; Bongert, *Rercherches*, pp. 228-51; M. J. Russell, 'Trial by Battle and the Writ of Right', 'Trial by Battle and the Appeals of Felony', *Journal of Legal History*, 1 (1980), pp. 111-64; J.-M. Carbasse, 'Le Duel judiciaire dans les coutumes meridionales', *Annales du Midi*, 87 (1975), pp. 385-403, Szeftel, 'Jugement de Dieu', pp. 267-93.

[2] As argued in Chapter 2 above.

[3] In the additions to the Salic law, *Pactus legis Salicae*, 131.2, ed. K. A. Eckhardt, MGH, *LL nat. Germ.* 4/1 (Hanover, 1962), p. 266, and as recorded in Gregory of Tours *Libri historiarum X*, 7.14, 10.10, ed. Henri Omont and Gaston Collon (rev. edn., Paris, 1913), pp. 263-5, 424-5.

[4] Heinrich Brunner, *Deutsche Rechtsgeschichte* (2 vols.: 1, 2nd edn., Leipzig, 1906, repr. Berlin, 1961; 2, rev. Claudius von Schwerin, Berlin, 1928, repr. Berlin, 1958), 2, p. 556.

widespread custom in this early period, *c.* 500-800, among most of the continental Germanic peoples.

There are some curious exceptions to this general rule. The Goths do not seem to have employed trial by battle. There is no reference to it in the Visigothic law and a letter of Cassiodorus, written on behalf of Theodoric the Ostrogoth, urges the inhabitants of Pannonia not to have recourse to battle among themselves, but to 'imitate our Goths, who practice warfare against foreigners but moderation at home'.[5] A celebrated duel that took place between two Goths in the reign of Lewis the Pious, which has usually been cited as proof that trial by battle was part of Visigothic law by the ninth century, may not illustrate that point at all.[6] As late as 1019 a plaintiff refused battle on the grounds that 'the Gothic Law does not prescribe that cases should be determined by battle'.[7]

An even clearer case of a Germanic people without judicial combat is provided by the Anglo-Saxons. The evidence is, of course, negative evidence, but the silence on the subject is deafening. There are no mentions of trial by battle in any pre-Conquest source. The earliest reference to the duel in England is that in the laws of William the Conqueror: 'If any Englishman challenges a Frenchman to combat on a charge of theft or homicide . . .'[8] and it is clear that the practice was introduced into the country by the Normans. The absence of trial by battle among the pre-Conquest English is somewhat puzzling and there has been no satisfactory explanation for it. 'Employed so extensively as legal evidence throughout their ancestral regions, by the kindred tribes from which they sprang,' mused Henry Charles Lea,[9] 'harmonizing, moreover, with their general habits and principles of action, it would seem impossible that they should not likewise have practised it [i.e. the duel].' The surprising fact should perhaps serve as a warning: there are limits to what can be deduced from Germanic ancestry and 'general habits'.

---

[5] *Variarum libri XII*, 3, *epistola* 24, *PL* 69, col. 589. The reference may, however, simply be to internecine strife.

[6] Iglesia Ferreirós, 'El proceso del conde Bera', pp. 2, 189-98.

[7] 'Eo quod lex Gothica non jubet ut per pugnam discutiantur negotia', Petrus de Marca, *Marca Hispanica*, ed. S. Baluze (Paris, 1688), app. doc. 181, col. 1013.

[8] *Willelmi articuli*, cap. 1, ed. Liebermann, *Gesetze*, 1, p. 483.

[9] *Superstition and Force*, pp. 114-15; the difficulty of explaining the absence of trial by battle among the Anglo-Saxons is graphically demonstrated by the feeble arguments to which even Pollock and Maitland were reduced, Frederick Pollock and Frederic W. Maitland, *The History of English Law before the time of Edward I* (2 vols., 2nd edn., reissued with an intro. by S. C. Milsom, Cambridge, 1968), 1, pp. 50-1.

A final conundrum in the geographical range of judicial combat is offered by the case of the Scandinavians.[10] The sagas present a world in which challenges to *hólmganga*–single combat (originally on an island, *holm*)–are frequent, and where elaborate procedural rules exist. The sagas were written, mainly, in the thirteenth century, but their action is set in a much earlier period, the tenth and eleventh centuries. According to the saga writers, who are supported in this by the twelfth-century chronicler Saxo Grammaticus,[11] the duel was abolished in Scandinavia in the early eleventh century. There is certainly no place for it in the lawbooks of the twelfth and thirteenth centuries. The picture would thus be perfectly consistent–if we can only accept the sagas as reasonable evidence for the customs of the time three centuries before their composition. Understandably, historians have often been unwilling to do this. Yet, if the sagas are not historically accurate, the most likely source for the social customs they describe must be the Icelandic society of their own day. It may well be the case, then, that duels continued in Scandinavia in the thirteenth century, despite the silence of the lawbooks.[12]

Trial by battle was, thus, a custom found widely, but not universally, among Germanic peoples, which could, of course, spread into new areas (as England after 1066 or Spain at some indeterminate date before 1000) or disappear from its former haunts (as, possibly, Scandinavia after the early eleventh century).

Trial by battle was thus a common heritage of the Germanic kingdoms of the early Middle Ages. The Carolingians regarded it as an essential and regular part of judicial procedure. They and their successors hoped, for example, that it might inhibit perjured oaths: 'It is better that they fight in the field with clubs than that they commit perjury'.[13] In 967 Otto I gave a ruling for Italy that pleas of land where the issue turned on the authenticity of documentary evidence could be decided in future only by battle, not by oath. The objection to the mere oath was 'that a detestable and wicked custom, which should not

---

[10] On the duel in Scandinavia, see Marlene Ciklami, 'The Old Icelandic Duel', *Scandinavian Studies*, 35 (1963), pp. 175-94, Olav Bø, '*Hólmganga* and *Einvígi*. Scandinavian Forms of the Duel', *Medieval Scandinavia*, 2 (1969), pp. 132-48; Konrad Maurer, *Vorlesungen über altnordische Rechtgeschichte* (5 vols. in 6 and index, Leipzig, 1907-38), 5, pp. 694-711.

[11] *Gesta Danorum*, 10.11.4, ed. J. Olrik and H. Raeder (2 vols., Copenhagen, 1931-57), 1, p. 282.

[12] For further discussion of the nature of the Scandinavian duel see below, pp. 114-15.

[13] MGH, *Capit.* 1, ed. Alfred Boretius (Hanover, 1883), p. 217 (799).

be imitated, has grown up in Italy, whereby those who do not fear God and are not afraid to perjure themselves, make acquisitions by their oaths with the appearance of legality'.[14] It has already been shown that the ordeals of fire and water were sometimes used to buttress the oath and the same is true of trial by battle. The parties to the dispute would still have to make an oath but would now have to back it up with combat.

The judicial combat was employed in a wide variety of cases. For instance, some texts of the eleventh-century Italian lawbook, the *Liber Papiensis*, include a list of twenty-three 'actions which may result in judicial duel'. The list includes treason, sexual offences like adultery and fornication, arson, poisoning, clashes of testimony, challenges to documentary evidence (in accordance with the ruling of 967), property cases, and thefts of property above a certain value.[15] The first impression this list makes is of the number and diversity of cases which involved duel: there are crimes against persons, crimes against property, cases criminal, civil, and political. Looked at more closely, however, certain identifiable categories emerge. There are the heinous and clandestine crimes, like treason, arson, and poisoning; the cases turning on disputed evidence; cases like theft, which are clandestine but not heinous; and trifling cases are excluded. This pattern is common in the legal arrangements of many European countries in the Middle Ages.

Treason was, essentially, a betrayal of one's lord and, since both parties, accuser and accused, would often be members of the military aristocracy, it is psychologically quite understandable that the issue would be resolved by battle.

> When Charles sees that they are false
> He bows his head in grief . . .
> But, behold, now stands before him a knight, Thierry . . .
> He speaks courteously to the emperor,
> 'Good lord king, do not lament so!
> You know I have served you long,
> By family descent I am bound to support your cause.
> Whatever wrong Roland did to Ganelon,
> A man must protect your service.
> Ganelon is a felon because he has betrayed that.
> He is perjured and foresworn towards you.
> For that I judge he should be hanged . . .

---

[14] MGH, *Const.* 1, ed. Ludwig Weiland (Hanover, 1893), no. 13, pp. 27-30.
[15] Ed. Alfred Boretius, MGH, *LL* 4 (Hanover, 1868), pp. 590-1.

Just like a felon who commits a felony.
If his relatives call me a liar,
With this sword I wear upon my belt
I will defend my judgement.'
The Franks respond, 'Well said!'[16]

Real knights as well as epic ones took this stand. In January 1095 at William Rufus' court at Salisbury 'Geoffrey Bainard accused William of Eu, the king's kinsman, of treason against the king, and maintained it against him in a trial by battle. After he was defeated the king ordered his eyes to be put out and then had him castrated'.[17] In 1163 another famous duel was fought after Robert de Montfort accused Henry of Essex of betraying the king during the Welsh expedition of 1157 by throwing down the royal standard and alarming the troops by proclaiming that the king was dead. Henry was defeated not only by Robert's 'many hard and manful blows' but also by the miraculous intervention of St Edmund, whom he had offended.[18] In 1294 William de Vescy appeared at Westminster on horseback and with full knightly arms to defend himself against the charge of uttering 'things against our lord the king and his estate' (*choses . . . encontre nostre seingnur le Rey e sun estat*).[19]

The link between accusations of treason and trial by battle was so strong that when Frederick II freed his southern Italian subjects from the judicial combat, he expressly excluded charges of treason. In his *Constitutions of Melfi* or *Liber Augustalis* of 1231 he made this a general rule: 'We wish single combat, commonly called duel, to have no place in cases between our subjects . . . We make an exception of charges of treason, for which we retain trial by battle'.[20] Duel was also retained, for such cases, in Frederick's German legislation.[21]

Men resorted to the judicial duel to decide charges of treason long

---

[16] *La Chanson de Roland*, canto 284, ed. F. Whitehead (2nd edn., Oxford, 1946), p. 112.

[17] *Anglo-Saxon Chronicle* (E), *s.a.* 1096, ed. Charles Plummer, *Two of the Saxon Chronicles Parallel* (2 vols., Oxford, 1892-9), 1, p. 232.

[18] Jocelin of Brakelond, *Chronicle*, ed. and tr. H. E. Butler (London, 1949), pp. 68-71; William of Newburgh, *Historia rerum Anglicarum* 2.5 and Robert of Torigny, *Chronica*, ed. R. Howlett, *Chronicles of the Reigns of Stephen, Henry II and Richard I* (4 vols., RS, 1884-9) 1, p. 108 and 4, p. 218.

[19] *Rotuli Parliamentorum* (6 vols., London, 1783), 1, pp. 127-33; *Calendar of Documents relating to Ireland*, ed. H. S. Sweetman (5 vols., London, 1875-86), 4, no. 147, pp. 71-3.

[20] J. L. A. Huillard-Bréholles, *Historia diplomatica Friderici secundi* (6 vols., Paris, 1852-61), 1, pp. 56, 376, 2, pp. 105-6; *Constitutions of Melfi*, 2.33, ibid. 4/1, pp. 105-6; *Die Konstitutionen Friedrichs II. für sein Königreich Sizilien*, ed. and tr. (into German), Hermann Conrad *et al.* (Cologne, 1973), pp. 220-2.

[21] MGH, *Const.* 2, ed. Ludwig Weiland (Hanover, 1896), no. 196, p. 246 (*Landfriede* of 1235, cap. 24 in the Latin version only).

after the custom had fallen into general disuse. The Court of Chivalry, which is attested in England from the mid-fourteenth century, had special cognizance of treasons committed outside the realm, and a regular form of proof in such cases was battle.[22] In 1380, for example, Sir John de Annesley fought and defeated Thomas Caterton on a charge of betraying one of the king's castles in Normandy to the French.[23] English law was in no way exceptional. From Catalonia to Scotland, from the sixth century to the sixteenth, charges of treason were settled by trial by battle.

Closely allied to treason were charges involving breaches of agreement, especially violation of truces. Such cases of *treuge violate* could lead to battle, as Henry (VII)'s ruling of 1234 shows in the case of Germany, or the charter of St Gaudens for the south of France, or the *Libellus de bataila facienda* for Catalonia.[24] The appropriateness of the duel for such charges is clear. Charges of treason, breach of truce, or perjury involved not only the imputation of a wrong, but also the implicit accusation of bad faith. In such circumstances an exculpatory oath was clearly not acceptable, for the charge implied that no trust could be placed in the word of the accused.

Battle was also a very common form of proof in ordinary civil and criminal cases. In thirteenth-century England, for example, battle was employed either for appeals of felony, when one man accused another of a serious crime, or in cases initiated by a writ of right, which attempted to determine the true ownership of a piece of property. In both cases battle was optional: the accused, in the first case, or the tenant in the second, could opt for a jury rather than battle. Naturally, careful consideration had to be given to the choice between jury and battle. Local conditions were obviously important. In 1287 the monks of Bury St Edmund's, involved in a dispute over the ownership of two Suffolk manors, wrote that 'After discussion of the case, since we were doubtful about the countryside, as friendly with and akin to our enemies, we decided that our right was to be defended by the duel'.[25]

[22] See George D. Squibb, *The High Court of Chivalry* (Oxford, 1959).

[23] J. G. Bellamy, 'Sir John de Annesley and the Chandos Inheritance', *Nottingham Medieval Studies*, 10 (1966), pp. 94-105.

[24] MGH, *Const.* 2 (as in n. 21), no. 318, p. 428; Paul Ourliac, 'Le Duel judiciaire dans le sud-ouest', *Revue du Nord*, 40 (1958), pp. 345-8, at p. 346, reprinted in *Études d'histoire du droit médiévale* (Paris, 1979), pp. 253-8, at p. 255; F. Valls-Taberner, 'Notes sobre el duel judicial a Catalunya', in *Obras selectas*, 2 (Barcelona, 1954), pp. 247-57, at p. 250.

[25] V. H. Galbraith, 'The Death of a Champion (1287)', in *Studies in Medieval History presented to F. M. Powicke*, ed. R. W. Hunt, W. A. Pantin, and R. W. Southern (Oxford, 1948, repr. 1969), pp. 283-95, quotation at p. 284.

Battle was not invoked for every civil or criminal plea. In civil cases or charges of theft the property involved had to be worth more than a specified amount.[26] Obviously it was thought that endangering a man's life for a few shillings was 'a wicked custom'.[27] It was sometimes laid down that battle could only take place when other forms of proof were not available. For example, in thirteenth-century Catalonia, 'if the accuser can prove his charge through authentic charters or through trustworthy witness, then that proof should be admitted and battle should not be adjudged . . . men may have recourse to the judgement of God only when human proof fails.'[28] In 1306, in his ordinance restricting trial by battle, Philip IV of France allowed duels in charges of homicide and other capital crimes only when these were committed secretly, when there were presumptions against the accused and when 'they could not be convicted by witnesses'.[29] Similar provisions can be found in England and Germany.[30]

Duels not only took place between accuser and accused, or between two parties in a civil dispute. It was possible for witnesses to be challenged; or a man accused of theft might claim that he had bought the item in question in good faith from a third party ('vouching to warranty') and, if the third party denied this, trial by battle might result; or, in France, a claim of default of justice against a lord might lead to battle. There were also rules about who could challenge whom. The unfree were generally not allowed to challenge the free: 'a serf may not fight a free man', in Beaumanoir's words.[31] Indeed, serfs had to be especially enfranchised before they were allowed to challenge free men.[32] In Germany a superior was permitted to refuse the

---

[26] For examples see Lea, *Superstition and Force*, pp. 147-8.

[27] *Ordonnances des roys de France de la troisième race*, 1, ed. E. de Laurière (Paris, 1723), p. 16: Louis VII's abolition of duel in Orleans for cases involving less than five sous, 1168.

[28] R. Otto (ed.), 'Die Verordnung für den gottesgerichtlichen Zweikampf zu Barcelona', *Zeitschrift für romanischen Philologie*, 13 (1889), pp. 98-114, quotation at p. 102.

[29] *Ordonnances*, 1 (as in n. 27), pp. 435-41.

[30] e.g. Thomas of Woodstock, *Ordenaunce and Fourme of Fighting within Lists*, ed. Travers Twiss, *Monumenta juridica. The Black Book of the Admiralty* (4 vols., RS, 1871-6), 1, pp. 304-5; MGH, *Const.* 2 (as in n. 21), no. 318, p. 428 (Henry (VII), 1234).

[31] Philippe de Beaumanoir, *Coutumes de Beauvasis*, cap. 63, ed. A. Salmon (2 vols., Paris, 1899-1900, repr. with vol. of commentary by Georges Hubrecht, Paris, 1970-4), 2, p. 414.

[32] *Ordonnances*, 1 (as in n. 27), p. 3-4, 5: 'servi sancti Fossatensis (Carnotensis) ecclesiae adversus omnes homines tam liberos quam servos, in omnibus causis, placitis et negotiis, liberam et perfectam habeant testificandi et bellandi licentiam' (Charters of Louis VI, 1118 and 1128).

challenge of an inferior–one 'worse born' than he[33]–and, if a knight challenged another knight, he had to prove his ancestry: 'the right of fighting the duel will not be granted to him unless he can prove that he, from of old, along with his parents, is a legitimate knight by birth.'[34] The apparent exclusivity should not delude us. The principle was that one could only challenge one's peers, not that challenges were in any way aristocratic. In the early and high Middle Ages the judicial duel was not a distinctive habit of the upper classes. It was only with the rise of the duel of chivalry in the later Middle Ages that trial by battle began to be a distinctively aristocratic activity.

Especially for the period after 1200 there are plenty of fairly detailed accounts of the procedure involved in judicial combat. Lawbooks such as the *Sachsenspiegel* and Beaumanoir, ordinances like those of Philip IV in 1306 and treatises like the Catalan *Libellus de bataila* or Thomas of Woodstock's *Ordenaunce and Fourme of Fighting within Lists* discuss the size and situation of the place of battle, the formalities, and the armaments involved.[35] A clearly demarcated spot–an island or specially marked-out lists–was chosen; rules were enforced regarding the behaviour of spectators; solemn injunctions and oath-swearing preceded the actual fight.

The weapons allowed were carefully regulated. Some traditions, such as the arming of the contestants with only a club and shield, were remarkably resistant to change: judicial combat was fought in this way–*cum fustibus et scutis*–in the Carolingian period and, still, seven centuries later, in the fifteenth century.[36] Ethnic and class distinctions

---

[33] *Sachsenspiegel, Landrecht*, 1.63.3, ed. Karl August Eckhardt, MGH, *Fontes iuris*, NS. 1/1 (2nd edn., Gottingen, 1955), p. 122.

[34] MGH, *Const.* 1 (as in n. 14), no. 140, p. 197 (*Landfriede* of Frederick Barbarossa, 1152, c. 10); compare the rules in the *Sachsenspiegel, Landrecht* (as in n. 33) which require a 'scepenbare vri man' to enumerate his four grandparents before he can challenge or receive the challenge of a peer, 1.51.4, 3.29.1, ed. cit., pp. 109, 211-12–see also 3.65.1, 3.79.3, pp. 251, 262.

[35] *Sachsenspiegel, Landrecht* (as in n. 33) 1.63.1-65.1, ed. cit., pp. 119-26; Beaumanoir, *Coutumes* (as in n. 31), caps. 61 and 64, ed. cit., 2, pp. 375-98, 427-35; *Ordonnances*, 1 (as in n. 27), pp. 435-41 (notes); *Libellus*, ed. Otto (as in n. 28); Thomas of Woodstock, *Ordenaunce* (as in n. 30), 1, pp. 301-29. See also Olivier de la Marche, *Le Livre de l'advis de gaige de bataille* and Hardouin de la Jaille, *Formulaires des gaiges de bataille*, ed. Bernard Prost, *Traicte de la forme et devis comme on faict les tournois* (Paris, 1878), pp. 1-54, 135-91; M. Pfeffer, 'Die Formalitäten des gottesgerichtlichen Zweikampfs im der altfranzösischen Epik', *Zeitschrift für romanische Philologie*, 9 (1885), pp. 1-74; M. J. Russell, 'Trial by Battle Procedure in Writs of Right and Criminal Appeals', *Tijdschrift voor Rechtsgeschiedenis*, 53 (1983), pp. 124-34; idem, 'Accoutrements of Battle', *Law Quarterly Review*, 99 (1983), pp. 432-42.

[36] For the Carolingian period, see, for example, MGH, *Capit.* 1 (as in n. 13), pp. 117,

were also important, however. Knights tended to acquire the right to fight on horseback, with knightly arms. Beaumanoir recounts an occasion when there was a lively debate before a battle 'in the wood of Vincennes' about the proper arming of a squire when he appealed a knight.[37] The custom (like most medieval customs) was clearly negotiable.

Despite the elaborate formalism of the proceedings, the battle itself was not a gavotte. Especially in criminal cases, where submission meant death, the fight was 'à outrance'. Gouging of eyes was common, and there is a famous line in Bracton, who advises that a man's front teeth 'help greatly to victory',[38] a point that is illustrated by a duel in Winchester in 1456, when one party took the other 'by the nose with his teeth' and thus won the fight.[39] The following is the account of a judicial combat fought in Flanders in 1127:

... both sides fought bitterly. Guy had unhorsed his adversary and kept him down with his lance just as he liked whenever Herman tried to get up. Then his adversary, coming closer, disemboweled Guy's horse, running him through with his sword. Guy, having slipped from his horse, rushed at his adversary with his sword drawn. Now there was a continuous and bitter struggle, with alternating thrusts of swords, until both, exhausted by the weight and burden of arms, threw away their shields and hastened to gain victory in the fight by resorting to wrestling. Herman the Iron fell prostrate on the ground, and Guy was lying on top of him smashing the knight's face and eyes with his iron gauntlets. But Herman, prostrate, little by little regained his strength from the coolness of the earth ... and by cleverly lying quiet made Guy believe he was certain of victory. Meanwhile, gently moving his hand down to the lower edge of the cuirass where Guy was not protected, Herman seized him by the testicles, and summoning all his strength for the brief space of one moment he hurled Guy from him; by this tearing motion all the lower parts of the body were broken so that Guy, now prostrate, gave up, crying out that he was conquered and dying.[40]

Such a bloody business could not be undertaken by everybody in person, and there were very common general rules about who could

180, 268-9, 283-4; for a fifteenth-century example, see the accounts of the duel at Valenciennes discussed below.

[37] Beaumanoir, *Coutumes* (as in n. 31), cap. 61, ed. cit., 2, pp. 397-8.

[38] *De legibus et consuetudines regni Angliae*, ed. George E. Woodbine, rev. and tr. Samuel E. Thorne (4 vols., Cambridge, Mass., 1968-77), 2, p. 410.

[39] Nielson, *Trial by Combat* (as in n. 1), p. 157.

[40] Galbert of Bruges, *De multro ... Karoli comitis Flandriarum*, cap. 58, ed. Henri Pirenne, *Histoire du Meurtre de Charles le Bon* (Paris, 1891), pp. 93-5, tr. James Bruce Ross, *The Murder of Charles the Good*, (rev. edn., New York, 1967), pp. 212-13.

offer a proxy. Women, the young, the old,[41] and the sick and maimed were almost universally excused. Clerics and Jews were frequently permitted to offer champions. These rules were not unvarying and uniform, of course: sometimes women seem to have fought in person; the Jews' right to have champions seems to have been established only gradually.[42] Nevertheless, a large number of those liable to be involved in suits did have the right to a representative or champion to fight their duel for them.

This was a right which spread over the course of time. One thirteenth-century Italian jurist commented, 'But today by custom anyone is allowed to have a champion.'[43] In England restrictions on the use of champions were eroded during the thirteenth century.[44] The natural outcome of this process was the birth of a class of professional champions. These were not always very savoury characters. The *Sachsenspiegel*, for example, categorizes them along with actors and bastards as 'unlaw-worthy' (*rechtelos*[45]). It was a trade in which foreign adventurers could make their mark. Several of the champions recorded in thirteenth-century England were from outside the realm, like Duncan the Scot, who was enlisted to fight duels on the writ of right in Dorset in 1229 and Middlesex in 1230.[46] But champions could be retained on a reasonably·regular financial basis, like Thomas of Bruges, who was paid 6s. 8d. a year by the bishop of Hereford 'so long as the said Thomas is able to perform the functions of champion'; payment of his retaining fee is recorded from 1276 to 1289.[47] In Italy professional champions were organized, regulated, and provided for litigants by the communes.[48]

---

[41] Sometimes the old were permitted to clear themselves by compurgation rather than by providing a champion, e.g. *Leges quatuor burgorum*, cap. 22, *Acts of the Parliament of Scotland*, 1, ed. T. Thomson and C. Innes (Edinburgh, 1844), p. 24 (336) and *Ancient Laws and Customs of the Burghs of Scotland*, 1 (Edinburgh, 1868), p. 11.

[42] Nottarp, *Gottesurteilstudien*, pp. 294-8; see also Eidelberg, 'Trial by Ordeal'.

[43] Roffredus of Benevento, *Summa de Pugna*, ed. Patetta, *Le ordalie*, pp. 480-92, quotation at p. 485.

[44] Finalized by the abolition of the requirement that champions be witnesses in the Statute of Westminster I, cap. 41, *Statutes of the Realm*, 1 (London, 1810), p. 37.

[45] *Sachsenspiegel, Landrecht* (as in n. 33), 1.38.1, ed. cit., p. 100.

[46] *Bracton's Notebook*, ed. F. W. Maitland (3 vols., London, 1887), nos. 328 and 400, 2, pp. 273-4 and 328-9; *Curia Regis Rolls*, 13 (HMSO, 1959), no. 1907, p. 400, and 14 (HMSO, 1961), no. 1186, p. 252; Nielson has a nicely patriotic interest in this as 'a bit of the history of a Scotsman', *Trial by Combat* (as in n. 1), p. 49 n. 5.

[47] *Roll of the Household Expenses of Richard de Swinfield, Bishop of Hereford, 1289-90*, ed. John Webb (2 vols., Camden Society, 59 and 62, 1853-4), 1 (= 59), pp. 125 and 201.

[48] Nottarp, *Gottesurteilstudien*, p. 302.

The least respectable and most despised of those who fought trial by battle were the 'approvers' of medieval England, men who had been accused of a felony and had turned Crown witness. They undertook to challenge their accomplices or other felons in the hope of eventual pardon. They were maintained at the Crown's expense and sometimes contracted to fight a fixed number of duels. In 1221, for example, it was recorded that Robert, son of Patrick, 'was captured at Kidderminster fleeing in company with thieves . . . he confessed that he is a thief . . . and he turns an approver to fight five battles' (*et devenit probator ad faciendum quinque duella*)'.[49]

The advantages of having criminals kill each other were clear to contemporaries: 'approvers . . . have a power, granted by the prince, to clean up the land (*ut terram purgent*) and win peace for the faithful . . . there are many who say that . . . it is licit for such accusers to accuse and convict the wicked'. This was not a position held by all: 'However, it is not safe to say this, both because the duel is prohibited by the sacred canons and because, according to divine law, a man convicted of or confessing to a crime ought not to have the right to accuse others'.[50]

Battle and Ordeal

Not all single combats fought in medieval Europe were ordeals. Some, of course, were simply private acts of violence. Others were more formally regulated, yet not judicial. Finally, there was trial by battle proper, the judicial combat. A passage from Beaumanoir illustrates some of these distinctions:

When there is a state of war between gentlefolk on account of some deed and some members of the lineage plead trial by battle for that deed, the state of war ceases, for it is clear that they wish to seek vengeance for the misdeed through judicial process, and this is why the state of war ceases. If anyone commits any outrage on the other party during this judicial process, he should be punished for the deed just as if there had never been a state of war . . .[51]

Beaumanoir has in mind three distinct types of combat that may exist. The first is the violent attack ('some deed') outside 'the state of war', an outrage which is simply wrong. Secondly, there are acts of violence committed during a state of war. In contrast to the first category, these

---

[49] *Select Pleas of the Crown (1200–25)*, ed. F. W. Maitland (Selden Soc., 1, 1887), no. 140, p. 92.
[50] Thomas of Chobham, *Summa confessorum*, 7.4.6.7, ed. F. Broomfield (Analecta mediaevalia Namurcensia, 25, Louvain and Paris, 1968), pp. 427-8.
[51] Beaumanoir, *Coutumes* (as in n. 31), c. 63, ed. cit., 2, p. 417.

are rule-bound, they are defined and regarded in the light of the state of war which now exists between the parties. In many countries, for example, an act of violence against those who were one's official enemies, that is, against those with whom a state of war existed, was punished quite differently from other acts of violence. Lastly, there was the judicial combat. Pledging trial by battle ends the state of war, because it is now clear that the wronged party 'wish to seek vengeance for the misdeed through judicial process' (*car il apert que l'en veut querre venjance du mesfet par justice*). The existence of this threefold gradation—ruleless acts of violence, rule-bound violence within the feud and judicial combat—makes it clear that, in Beaumanoir's France at least, the duel was judicial and was not simply 'private war under regulations'.[52] Such private war did exist, but was explicitly distinguished from the *justice* of the duel. The same point could be made about the duel of honour of modern times. It was certainly formal and minutely regulated, but it was not judicial and, indeed, was illegal in most countries. Regulated private combat is thus not the same thing as trial by battle.

Even if judicial, however, the duel did not have to have the character of a *iudicium dei*. It is possible to imagine it as simply a device for reaching a decision, and German scholars, in particular, enjoy the distinction between 'a means of obtaining a decision' (*Entscheidungsmittel*) and 'a means of obtaining proof' (*Beweismittel*).[53] Although abstract, this distinction is important. The idea of 'letting them fight it out' is at least as strong as the sentiment 'may the best man win' (even given that 'best' means 'with the best case'). The Scandinavian duel, the *hólmganga*, for example, seems to have been a formal *Entscheidungsmittel*, rather than a judgement of God, and the Norsemen had few illusions about the causes of success or failure in the duel. In *Njal's Saga*, for instance, when the Icelander Mord is challenged to the duel by Hrut, he 'took counsel with his friends as to the advisability of accepting the challenge. The *godi* Jorund spoke: "You don't need any advice from us in this matter, for you know that you will lose both your life and your money if you fight with Hrut. He is a formidable opponent; he is powerful and brave." '[54] There is no mention here of

---

[52] Pollock and Maitland, *History of English Law* (as in n. 9), 1, p. 39 n. 7, quoting Sir James Stephen, *A History of the Criminal Law of England* (3 vols., London, 1883), 1, p. 61.
[53] e.g. Nottarp, *Gottesurteilstudien*, pp. 269-70.
[54] Cap. 8, tr. C. F. Bayerschmidt and L. M. Hollander (London, 1956), p. 34; cf. the remark of Ciklamini, 'Old Icelandic Duel' (as in n. 10), p. 190: 'The duel was not

divine intervention or even of the justice of the case. Similarly, the duel of honour of modern times was fought between aristocrats and officers over insults and contained scarcely a hint of the idea that God was revealing the truth in the outcome.

These distinctions, between ruleless, rule-bound, and judicial combat, and between the duel as a means of determining a case and as a proof, may help us define our subject. If we are considering trial by ordeal, the form of duel that concerns us is the judicial *iudicium dei* – a judicial process designed to obtain proof by a direct verdict of God. Already, in the earliest law codes, trial by battle is termed 'judgement of God'. In the Burgundian laws of *c.*500, for instance, when the oath of witnesses was challenged, 'permission to fight should not be denied, so that one of those witnesses who have assembled to swear oaths should fight, with God as judge'.[55] The phrase 'judgement of God' is a synonym for the duel in both Lombard and Bavarian law.[56] When Gundeberga, the Frankish wife of the Lombard king Charoald (626-36), was accused of treason, a deputation from her relatives suggested, 'Order the man who brought this charge to arm himself and let another man of Queen Gundeberga's party proceed to single combat with him. By the conflict of these two the judgement of God will be made known, whether Gundeberga is innocent or guilty of this charge.'[57] Leaping the centuries, the same underlying concept, refined now by scholastic analysis, can be found in the definition advanced by the learned men of the thirteenth century: 'A duel is a single combat between two persons with the purpose of proving the truth of some hidden thing through the victory of one of them, by, as it were, a sign of divine judgement, which otherwise cannot be made clear by human judgement.'[58] The components, in the fifth century as in the thirteenth, are clear: the absence of other means of proof, divine judgement, single combat, a means of proof.

It is apparent, then, that in some respects trial by battle was an ordeal in the same sense as trial by fire and water. It was a means of

considered a judgement of God'. See also Gwyn Jones, 'The Religious Elements of the Icelandic *Hólmganga*', *Modern Language Review*, 27 (1932), pp. 308-13.

[55] *Leges Burgundionum*, 45, ed. L. R. von Salis, MGH, *LL nat. Germ.* 2/1 (Hanover, 1892), pp. 75-6; cf. 80.2, p. 104.

[56] *Leges Langobardorum, Edictus Rothari*, 198, *Liutprandi leges, Anni IX*, 21. III, ed. Franz Beyerle (2nd edn., Witzenhausen, 1962), pp. 53-4, 111; *Lex Baiwariorum*, 2.1, ed. Ernst von Schwind, MGH, *LL nat. Germ.* 5/2 (Hanover, 1926), p. 292.

[57] *The Fourth Book of the Chronicle of Fredegar*, cap. 51, ed. and tr. J. M. Wallace-Hadrill (London, etc., 1960), pp.41-3.

[58] Henry of Ghent, *Quodlibeta*, 5.32, (2 vols., Paris 1518), I, ff. 210-11.

proof which relied upon God's intervention when normal human procedures were not available. It could be deeply enmeshed in that axiomatic providentialism which was the psychological and intellectual framework of the Middle Ages: 'Why is it that causes between kingdoms and peoples and even between individuals are, by the divine judgement, committed to the settlement of battle? And that victory goes to the party with the more just case?'[59]

Yet, despite this fundamental similarity, which links trial by battle with the other ordeals in a tight sibling group within the wider extended family of oaths, sortilege, and divination, there are also crucial differences. Unlike trial by fire or water, the judicial combat was bilateral, involving both the parties, did not demand a response from the physical elements, and led to bloodshed. The existence of these distinguishing features meant that the history of trial by battle was not simply a parallel to that of the other ordeals.

The simple fact that the mode of trial by battle was single combat had important consequences. Medieval men had plenty of experience of fighting and were well aware of the physical, psychological, and technical factors that determined defeat or victory. The idea that the justice of the cause was, therefore, the single relevant datum for victory in the ordeal was, perhaps, not always entirely convincing. Certainly, very early scepticism about the verdicts of trial by battle is recorded. As has been mentioned, Liudprand, king of the Lombards (713-44), wrote, 'We are unsure about the judgement of God and have heard of many men who have lost their case unjustly through trial by combat'.[60]

It was, of course, possible to dismiss trial by fire and water in the same way, by claiming that the outcome of such tests was determined by physical conditions (such as the retention of air by the person undergoing trial by cold water). Claims of this sort were harder to maintain, however, since the very idiosyncrasy of trial by fire and water rendered it less vulnerable to casual scepticism. Trial by battle was a ritual form of an activity that men frequently saw around them in a non-ritual form. They might well wonder why the result of the ritual form should be determined by forces so irrelevant to the non-ritual

---

[59] Words attributed to King Gundobad of the Burgundians, Agobard of Lyon, *Liber adversus legem Gundobadi*, 13, ed. cit., p. 27.

[60] *Leges Langobardorum, Liutprandi leges, Anni XIX*, cap. 118 (II), ed. Beyerle (as in n. 56), pp. 155-6.

form. Trial by fire and water existed *only* in a ritual form and was, therefore, relatively immune from doubts of this kind.

Moreover, the possibility of scepticism about the results of the duel reinforced, and was reinforced by, clerical criticism of trial by battle on the grounds that it involved the shedding of Christian blood. It gave ammunition to those who thought trial by battle was wrong. Here, again, a distinction can be drawn between battle and fire and water. Clerical opinion and canon law were far more consistently and explicitly opposed to the duel than to the ordeals of fire and water. There were no ecclesiastical apologists like Hincmar of Rheims; no church councils prescribed the duel, no canonists endorsed it.[61] It had, it is true, permeated local custom to such an extent that prelates and ecclesiastical corporations had to preside over it or fight their causes by its means, but there was never that uncertainty of principle found in clerical attitudes to ordeal by fire and water.

From the very earliest days of the recorded history of trial by battle, clerics raised against the simple providentialism of those who equated 'battle' and 'divine judgement' a more sophisticated theodicy, in which the ultimate rather than the immediate sense of providence was stressed and full allowance was given to man's inability to know very much of God's long-term plans:

Can it really be that the Highest Justice requires spears and swords to judge cases? We often see that the rightful tenant or claimant fighting in battle is overcome by the superior strength or some underhand trick of the unjust party.

We do not deny that God's providence sometimes clears the innocent and condemns the guilty, but it is in no wise ordained by God that this should happen in every case, except at the Last Judgement.[62]

Agobard of Lyons (d. 840), who wrote these words, was even harsher in his criticisms of the duel than of the other ordeals. He believed, to borrow the words of Schwentner's admirable summary, that 'the duel was opposed to Christian charity, to reason and to experience, which teaches us that the outcome of duels is often unjust and wrong, and which is confirmed by many examples from Holy Scripture showing that even the just man can be defeated in battle; finally, the duel was

---

[61] For (quite minimal) exceptions to this statement see Bernhard Schwentner, 'Die Stellung der Kirche zum Zweikampfe bis zu den Dekretalen Gregors IX.', *Theologische Quartalschrift*, 3 (1930), pp. 190-234, at pp. 212-19.

[62] Agobard, *Liber adversus legem Gundobadi*, 13, ed. cit., p. 27 (citing Avitus, sixth-century bishop of Vienne) and 9, p. 24.

opposed to the nature of judgement, which consists in wise investigations not brutal power'.[63] Here the bilateral and combative nature of trial by battle was clearly important: duels were brutal and offended against Christian charity. Such objections did not apply to the other ordeals.

The Teutberga case of the 850s and 860s, which prompted Hincmar's defence of the ordeal, also occasioned some discussion of trial by battle, for this, too, was at one point canvassed as a possible means of resolving the case. The reigning pope, Nicolas I, was unambiguous in his response: 'We know of no precept that commands single combat to be allowed as a proof, although we read that some have entered into it, as Holy Scripture tells us of the blessed David and Goliath. Nevertheless, divine authority has never sanctioned it as a law, for this and those who practise it are only tempting God.'[64] This ruling, *Monomachiam*, passed via the canonists Regino, Buchard, and Ivo into Gratian's *Decretum* and thus became an integral part of the universal canon law of the twelfth and thirteenth centuries.[65] It shows that the objections made against the other ordeals–their uncanonical basis and their 'tempting of God'–were also raised against trial by battle. The case of David and Goliath had to be skirted by skilful interpretation, but, as an ordeal, judicial combat was obviously sensitive to the same kind of clerical disapproval as was applied, increasingly, to trial by fire and water.

Clerical opposition to the judicial combat was only heightened over the course of the eleventh and twelfth centuries as ecclesiastical thinkers and polemicists came increasingly to define the clerical order by its distance from, and lack of implication in, acts of blood. As Ivo of Chartres put it, 'The duel can rarely or never take place without the shedding of blood, but the authority of the Fathers, which should be followed, forbids clerics to exercise judgement of blood, and the Roman Church does not receive it as law.'[66] The provision of Lateran IV dealing with the duel was placed under the rubric 'Prohibition to clerics of judgement of blood and of the duel'.[67]

[63] Schwentner, 'Die Stellung der Kirche' (as in n. 61), p. 199.

[64] MGH, *Epp.* 6, ed. E. Perels (Berlin, 1902-25), pp. 330-1.

[65] Regino, *De ecclesiasticis disciplinis et religione christiana*, 2.77, *PL* 132, col. 300; Burchard, *Decretum*, 9.5, *PL* 140, col. 823; Ivo of Chartres, *Decretum*, 8.187, *PL* 161, col. 623; idem, *epistolae* 74, 205, 247, 280, *PL* 162, cols. 96, 213, 254, 281; Gratian, *Decretum*, C. 2, q. 5, c. 22.

[66] *Epistola* 247, *PL* 162, col. 254.

[67] For the rubrics, see A. García y García (ed.), *Constitutiones Concilii quarti Lateranensis una cum Commentariis glossatorum* (Vatican City, 1981), p. 147.

Clerical opposition to the duel was expressed most urgently and most generally in the campaign to obtain exemption for clerics. As in the case of the other ordeals, this goal was pursued more vigorously and with earlier success than any attempt at general abolition. Popes of the twelfth century used the weight of their authority and their rhetoric against any clerical involvement in duels. On the one hand they negotiated with, or denounced, the secular authorities. In 1176, for example, Henry II of England was induced to grant 'that clerics shall not be forced to fight duels'.[68] In 1216 Innocent III was threatening anathemas against anyone in the province of York or the kingdom of Scotland who forced clergy to 'undergo the duel in person'. Such a custom was 'pestiferous and corrupt'.[69] One of the standard accusations against tyrannical rulers was that they had forced clerics to fight duels.[70] On the other hand, canonical penalties were enforced against the clerical participants. The papacy adopted the strict view that participation in judicial combat was enough to render a clerk irregular, that duels should not be fought even to defend ecclesiastical property, and that killing in a duel was simply homicide.[71] The position affirmed and elaborated by the popes and canonists of the twelfth and early thirteenth centuries was given universal legislative force in the *Decretals* of Gregory IX in 1234.[72] It became fundamental.

Clerics were not the only group to struggle for exemption from the duel in the eleventh, twelfth, and thirteenth centuries. Burgesses, too, clearly aimed at such a privilege. As has been argued, the assumption that townsmen sought exemption from trial by ordeal in general is a weak one, but their aversion to trial by battle cannot be doubted. As early as 1081 the Emperor Henry IV granted exemptions to the citizens of Pisa and Lucca, reserving, like his descendant Frederick II, cases of treason.[73] A similar exemption, with a similar proviso, was granted by Henry I of England to the burgesses of Newcastle.[74] His

---

[68] Ralph of Diceto, *Imagines historiarum* in *Opera historica*, ed. William Stubbs (2 vols., RS, 1876), 1, p. 410.

[69] *Registrum episcopatus Glasguensis*, ed. C. Innes (2 vols., Bannatyne Club, 1843), no. 110, p. 94; Po. 5092; see Neilson, *Trial by Combat* (as in n. 1), pp. 123-4.

[70] MGH, *Const.* 2 (as in n. 21), no. 400, p. 511 (one of the charges in Innocent IV's deposition of Frederick II, 1245).

[71] Schwentner, 'Die Stellung der Kirche' (as in n. 61), pp. 222-34.

[72] X.1.20.1, 3.50.9, 5.14.1-2, 5.25.1-2.

[73] MGH, *DD Heinrici IV*, ed. D. von Gladiss and Alfred Gawlik (Berlin, Weimar and Hanover, 1941-78), nos. 334 and 336, pp. 437-9, 442-3.

[74] W. Stubbs (ed.), *Select Charters* (9th edn., rev. H. W. C. Davis, Oxford, 1913), p. 134; cf. *Leges quatuor burgorum* (as in n. 41), cap. 12, ed. (1844), p. 23 (335), (1868), p. 8.

father had introduced trial by battle, Henry now began to limit its scope. The spread of urban exemptions across the British Isles can be followed conveniently in the charters analysed by Ballard and Tait.[75] Newcastle and London, both granted exemption in the early twelfth century, were the models for boroughs throughout England, Scotland, and Ireland. In a charter of 1196-7 William the Lion freed the burgesses of Inverness from the duel.[76] About the same time those of Dublin were granted the same right by their lord, John, lord of Ireland (later king).[77] By the early thirteenth century exemption from trial by battle was one characteristic of the privileged status of burgesses in the British Isles.

It is paradoxical that, despite the unremitting hostility of the papacy and the clamorous demands for exemption from townsmen, the duel continued in use longer and more generally than the ordeals of fire and water. Moreover, there was never a clear-cut, clerically inspired prohibition of the kind issued against unilateral ordeals in Denmark in 1216 and England in 1219. Instead, we find a gradual decline of trial by battle in the later Middle Ages, punctuated by local and partial abolitions such as those of Frederick II in 1231, Louis IX in 1258,[78] and Philip IV in 1306. It is notorious that trial by battle in certain criminal appeals was not removed by statute in England until 1819.[79]

The rather gradual disappearance of trial by battle highlights an important point in which it contrasted with the other ordeals. Trial by fire and water was deeply involved in priestly and liturgical ritual. The numerous liturgical manuscripts surviving from the Middle Ages show how essential priestly benediction and supervision was. Trial by battle, on the other hand, despite its status as a *iudicium dei* and the

---

[75] A. Ballard, *British Borough Charters, 1042-1216* (Cambridge, 1913), pp. 132-4; idem and James Tait, *British Borough Charters, 1216-1307* (Cambridge, 1923), p. 184. See also *Borough Customs*, ed. Mary Bateson (2 vols., Selden Soc. 18 and 21, 1904-6), 1 (= 18), p. 32, and Charles Gross, 'Modes of Trial in the Medieval Boroughs of England', *Harvard Law Review*, 15 (1902), pp. 691-706.

[76] *Regesta regum Scottorum*, 2, ed. G. W. S. Barrow (Edinburgh, 1971), no. 388, pp. 379-80.

[77] *Historic and Municipal Documents of Ireland 1172-1320*, ed. J. T. Gilbert (RS, 1870), no. 6, p. 52.

[78] *Les Établissements de S. Louis*, ed. Paul Viollet (4 vols., Paris, 1881-6), 1, pp. 487-93; see J. Tardif, 'La Date et le caractère de l'ordonnance de S. Louis sur le duel judiciare', *Revue historique de droit français et étranger*, 11 (1887), pp. 163-74; for some further discussion see W. C. Jordan, *Louis IX and the Challenge of the Crusade* (Princeton, 1979), p. 204 and the references given there.

[79] Stat. 59 Geo. III, cap. 46, *Statutes of the United Kingdom (from 1801)*, ed. T. E. Tomlins, etc., 7 (London, 1817-19), p. 723.

ritual solemnity that surrounded it, could be, and was, conducted with minimal priestly involvement. We know that 'according to the custom of some places, priests make blessings and imprecations over the champions, just as there used to be adjurations over the hot iron or cold water',[80] but such practices cannot have been essential. To set beside the numerous rituals for blessing the hot iron or the ordeal pool, there is a solitary liturgical manuscript containing a blessing for the weapons of the duel.[81] The priest's role in the judicial combat was ancillary. He might bring relics or gospels to the scene of combat on which the parties or their champions would swear. York Minster, for example, had a monopoly on providing such books or relics in York,[82] and Peter the Chanter, in his attack on duels, asserted, 'As a priest I would not provide relics and holy things for a man about to fight a duel to swear upon, lest through that authority and pretext I should be guilty of the shedding of blood'.[83] But the oath, although relying for its ultimate sanction on God's active interest in the proceedings of human lawcourts, was not intrinsically ecclesiastical. Roman law offered the example of a legal system where religious, but non-ecclesiastical, oaths had an important role. In the procedure for appeal of felony in England oaths were sworn before the justices.[84] According to Philip IV's ordinance of 1306, although a priest should be present to exhort the combatants, it was the marshal who administered the oath, and the priest left before the battle.[85] At Valenciennes in 1455 the oaths were sworn on a missal brought by *ceux de la loy*, presumably secular law officers.[86] In a word, the judicial combat was a less sacral ordeal than trial by fire and water.

The relative unimportance of liturgical ritual and priestly involvement is obviously connected with the fact that the judicial combat did not claim or require a miraculous intervention in the physical elements. It claimed, in theory, that a weak, just man would defeat a strong, unjust man, but it did not anticipate a ritually-effected change

[80] William of Rennes, gloss on Raymond of Peñaforte's *Summa* on the *Decretals*, printed Browe, *De ordaliis*, 2, no. 108.
[81] Liebermann, *Gesetze*, 1, pp. 430-1.
[82] *Regesta regum Anglo-Normannorum*, 3, ed. H. A. Cronne and R. H. C. Davis (Oxford, 1968), no. 975, p. 361 (1136).
[83] *Verbum abbreviatum*, 78, *PL* 205, col. 232.
[84] Russell, 'Trial by Battle Procedure' (as in n. 35), p. 132.
[85] *Ordonnances*, 1 (as in n. 27), pp. 439-40, notes.
[86] Olivier de la Marche, *Mémoires*, 1.32, ed. H. Beaune and J. d'Arbaumont (4 vols., 1883-8) 2, p. 404; see Otto Cartellieri, 'Ein Zweikampf in Valenciennes im Jahre 1455', *Festschrift Johannes Hoops* (Heidelberg, 1925), pp. 169-76.

in iron or water, the material of the world. It was the most natural as well as the least liturgical of the ordeals. Aquinas, among others, recognized this. In the context of a general discussion of lots, he observed that while the trials of fire and water resembled lots in that they sought to discover secrets by human action, they differed from them in that 'they anticipate a miraculous effect'. The same point applies also to trial by battle,' he continues, 'except that they function more like lots, since they do not anticipate a miraculous effect; except in the case where the champions are extremely unequal in strength or skill.'[87]

Because the duel was non-sacral and natural, the withdrawal of clerical participation was not so definitive as in the case of the other ordeals. If priests could be found willing to provide relics for oaths–or even if a gospel book could be procured from any source–the duel could continue. It was not shackled, like trial by fire and water, by clerical opposition.

Thus, clerical disengagement from the duel did not deal it a death blow. In the thirteenth century it was frequently employed, not only in the wild lands of the Anglo-Scottish borders,[88] but in the great cities of Italy.[89] Dante defended it in his *De Monarchia*.[90] The lawbooks of England, France, and Germany presume that duels are a usual part of the judicial process. The *fueros* of Spain and the laws of eastern Europe mention it. Only over the course of the fourteenth and fifteenth centuries did it decline. The 'last judicial duel fought on English soil' took place in 1492.[91] One of the inducements that brought Philip the Good, duke of Burgundy, to witness a duel in Valenciennes in 1455 was the fact that 'such things do not happen often'.[92] By the fifteenth century trial by battle was thus an oddity.

If clerical hostility is an inadequate explanation for the decline of trial by battle, no single alternative explanation is absolutely con-

---

[87] *Summa theologica*, 2.2.95.8, Blackfriars edn., ed. T. Gilby *et al.* (60 vols., London, 1963-76), 40, p. 66.

[88] The duel is a common resort in the *Leges Marchiarum*, ed. *Acts of the Parliament of Scotland*, 1 (as in n. 41), pp. 413-16 (83-86), tr. and discussed by George Neilson in *Miscellany*, 1 (Stair Soc. 26, 1971), pp. 12-77.

[89] Antonio Pertile, *Storia del diritto italiano* (2nd edn., 7 vols. in 9, Bologna, 1892-1902, repr., 1966), 6/1, pp. 337-46, cites many civic statutes of the thirteenth century regulating the duel.

[90] 2.7, 9-10, ed. P. G. Ricci (Milan, 1965), pp. 196-9, 204-12: 'Quod per duellum acquiritur, de iure acquiritur.'

[91] Nielson, *Trial by Combat* (as in n. 1), p. 203.

[92] De la Marche, *Mémoires* (as in n. 86), 1.32, ed. cit., 2, p. 403.

vincing. Certainly, the growth of Roman law was important, for, although some legists managed to argue that the duel 'was not prohibited by Roman law',[93] this was an extremely tendentious position. In general, study of Roman law led to distrust of battle as a form of proof.

The indirect influence of clerical opinions was also important. Rather than ecclesiastical condemnation leading to priestly withdrawal and so directly to the decline of the proof, as in the case of trial by fire and water, it might have to work through the consciences of secular rulers. In the *Siete Partidas*, for example, Alfonso the Wise cited two objections to trial by battle, one of which was 'that he who desires to venture this proof seems to be tempting Our Lord God'.[94] According to one of his Dominican biographers, St Louis was moved to prohibit trial by battle in the royal demesne in 1258 because 'he came to understand that judicial combat could not be employed without mortal sin, for it is not justice but rather a temptation of God'.[95]

The mixture of motives at work in a princely decision to end the duel is well illustrated by Frederick II's prohibition in the *Constitutions of Melfi* of 1231. Battle, he claimed, 'should be termed a form of divination rather than a genuine proof. It is not in harmony with nature, it deviates from universal law and it is opposed to the processes of equity'. When Frederick condemned trial by battle as a form of divination, he meant that it sought to reach a decision on the basis of a process which had no real connection with the point at issue. Those who turned to this, as to other, forms of ordeal were guilty of superstition by attributing to the fortuitous a significance it did not have. But he excepted from his general prohibition those accused of treason or secret homicide (including poisoning), when usual proofs were lacking. Battle in these cases was employed 'not so much as a proof as a deterrent. Not that Our Serenity deems just in these cases that which is unjust in others, but we wish such killers to be subjected to this fearful kind of proof publicly in the sight of men, as a punishment to them and an example to others.'[96] Frederick's reasoning is not entirely

[93] Nottarp, *Gottesurteilstudien*, p. 49.

[94] 3.14.8, ed. Real Academia de la Historia (3 vols., Madrid, 1807, repr., 1972), 2, p. 507.

[95] William of Chartres, *De Vita ... Ludovici, Recueils des historiens des Gaules et de la France*, 20 (Paris, 1840), p. 34; compare the alternative explanation of his motives in *Les Grands chroniques de France*, 'Saint Louis', cap. 116, ed. Jules Viard, 7 (Paris, 1932), p. 281.

[96] 2.33 (as in n. 20). For some discussion of this passage, see Conrad, 'Das Gottesurteil'.

consistent. If battle was not a true proof, then subjecting accused killers to it would itself be 'opposed to the processes of equity'. A fearful *punishment* as a deterrent to others is a common feature of many judicial systems; a fearful *proof* is not.

Another ground which Frederick cited for his prohibition was the impossibility of having two absolutely equally matched combatants; if the champions were not equally matched, he presumed, the contest would be unfair. Here, too, there is some misunderstanding. Those who defended trial by battle argued that, in the struggle, God was showing his judgement: the relative strength and skill of the combatants was, strictly speaking, irrelevant.[97] Frederick's objection to inequality between combatants thus applied only if the duel is viewed as a conscious lottery–if one has decided to let chance decide, then absolute initial parity between the parties is essential, for no one should have a double-headed coin. Frederick was thus advancing incompatible arguments when he objected to battle both on the grounds that it was a form of divination and because of the impossibility of matching the combatants equally: as if he objected to dicing both because gambling was wrong and because the dice were loaded.

The prohibition of trial by battle in the *Constitutions of Melfi* is absolutely characteristic of Frederick II's mind, in its authoritarianism, in its invocation of highly abstract principles of nature and justice, and in its self-contradiction. He retained the duel as an instrument of executive terror, despite his dismissiveness about it as an unnatural and unjust proof. His motives contrast strongly with those of his contemporary, St Louis, at least as his biographers record them.

The fact that the king renowned for his piety and the emperor whose opponents dubbed him Antichrist both took steps to prohibit trial by battle may suggest that the situation of rulers in the thirteenth century predisposed them towards a limitation of the duel, regardless of their professed motives. Already Henry II of England, in the second half of the previous century, had introduced the Grand Assize as an alternative to battle. Alfonso the Wise of Castile, Rudolf I of Germany, and Philip IV of France also imposed limitations on battle over the ensuing 150 years.

Just as there is evidence for monarchical hostility to the duel, so there are some grounds for positing an aristocratic preference for it. There were probably two separate issues involved here. The first was

---

[97] See, for example, Dante's comments 'de imparitate virium', *De monarchia* (as in n. 90) 2.9, ed. cit., p. 207.

a simple defence of the judicial rights of those lords who had high justice–they wished to retain their right to hold battles in their courts. Limitation of battle could mean erosion of aristocratic judicial power, as in England, where the option of the Grand Assize was 'a royal benefit'[98] which removed cases into the royal court. In France, St Louis's prohibition of 1258 applied to the royal demesne only and not to the 'courts of his barons',[99] but Philip IV's prohibitions were more general, prompting protests after his death. During the agitation of 1315 Louis X had to concede the right to employ trial by battle to the nobles of Burgundy, Amiens, and Vermandois, who had complained about the erosion of their liberties. 'As for the wager of battle,' reads one act, 'we wish that they may use it, as they did of old.'[100] For the upper strata, from the French knight who had been accustomed to guard the lists in one of the royal courts and brought suit against St Louis in 1260 for loss of occupation and income,[101] to the abbot of Peterborough, asserting his right to 'judicial combat in all his hundreds and all lands of his fee' in *Quo Warranto* proceedings in 1329,[102] trial by battle represented a present interest, which would be limited only at their expense and in the face of their protests.

There is the further point, however, that the right to settle one's disputes by battle had always been associated with free status. It had often been ruled that, in circumstances where the unilateral ordeal was the proof of the unfree, battle should be the proof of the free. Such arrangements persisted into the thirteenth century. At Brescia in 1277, for example, those appealed of homicide and other serious crimes had 'to clear themselves by battle if free, by ordeal if unfree'.[103] The right to bear arms had often been taken as a mark of status. In Germany a two-tiered system based on an armed knightly class and a disarmed peasantry had been, if not a reality, at least a vivid legal idea in the twelfth and thirteenth centuries.[104]

In the later Middle Ages, as trial by battle became less frequent in the courts, aristocrats insisted that they could still vindicate themselves

---

[98] *The Treatise on the Laws and Customs of England commonly called Glanvill*, 2.7, ed. G. D. Hall (London, etc., 1965), p. 28.

[99] Beaumanoir, *Coutumes* (as in n. 31), cap. 61, ed. cit., 2, p. 380.

[100] *Ordonnances*, 1 (as in n. 27), pp. 557-60, 561-7.

[101] *Les Olim*, ed. A.-A. Beugnot (4 vols., Paris, 1839-48), 1, p. 491.

[102] *The Eyre in Northamptonshire, 1329-30*, ed. Donald W. Sutherland (2 vols., Selden Soc. 97-8, 1981-2), 1, p. 41.

[103] Cited by Pertile, *Storia del diritto* (as in n. 89), 6/1, p. 338 n. 9.

[104] Hans Fehr, 'Das Waffenrecht der Bauern im Mittelalter', *ZRG, Germanistische Abteilung*, 35 (1914), pp. 111-211, 38 (1917), pp. 1-114, esp. 35, pp. 137-62.

by combat, especially in cases touching their honour. Despite the general hostility to battle Alfonso the Wise expressed in the *Siete Partidas*, he ruled that a nobleman impeached of treason or perfidy retained the option of defending himself by battle.[105] The duel of chivalry in later medieval England was also mainly an aristocratic affair. Until the thirteenth century trial by battle was a common judicial procedure for the freeborn. From the sixteenth century onwards formal duels were non-judicial and usually turned on matters of aristocratic honour. The later Middle Ages seem to have an intermediate position, during which the duel was frequently aristocratic, but still judicial.

There are, then, signs in this period of a clash between rulers seeking to limit the duel and aristocracies jealous of their judicial authority and individual honour. This makes our picture of the abolition of the duel very different from that of the demise of unilateral ordeals. Paradoxically, clerical hostility to the judicial combat was stronger, earlier, and more unanimous then clerical hostility to the trials of fire and water, but also far less important as an explanation for its disappearance.[106] This least sacral and most natural of ordeals outlived the scholastic and papal assaults of the twelfth and early thirteenth centuries and only succumbed to princely prohibitions and other legal changes of the later Middle Ages. Perhaps the indirect influence of clerical opinion on the princes may have had some importance, but it was not decisive.

Clerical policies may, however, have had an even more mediated, but also more important, impact on the duel by way of their impact on the unilateral ordeal. For it is highly likely that the most important reason for the decline of trial by battle was the growth, from the thirteenth century, of alternative judicial procedures, of new ways of seeking results in the courtroom, which developed as a consequence of that lethal blow struck against trial by fire and water by the clerical critics of the age of Innocent III.

---

[105] 7.3 (as in n. 94), 3, pp. 543-9.
[106] Compare the remarks in Bongert, *Recherches*, p. 210.

7

Aftermath

Disappearance

THE slow communications and the undeveloped local administration characteristic of thirteenth-century Europe meant that legislative changes took effect only very gradually. The decision of
Lateran IV in 1215 thus represented not only the culmination of a
century and a half of debate, but also the beginning of a long effort to
implement the new ruling. The speed and thoroughness with which
the ordeal was abolished varied according to local conditions. The
earliest and most clear-cut prohibitions occurred in those smaller and
precociously centralized kingdoms in close relations with the papacy.
In Denmark and England the abolition of trial by ordeal was recognized in royal ordinances of 1216 and 1219 respectively.[1] Both kingdoms had close ties with the papacy; both, for example, being among
the limited number of realms that paid Peter's Pence, and in 1219
England, a papal fief 'whose lordship belonged to the Roman
Church',[2] was ruled by a regency government containing the papal
legate, Pandulf.

Other monarchies followed suit rather more slowly. Prohibitions in
the kingdoms of Scotland and Sicily were enacted in 1230 and 1231.[3]
Birger Jarl, the regent of Sweden (1248-66), abolished the ordeal there,
though his ruling was not entirely effective in every part of Sweden, for
the prohibition had to be repeated in Helsingeland in 1320.[4] When the

---

[1] *Diplomatarium Danicum*, ed. N. Skylum-Nielsen, 1st ser., 5 (Copenhagen, 1957),
no. 96, pp. 137-43; *Patent Rolls of the Reign of Henry III (1216-32)* (2 vols., HMSO, 1901-3),
1, p. 186.
[2] Letter of Innocent III, 1216, Po. 4990, ed. C. R. Cheney and W. H. Semple, *Selected
Letters of Pope Innocent III concerning England* (London, etc., 1953), no. 82, p. 215.
[3] *Statuta regis Alexandri II*, 6, *Acts of the Parliament of Scotland*, 1, ed. T. Thomson and
C. Innes (Edinburgh, 1844), p. 70 (400); *Constitutions of Melfi*, 2.31, ed. J. L. A. Huillard-
Bréholles, *Historia diplomatica Friderici secundi* (6 vols., Paris, 1852-61), 4/1, p. 102; *Die
Konstitutionen Friedrichs II. für sein Königreich Sizilien*, ed. and tr. (into German), Hermann
Conrad *et al.* (Cologne, 1973), pp. 216-18.
[4] Östgötalagen, 'kunungs ethsöre', 17. German tr. D. Strauch, *Das Ostgötenrecht*
(Cologne and Vienna, 1971), p. 65; Helsinge-Lagen, 'Aerftha balken', 16, ed. D. C. J.
Schlyter, *Corpus iuris sueo-gotorum antiqui*, 6 (Lund, 1844), pp. 39-40.

Norwegian provincial laws were codified by Magnus VI in 1274,[5] the ordeal, which had figured prominently in earlier versions, was silently omitted. In France unilateral ordeals were a rarity in the thirteenth century. In the Spanish kingdoms, James I of Aragon (1213-76) 'can be considered the chief enemy of ordeals in the peninsula'.[6]

The disappearance of trial by ordeal can occasionally be glimpsed in court records, which reveal actual judicial activity rather than legislative prescription. The English plea rolls, for example, contain dozens of cases of trial by ordeal between 1194 and 1219, but none thereafter. The Varad register,[7] which contains accounts of cases settled at the Hungarian church of Varad between the years 1208 and 1234, can also be analysed for this purpose. As the records are so fragmentary it would be meaningless to compare total figures from year to year. A worthwhile gauge of the relative frequency of ordeals can, however, be obtained by comparing the number of cases involving the ordeal in any given year with the total number of cases for which record has survived for that year. The result is shown in Figure 1. Before 1223 cases involving the ordeal (including those where it was ordered but not undergone) hardly ever fell below three-quarters of the total. Isolated data for the later 1220s show that ordeal cases then fell to half or less of the total. In 1234 about one quarter of the cases involved ordeal; and in 1235, the last year for which there are records, no ordeal cases are mentioned. Another important statistic is the relationship between total individual ordeals actually undergone and the total number of cases recorded. Here, too, the trend is downwards between the period before 1223, the late 1220s, and the 1230s.

Such statistics have to be treated with caution. The total numbers involved are small, especially in the later years. In 1234 and 1235 there are records of only eleven and seven cases respectively. Nevertheless, there is no good reason to believe that the records have survived on any other than a random basis. Hence a drop from 75 per cent to 50 per cent to 25 per cent or less over the years 1208 to 1235 is significant. It may also be noted that, before 1226, the lowest frequency of ordeals occurs in 1216, the year after the Lateran Council. We may well, then, envisage the Varad figures as evidence for a busy ordeal

---

[5] *Landrecht des Königs Magnus Hakonarson*, ed. with German tr. Rudolf Meissner (Weimar, 1941).
[6] Iglesia Ferreirós, 'El proceso del conde Bera', p. 169.
[7] *Regestrum Varadinense*, discussed in Chapter 4.

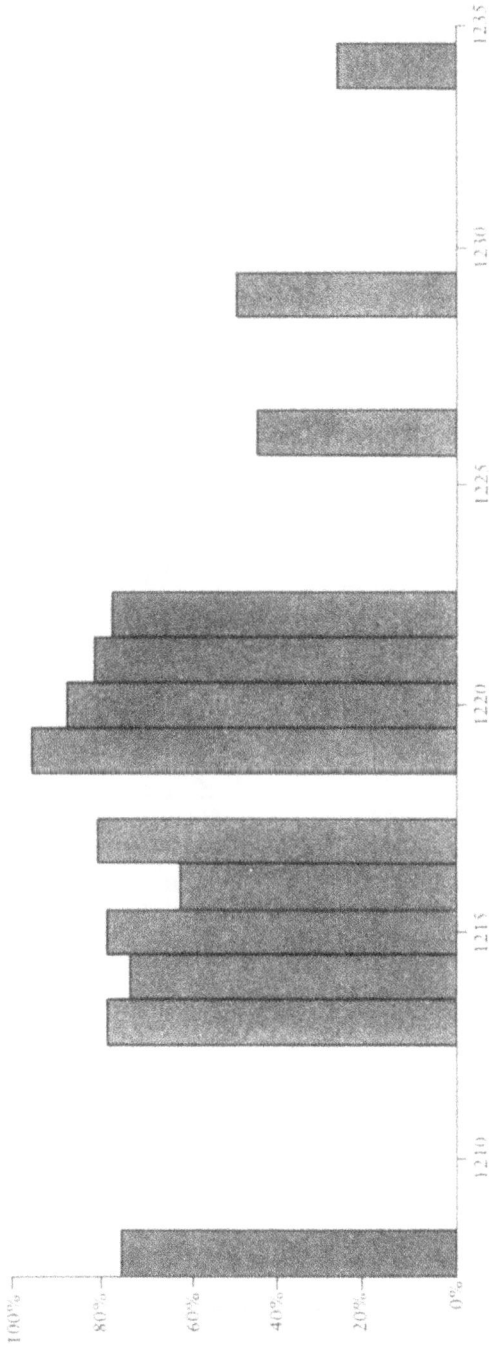

Figure 1. The Varad Register. Cases involving the ordeal as a percentage of total cases recorded. (Note that cases are recorded for 1235, but none involved the ordeal.)

church where 1215 made an immediate, but short-lived dent, but which found the long-term pressure against ordeals irresistible.

There is plenty of evidence for such continued pressure. The ruling of Lateran IV was not only included in the *Decretals*,[8] but was reiterated by numerous ecclesiastical councils over the course of the thirteenth and fourteenth centuries. In Spain, for example, prohibitions were included in the canons of Valencia (1255), León (1288), and Valladolid (1322).[9] Similar rulings were made by councils in France, Germany, and Hungary, sometimes in the very words of Lateran IV.[10] The thirteenth century saw an intensification of synodal activity, much of it deeply marked by the legislation of Innocent III's great council, and the abolition of the ordeal thus came to form part of a programme of reform gradually being implemented at an ever more effective and ever more local level.

This did not mean, of course, that the ordeal disappeared completely. It is not surprising to find cases in the 1230s in Germany or even in France.[11] In the 1250s even as important an ecclesiastic as the dean of Hamburg cathedral was still submitting men to the ordeal.[12] The lawbooks, too, often continued to include provision for trial by ordeal. The Scottish lawbook *Regiam majestatem*, for example, repeated Glanvill's rules about trial by ordeal and also the passage on ordeals from the so-called 'Assize of William the Lion'.[13] This may have been mere antiquarianism, but, nevertheless, it meant that a reasonably authoritative lawbook of *c.* 1300 was still talking of ordeals in the present tense.

The German lawbooks show a far more striking survival of the ordeal, and it is hard not to believe that this reflects contemporary German practice. Ruprecht of Freising, in the *Freisinger Rechtsbuch* of *c.* 1325, though he regarded the hot iron and cauldron as *verbotene Gerichte*, nevertheless admitted that they might take place with the

---

[8] X.3.50.9.

[9] Mansi, 23, col. 893; José Sánchez Herrero, 'Los sínodos de la díocesis de León en los siglos XIII al XV', published separately from *León y su Historia* 3 (León, 1975), pp. 165-262, quotation at pp. 227-30; Mansi, 25, col. 722.

[10] e.g Synod of Buda (1279), Mansi, 24, col. 276; Synod of Bayeux (1300), ibid., 25, col. 67.

[11] e.g. *UB des Hochstifts Halberstadt*, ed. G. Schmidt (4 vols., Leipzig, 1883-90), 1, no. 620 (1231); *Actes du Parlement de Paris*, ed. E. Boutaric (2 vols. in 4, Paris, 1863-7), 1, p. cccv.

[12] *Hamburgisches UB*, ed. I. M. Lappenberg, 1 (Hamburg, 1842), no. 617; Po. 16860 (1257).

[13] 4.3.4 and 4.17.1, ed. T. M. Cooper (Stair Soc. 11, 1947), pp. 252, 263-4.

consent of the accused.[14] Most of the lawbooks dependent on the *Sachsenspiegel* admitted some place to trial by ordeal. Indeed, one of the grounds on which Pope Gregory XI solemnly condemned the *Sachsenspiegel* in 1374 was its 'erroneous' ruling that 'whoever has lost his law due to theft or rapine, if he is again accused of the same charge, cannot clear himself by oath but has choice of hot iron, boiling water or duel'.[15] This objectionable provision was still being cited, as current law, by the Hanover town council in 1436.[16] One of the latest ordeal rituals, from the fourteenth century, is from the Rhineland.[17] The customs of Lorsch, which were drawn up in 1423, specify the cold water as proof in forest offences.[18]

Clearly Germany was one area where the ordeal lingered, not, probably, as a very important part of current judicial practice, but as a possibility in the minds of litigants and judges. Another, quite different, region where the ordeal seems to have thrived in the later Middle Ages, was south-east Europe. Trial by ordeal entered the Greek world in the thirteenth century; a case is recorded in Epirus in (probably) 1228,[19] another at the court of the Nicaean emperor in 1252.[20] It has been suggested that the ordeal entered Byzantium via the crusader states,[21] and this is highly likely. The Assizes of Jerusalem and Cyprus contained provision for the ordeal[22] and both were current in some parts of the eastern Mediterranean down to the sixteenth century. Here, in the cosmopolitan amalgam of Greek, Frank, Slav, and Italian, in the eastern Mediterranean and south-east Europe, the ordeal survived in various cultural contexts: a woman cleared herself

---

[14] Caps. 271 and 273, ed. Hans-Kurt Claussen (Weimar, 1941) pp. 312-17.

[15] Mansi, 23, col. 158; Browe, *De ordaliis*, 1, no. 44.

[16] C. U. Grupen, *Observationes rerum et antiquitatum Germanicarum et Romanicarum* (Halle, 1763), cited in Nottarp, *Gottesurteilstudien*, p. 204.

[17] Zeumer, *Formulae*, p. 687.

[18] Jacob Grimm, *Weisthümer* (7 vols., 1840-78, repr., Darmstadt, 1957) 1, 465-6.

[19] A. Papadopoulous Kerameus, 'Synodika gramata Ioannou tou Apokaukou', *Byzantis*, 1 (1909), pp. 27-8.

[20] George Acropolites, *Opera*, ed. A. Heisenberg (2 vols., Leipzig, 1903), 1, pp. 92-100; George Pachymeres, *De Michaele et Andronico Palaeologis*, ed. I. Bekker (2 vols., Bonn, 1835),1, pp. 21-3.

[21] Angold, 'The Interaction of Latins and Byzantines'; Geanakoplos, 'Ordeal by Fire', claims that the ordeal probably entered Byzantium via westerners settled in the Latin Empire and following the *Assises of Romania* (p. 152); however, despite his reference to *Les Assises de Romanie*, ed. G. Recoura (Paris, 1929), pp. 146-53, the *Assises* have no mention of trial by ordeal.

[22] *Livre des assises de la cour des bourgeois*, caps. 135, 265-7, 286-7, ed. A.-A. Beugnot, *Recueil des historiens des croisades, Lois*, 2 (Paris, 1843), pp. 93, 200-3, 217-18. The Assizes of Cyprus were edited by K. N. Sathas in *Bibliotheca graeca medii aevi*, 6 (Paris, 1877).

of adultery by the hot iron in a Thracian town in 1341;[23] Stephan Dushan's codes of 1349 and 1354 regulated the place of the ordeal of hot iron and the cauldron in Serbian law;[24] in the sixteenth century the ordeal was employed by Epirots settled in Italy or in Venetian service.[25]

Some of the evidence for the survival of trial by ordeal is very hard to weigh. For instance, it was common charter form in many parts of the British Isles that grants of higher jurisdiction should include *furca et fossa*–that is,'the gallows and the [ordeal] pit'. These grants continued well into the thirteenth century. Alexander II of Scotland, who had formally abolished trial by ordeal in 1230, granted land to Holyrood abbey four years later *cum furca et fossa*.[26] There are many other examples from thirteenth-century Scotland, England, and Ireland. The first impulse would be to see these as merely formulaic, archaic survivals preserved only by the conservatism of the law, but this is only a presumption, and one recent writer has warned 'historians have been too ready to assume these are merely empty formulae'.[27]

The chronology and geography of the abolition of the ordeal reflects, more than anything else, the relative authority of the central power and the intensity of papal influence. The general socio-economic environment was less significant, except where it shaped the other two factors. The ordeal was abandoned in rural Denmark long before the urban Rhineland, because Denmark was ruled by a strong central monarchy receptive to papal policies. The politically de-centralized regions of Europe, such as Germany, saw a relatively late survival of trial by ordeal. In the Balkans and the eastern Mediter-ranean, where the political map was kaleidoscopic, neither decisive state intervention nor strong papal influence existed; here the ordeal

---

[23] John Cantacuzenus, *Historiarum libri IV*, ed. L. Schopen (3 vols., Bonn, 1828), 2, pp. 171-3.

[24] *The Code of Stephan Dushan*, arts. 84, 106, 150, tr. M. Burr, *Slavonic and East European Review*, 28 (1949-50), pp. 214, 517.

[25] Giulio Ferretti, *Aureae additiones in Bartholum de Saxoferrato ... de differentiis ac varietatibus iuris Romanorum et Langobardorum* (Venice, 1599), p. 117; F. P. Canciani, *Barbarorum leges antiquae* (5 vols., Venice, 1781-92), 2, p. 565.

[26] *Liber cartarum sancte Crucis* (Ballantyne Club, 1840), no. 65, pp. 51-2.

[27] K. W. Nicholls, 'Anglo-French Ireland and After', *Peritia*, 1 (1982), pp. 370-403, quotation at p. 377. He interprets *fossa* in the phrase 'in judicio aque et ferri et fossa et furcis et duella' as 'dungeon', p. 377 n. 2. It should be noted, however, that the Scots version of Alexander II's prohibition of the ordeal (as in n. 3) gives 'thruch dykpot na yrn' as the equivalent of *per fossam vel ferrum*.

was being employed four centuries after Lateran IV. Ordeals sometimes survived in remote places (Frisia, for example) because it was
harder to enforce anti-ordeal legislation there.

Just as, in the early Middle Ages, ordeals had spread out slowly
from their Frankish home, only penetrating the peripheries of
Christendom in the eleventh and twelfth centuries, so now the abandonment of the ordeal proceeded slowly, being most effectual in the
most centralized and disciplined polities, such as England and Sicily,
and most gradual in the decentralized ones. One curious consequence
of this pattern of diffusion and decline was that in some areas,
Scandinavia for example, there was probably little distance in time
between the introduction of trial by ordeal and the beginnings of the
clerical crusade against it. In Sweden the thunders of Pope Alexander III against putting clerics to the ordeal[28] must have resounded
in a world which was only beginning to get used to the practice, which
had probably entered the country as part of the conversion of the
eleventh and twelfth centuries. It was as if a slow-moving wave dif-
fusing Carolingian influence had been overtaken by a more urgent
flood of Gregorian exhortation.

Gregorian exhortation, in the end, won a clear victory. By 1300 the
ordeal had virtually disappeared. In the south-west of France 'the last
mention of ordeals appears to be that in the customs of Alzen in the
county of Foix in 1309'.[29] The last ordeals in the north of France were
probably much earlier. In the British Isles, with the exception of
archaizing lawbooks and charter formulae, the ordeal was as good as
extinct. Roger Bacon, writing *c.*1260, mentioned the continued
existence of sacerdotal ordeals 'in many regions',[30] but these regions
probably did not include his own homeland. The author of the *The
Mirror of Justices*, writing in the reign of Edward I, so misunderstood
the practice that he believed that, in the days of the ordeal, the accused
might have to put his *foot* in boiling water![31]

Both cases of ordeals and legislation concerning them can, however, be found in the centuries after 1300. In 1329, for instance, while

---

[28] Letter to the archbishop of Uppsala and the bishops of Sweden, JL 12117; *PL* 200,
cols. 854-60 (1171-2).
[29] Paul Ourliac, 'Le Duel judiciaire dans le sud-ouest', *Revue du Nord*, 40 (1958),
pp. 345-8, at p. 345 n. 1, repr. in *Études d'histoire du droit médiévale* (Paris, 1979), pp. 253-8,
at p. 254 n. 1.
[30] *De potestate artis et natura (De nullitate magiae)*, ed. J. S. Brewer, *Opera quaedam
hactenus inedita* (RS, 1859), p. 526.
[31] 3.23, ed. W. J. Whittaker (Selden Soc. 7, 1893), p. 110.

Lewis the Bavarian's German soldiery were encamped at Modena, a dispute between the local citizens and the soldiers went to trial by ordeal: 'the men of Modena denied the charge and, in order to uncover the truth of the matter, they offered to carry the iron bar heated in the fire and bore it without any harm.'[32] A century later a synod at Riga condemned the ordeal, which, the assembled clergy asserted, 'continued to be practised, most reprehensibly, in certain dioceses of our province more than in other parts of the world'.[33] Even in 1541, episcopal visitation in a remote diocese of Galicia in northwest Spain revealed that 'many men . . . suspecting that their wives or mistresses have bewitched them . . . in order to find this out . . . take them to the church to swear on the holy sacrament or place their hands on a bar of hot iron . . .' The authorities concluded, 'Since this is against the commandment that we should not tempt God, and is a diabolical superstition, we anathemize them.'[34]

As might be expected, isolated practices survived. Knowledge of the ordeal might be dimmed but never disappeared. Literary and pictorial allusions kept the custom alive in the imagination. Criseyde offered to allay Troilus' jealous suspicions 'by ordal or by othe',[35] and certain legendary ordeals were commonly represented in painting and sculpture in the later Middle Ages.[36]

Nevertheless, it is worth stressing that the thirteenth century truly was a turning point. Isolated cases of ordeals, and literary and antiquarian reference in the fourteenth and fifteenth centuries, are not of great significance. The campaign against trial by ordeal, which had reached a zenith of intention in 1215, attained a zenith of effect by 1300. A form of proof that had been a regular and functioning part of the judicial process across Christendom in 1200 was vestigial, rare, and local in 1300. The decisions of the twelfth-century schools and the

[32] Boniface of Morano, *Chronicon Mutinense*, ed.L. A. Muratori, *Rerum Italiarum Scriptores* (25 vols.,Milan, 1723-51), 11, col. 119.
[33] *Liv-, Est- und Kurländisches UB*, 7, ed. F. G.von Bunge (Riga, 1881), p. 491 (cap. 44).
[34] Synod of Mondoñedo, cap. 13, ed. Arturo Bernal Palacios *et al.*, *Synodicum Hispanum 1. Galicia* (Madrid, 1981), p. 76.
[35] Geoffrey Chaucer, *Troilus and Criseyde*, bk. 3, line 1046, ed. B. A. Windeatt (London, 1984), p. 302.
[36] e.g. Dieric Bouts' *The Judgement of the Emperor Otto*, commissioned by the town of Louvain in 1468 and now in the Musées Royaux des Beaux-Arts de Belgiques, Brussels (reproduced as the frontispiece to Bongert, *Recherches*); for a good example of the way that the ordeal lived on in popular literature see the poems and dramas of Hans Sachs, several of which, notably *Das heiss Eysen* of 1551, treat this theme, ed. Adalbert von Keller and Edmund Goetz (26 vols., Bibliothek des litterarischen Vereins in Stuttgart, Tübingen, 1870-1908), 9, pp. 85-95.

power of the thirteenth-century papacy had transformed the courts of Europe.

Replacement

The argument advanced in Chapter 3 of this book is that the function of the ordeal was not latent or implicit, but something which was quite clear to contemporaries, the men who employed the ordeal. Its function was to secure proof in circumstances where the normal modes could offer none. It is natural, then, to ask how this function was fulfilled after the abolition of the ordeal in the thirteenth century. There were still hard cases that demanded resolution. If the ordeal was no longer available other methods had to be employed.

There were three main developments in the area of proof in response to the demise of the ordeal: the extension of existing proofs into cases previously resolved by the ordeal; the swift progress towards the trial jury in England and some other countries; and, most important of all, the rise of torture to replace the ordeal.

The first process, the extension of existing proofs, can be illustrated by the curious case of the charters of Tournai and Péronne. The Tournai charter granted in 1188 prescribed the trial of cold water in two circumstances: homicide without witnesses, and wounding without witnesses at night. The second ruling is particularly instructive. The text of the relevant clause reads:

If an armed man wounds someone, by night or by day, and the wounded man can produce witnesses to this, the assailant must pay ten pounds . . . but if he cannot produce witnesses and the deed took place by day, the accused shall clear himself by a sevenfold compurgation. If the deed took place at night, however, he shall clear himself by the ordeal of cold water.[37]

There is here a sensitive gradation of forms of proof, according to the degree of certainty allowed by the circumstances. The production of witnesses was obviously decisive and clinched the case. In the absence of witnesses, the situation was more difficult, but, even so, rational distinctions could be made. A daytime assault was different from a nighttime assault, and, in the case of a daytime assault, it seemed reasonable to allow compurgation. The co-jurors would be attesting the good reputation of the accused and might even have good circumstantial grounds for believing in his innocence. The nighttime

---

[37] Ed. Mina Martens in *Elenchus fontium urbanae*, 1, ed. C. van de Kieft and J. F. Niermeijer (Leiden, 1967), pp. 349-53.

wounding was trickier. In the case of an attack in the dark with no witnesses, there really might be the temptation to wonder who could
know the truth of the matter. The ordeal offered a solution at just this
point. God knew the truth–and could be asked.

The privileges of Tournai formed the model for those of Péronne
and some other north French towns. This Péronne family of charters,
twenty or more years later than their Tournai exemplar, show, however, a few striking divergences from their model, most notably, for
our purposes, in that they exclude the ordeal. While the Tournai
charter prescribed the ordeal for unwitnessed homicide, the later
charters simply specified that the accused 'shall clear himself through
the right judgement of the urban magistrates (*échevins*)'–a vague
formula which left much to the court's discretion. In the other case
where the Tournai charter prescribed the ordeal, unwitnessed
wounding at night, the omission of the ordeal left both a grammatical
and a procedural lacuna. A comparison of the Péronne regulation with
that of Tournai cited above brings this out clearly:

> If an armed man wounds someone, by night or by day, and the wounded man
> can produce witnesses to this, the assailant must pay ten pounds . . . but if he
> cannot produce witnesses and the deed took place by day, the accused shall
> clear himself by a sevenfold compurgation. If the deed took place at night,
> however, he shall likewise clear himself by a sevenfold compurgation.[38]

The inconsistency and awkwardness of this formulation show the gap
where the ordeal had been removed. One consequence of this removal
was that circumstances which had previously been distinguished–
unwitnessed assult by day and by night–were now treated identically.
A subtly graded scale of proof had been made cruder.

There are many other examples where the removal of the ordeal
simply widened the scope of compurgation. Especially in ecclesiastical and urban courts, but also more generally, compurgation must
have been one of the commonest forms of proof in the period after the
condemnation of the ordeal. Already in some twelfth-century urban
charters, as we have seen, there was a move to replace ordeal by compurgation. The system of proof by compurgation was, in fact,
important throughout the Middle Ages. Historians have been inclined

[38] The charter of Péronne itself is printed by M. A. Teulet, *Layettes du trésor des chartes*,
1 (Paris, 1863), pp. 337-9. The charters of Hesdin and Athies belong to the same family.
The former is printed by G. Espinas (ed.), *Recueil des documents relatifs à l'histoire du droit
municipal. Artois*, 2 (Paris, 1934), pp. 588-94 (cf. p. 596), the latter by R. Fossier, *Chartes du
Coutume en Picardie (XIe-XIIIe s.)* (Paris, 1974), pp. 310-16.

to pre-date its decline and to associate it with the ordeal under the heading 'irrational and formal proofs',[39] supposedly replaced by rational proofs over the course of time. This obscures the fact that sometimes, compurgation replaced ordeal: 'If a woman is accused on some charge and it cannot be proved, I order that she should clear herself by oath and not by the hot iron.'[40]

The abolition of the ordeal might put greater discretionary power in the hands of judges–in one Flemish town the ordeal was replaced with a proof 'which, in the opinion of the judges, can be compared to the ordeal of hot iron'[41]–but there was also a development which gave even greater power to another group of men in court–the emergence of the criminal trial jury. Juries were developing in several European countries in the twelfth and thirteenth centuries but the best known instance, and the one with the greatest historical consequences, was the English jury.[42]

Juries of presentment already existed in twelfth-century England (and were possibly ancient). Their task was to indict felons, that is, to testify that named individuals were generally believed to have committed felonies. They did not, however, decide the guilt or innocence of those indicted. This was done either through 'inquests and inquisitions before the judges'[43] or through the ordeal. Juries of presentment were thus not trial juries. However, over the course of the early thirteenth century, they developed into trial juries. The indicted felon could now 'put himself on the country', that is, agree to accept the verdict of a jury. The process, as it eventually crystallized, is described by Bracton in the following way: the justices address the jurymen, 'such a one . . . charged with the death of such a one . . . denies the death . . . and on this matter puts himself for good and ill upon the words of your mouth . . . And therefore we tell you that on the faith that binds you to God and by the oath that you have taken you are to let us know the truth thereof.' 'Discharge or condemnation' immediately followed the verdict.[44]

---

[39] e.g. R. C. van Caenegem in *La Preuve, passim.*

[40] *Fuero de Cuenca*, ed. R. de Ureña y Smenjaud (Madrid, 1935), p. 863 (A modification of the *fuero* by Sancho IV of León and Castile, 1285).

[41] Henri Platelle, *La Justice seigneuriale de l'abbaye de S. Amand* (Louvain and Paris, 1965), p. 316.

[42] There is a large literature. A good short account is provided by T. F. T. Plucknett, *A Concise History of the Common Law* (5th edn., London, 1956), pp. 106-38.

[43] *The Treatise on the Laws and Customs of England commonly called Glanvill*, 14, ed. G. D. Hall (London, etc., 1965), p. 171.

[44] *De legibus et consuetudines regni Angliae*, ed. George E. Woodbine, rev. and tr. Samuel

The close connection between the abolition of ordeals and the rise of the trial jury has been commented upon by many legal historians. They argue that the 1215 decision 'left a gap', 'disturbed all [the law's] arrangements',[45] and caused 'practical and intellectual disarray'.[46] The jury filled this gap: 'The path of inclination for the English was thus to extend jury procedure to fill the enormous gap left by the abolition of ordeals'.[47]

The initial confusion caused by the abolition of ordeals is reflected by the royal mandate of 1219 to the justices. After prohibiting ordeals, it went on to suggest some *ad hoc* measures for dealing with accused criminals and concluded: 'Since our council will not make any more definite arrangements on this issue at present, we leave it to your discretion how you will follow these instructions in your eyre. Proceed in this matter according to your discretion and your conscience, ascertaining as far as you can the character of the individuals involved, the nature of the crime and the truth of the matter.'[48]

Here, as we have already observed in other countries, the removal of this mode of proof left, at least temporarily, great discretionary power in judges' hands. The development of the trial jury over the course of the reign of Henry III (1216-72) limited this power again, as a new independent source of a verdict, the jury, replaced the old independent source, the ordeal. In 1231 the seneschal of the abbey of Bury St Edmunds explained that the empanelling of juries in the abbot's court 'has been customary since the war [i.e. the civil war of 1215-17], because before the war they had the ordeal of fire and water'.[49] The years around 1215 stood in this man's mind as the moment of transition from the age of the ordeal to the age of the jury.

It was not only in England that the demise of the ordeal led directly to the trial jury. A very similar development occurred in Denmark too, and here there is unambiguous documentary evidence for the fact that the trial jury was actually devised to replace the ordeal. In an instruction of Valdemar II, issued in 1216 or soon after, we read

E. Thorne (4 vols., Cambridge, Mass., 1968-77), 2, p. 405.

[45] Frederick Pollock and Frederic W. Maitland, *The History of English Law before the time of Edward I* (2 vols., 2nd edn., reissued with an intro. by S. C. Milsom, Cambridge, 1968), 2, pp. 619 and 650.

[46] S. F. C. Milsom, *Historical Foundations of the Common Law* (London, 1969), p. 359.

[47] John H. Langbein, *Torture and the Law of Proof* (Chicago, 1977), p. 75.

[48] *Patent Rolls* (as in n. 1).

[49] *Bracton's Notebook*, ed. F. W. Maitland (3 vols., London, 1887), 2, p. 457, no. 592; *Curia Regis Rolls*, 14 (HMSO, 1961), p. 370, no. 1737.

Since the lord pope has prohibited trial by hot iron for all Christians, we do not wish to, and cannot, except ourselves from this general rule. So we have pondered for a long time, taking counsel with our chief men, as to what more generally acceptable form of proof we should decree instead of the verdict of the hot iron . . . We have decreed that anyone accused of homicide should be brought before the court and the accuser should name fifteen men from the region of the accused; the accused may object to three; the remaining twelve will swear, after fifteen days, either that he deserves to be outlawed for killing without cause or that he should pay compensation for killing an enemy or they should clear him absolutely with their oath.[50]

Such clear evidence of the creation of new legal procedures to fill the gap left by the decision of 1215 must make it even harder to maintain the view that the ordeal was already withering or atrophying in the twelfth century.

There is one last point to be made about the replacement of the ordeal by the jury. There is a sense in which the jury not only fulfilled the same function as the ordeal, but also partook of the same nature. In particular, the inscrutability of the jury's verdict was reminiscent of ordeal procedure. As F. Joüon de Longrais puts it, 'Their verdict is accepted without discussion and formalistically. It has all the archaic firmness of the old proofs. It acts on the material question, the matters of fact, like a kind of ordeal. One cannot ask its reasons, still less begin it over again.'[51] It bound the judges, just as the ordeal had bound them. It is this inscrutable and binding quality that makes sense of the claim that 'the jury was first seen as a new ordeal'.[52]

This 'newer sort of ordeal',[53] the trial jury, developed in only a few countries, however. The procedure that really blossomed in the thirteenth century, filling the role earlier played by the ordeal, was judicial torture.[54] The first legislative reference to torture, in the *Liber juris civilis* of Verona in 1228,[55] shows how it was explicitly regarded as an alternative to trial by ordeal. As the thirteenth century progressed, judicial torture was employed increasingly frequently, at first against

---

[50] *Diplomatarium Danicum* (as in n. 1).

[51] *La Preuve*, p. 206.

[52] Milsom, *Historical Foundations* (as in n. 46), p. x; see also van Caenegem in *La Preuve*, p. 729; Langbein, *Torture and the Law of Proof* (as in n. 47), p. 77.

[53] Plucknett, *Concise History* (as in n. 42), p. 125.

[54] In general, see P. Fiorelli, *La tortura guidiziaria nel diritto comune* (2 vols., Rome, 1953-4); Langbein, *Torture and the Law of Proof* (as in n. 47); Edward Peters, *Torture* (Oxford, 1985); Lea, *Superstition and Force*, pp. 429-590, relevant sections reissued as *Torture*, ed. Edward Peters (Philadelphia, 1973).

[55] Ed. Bartolomeo Campagnola (Verona, 1728), p. 61, cap. 75.

suspected criminals in the Italian cities, later by the Inquisition and by royal judges in St Louis's France.

One important stimulus to the rise of torture was the ever-growing authority and familiarity of Roman law. Unlike the customary laws of earlier medieval Europe, Roman law had a definite and regulated place for the judicial torture of both witnesses and suspects–'it is customary for torture to be applied for the purpose of detecting crime'.[56] For the most part, this meant torture of slaves only, but, in certain circumstances, free men too might be tortured.

Just as the absence of the ordeal from the Roman law seriously damaged its credibility in the twelfth and thirteenth centuries, so the law's prescriptions concerning torture encouraged the revival of this practice in the same period. Academic jurists, canon lawyers, and secular legislators alike agreed in approving even this component of the law they revered. Their reading of the text of the Roman law convinced them that 'the wise men of ancient times held it good to torture men to know from them the truth'.[57]

The revival of torture in the thirteenth century cannot, however, be attributed solely to the allure of Roman law. Torture was not only prescribed in the texts, it was also necessary for the functioning of the newly developing inquisitorial procedure, especially after the completion of its elaborate theory of proofs. For the twelfth and thirteenth centuries saw, alongside the academic study of Roman law, the rise of new judicial procedures, which significantly shifted the balance of power in the court. Until that period both criminal and civil cases had usually been raised and pursued by the injured party; the court then decided which proof should apply; and the accuser could suffer if the case went against him. With the development of inquisitorial techniques, officers of Church and State began to assume, to a much greater degree, the right to initiate proceedings and to take a much more active role in the court. 'The most significant aspect of the inquisitorial procedure', writes Edward Peters, 'was the elimination of the liable accuser and the increased latitude and power of the courts and of the authorities they represented.'[58] Thus an active inquisitorial judge now confronted a suspect in circumstances which made it easy to probe, to intimidate, and to harry him.

[56] *Digest*, 48.18.1. Important Roman Law references to torture are also found in ibid., 22.5, 29.5, 48.19, *Code*, 6.35, 9.8, 9.41, 'Opinions of Paulus', 5.14-16, and *Novels*, 90.1.

[57] *Las Siete Partidas*, 7.30, preamble, ed. Real Academia de la Historia (3 vols., Madrid, 1807, repr., 1972), 3, p. 701.

[58] *The Magician, the Witch and the Law* (Philadelphia, 1978), p. 189.

Inquisitorial procedure, which spread into the ecclesiastical and secular courts of most of Europe in the later Middle Ages, thus created a court situation amenable to the torturing of suspects. The final impetus, however, was given by the associated Romano-canonical system of proofs, for, despite the increased power of the judge in inquisitorial procedure, he was still bound by quite strict rules of proof.[59] The common opinion of Romanists and canonists was that 'in criminal cases proofs should be clear and manifest',[60] and, in the mature system, this meant that, if more than one eye-witness to a crime could not be produced, then only the suspect's confession counted as full proof. Moreover, in many systems, capital punishment could only be inflicted if the suspect confessed. The stringent application of so-called 'legal proof' thus placed enormous emphasis on extracting a confession: 'The jurists who devised it had solved one problem by creating another. They had constructed a system of proof that could handle the easy cases but not the hard ones. Their system could deal with most cases of overt crime but seldom with cases of covert crime ... the Roman-canon law of proof was unworkable standing alone.'[61] Because it was unworkable standing alone, it was supplemented by torture. In the 'hard cases', as long as the suspect were notorious or circumstantial evidence existed, torture was the usual judicial recourse of most of Europe in the later Middle Ages and early modern period.

This new solution to hard cases differed from the old one, the ordeal, in several ways. It was designed to extract a confession, rather than swiftly reveal guilt or innocence. It made no appeal to God and did not depend on priestly involvement (though the instruments of torture might be blessed). It was heavily biased against the accused, since his only recourse was to endure the torture, which could often be repeated. In contrast, when the accused underwent the ordeal, it was, almost invariably, a single test which could lead to an unambiguous declaration of innocence if it were passed. Torture, a judicial procedure in human hands, was more unrelenting than the judgement of God.

[59] See, in general, Jean-Philippe Lévy, *La Hiérarchie des preuves dans le droit savant du moyen âge* (Annales de l'Université de Lyon, 3ᵉ ser., Droit, 5, Paris, 1939); idem in *La Preuve*, pp. 137-67; Langbein (as in n. 47).

[60] Tancred, *De iudiciorum ordine*, 2.7.8, ed. F. Bergmann, *Pillii, Tancredi, Gratiae libri de iudiciorum ordine* (Göttingen, 1842, repr.,Aalen, 1965), p. 161.

[61] Langbein, *Torture and the Law of Proof* (as in n. 47), p. 7.

Despite these differences, it is reasonably clear that in the period 1200-1700 judicial torture fulfilled the same function as ordeals had done in the period 800-1200. There is, for example, a striking similarity between these cases in which the ordeal was employed before 1200 and those in which torture was used after 1200. Like the ordeal, torture was a last resort: 'Men are tortured in civil and criminal cases when the truth may not be discovered in any other way.'[62] It was used for the 'invisible' crimes of belief like heresy. The heresy trials of the twelfth century had frequently culminated in a dramatic trial by fire or water; those of the later Middle Ages led to the privacy of the Inquisitors' rooms and the torture chambers. Treason, too, once frequently tried by ordeal, was commonly dealt with by torture, even in countries like England, where torture was otherwise rare.[63] Witchcraft trials, which will be discussed more fully below, are another example.

One good example of the way the ordeal was superseded by torture is provided by the *Liber Augustalis* or *Constitutions of Melfi*, issued by Frederick II for his Sicilian kingdom in 1231. In this code, deeply marked by Roman law, Frederick contemptuously criticized and prohibited trial by ordeal. He also made provision for the torturing of suspects in certain circumstances:

> If, through the remedies provided by our imperial care, we have rightly relieved those who suffer clandestine losses or injuries when the perpetrators cannot be discovered by clear proofs ... much more strongly do we believe it unworthy to leave outside our care those whose fathers or sons or relatives on either side have been killed anywhere by secret homicides, when the perpetrators of such a heinous crime cannot be discovered by any investigation, however probing ... [After specifying an inquisition, Frederick's ruling continues] But if, during this inquisition any unrespectable persons (*leves persone*) are blamed for that homicide, even if the inquisition does not prove it fully against them, we decree that one should proceed to torture those unrespectable persons of the lower orders (*persone leves et viles*) ... We decree that this procedure, of inquisition, proof and, eventually, torture, shall be observed in the case of other clandestine or nocturnal injuries.[64]

[62] Albertus Gandinus, *Tractatus de maleficiis*, ed. Hermann Kantorowicz, *Albertus Gandinus und das Strafrecht der Scholastik*, 2 (Berlin and Leipzig, 1926), p. 159; Azo, *Summa super Codicem (Summa Aurea)*, 9.41 (Lyons, 1557, repr. Frankfurt am Main, 1968), fol. 236, drawing on *Digest*, 48.18.9 (but out of context).

[63] For torture in England see Langbein, *Torture and the Law of Proof* (as in n. 47) and James Heath, *Torture and English Law* (Westport, Conn., 1982).

[64] 1.28 (32), ed. J. L. A. Huillard-Bréholles, *Historia diplomatica Friderici secundi* (6 vols., Paris, 1852-61), 4/1, pp. 29-32; *Die Konstitutionen Friedrichs II. für sein Königreich Sizilien*, ed. and tr. (into German), Hermann Conrad *et al.* (Cologne, 1973), pp. 40-2.

The functional parallel between the ordeal and torture is here patent, especially in a code which abolished the former and introduced the latter. Both were a solution to the judicial problem of cases where full and acceptable proof was lacking but some presumption against the accused existed (much of the legal literature of the later centuries was, in fact, concerned with estimating exactly how much presumptive evidence–*indicia*–was necessary before torture was permissible). The early fourteenth-century *Très ancienne coutume de Bretagne* prescribed, 'if full proof cannot be obtained, but there is common report or apparent presumptions against the accused, then he must undergo ordeal or be submitted to torture.'[65] Both ordeal and torture were forms of proof frequently employed against the lower orders and against 'clandestine and nocturnal' crimes. 'The ordeal left a gap and it was filled by torture.'[66]

Even the exceptional case of England helps make the point. For there was one rare situation in which trial by jury did not work. This was when an indicted criminal refused to 'put himself on the country' (i.e. accept a jury verdict). To meet this problem the lawyers and rulers of the later Middle Ages developed a solution: the accused man would be subject to *la peine forte et dure*, a form of torture designed to make him plead before a jury.[67] It was not exactly the continental form of torture, intended to elicit a confession, but it shows how natural it was to have resort to torture in those few special cases which the jury could not handle. The gap left by the ordeal had to be closed, even to some extent in England, by torture–'in the place of fire and water, entered torture'.[68] In this way the world of the ordeal gave place to the world of inquisition and torture, or, in a few places, the world of jury trial. Appeals to God now had little place in human justice. The result was that some men–inquisitors, torturers, or jurymen–had greater power over other men than they had done before. By drawing new lines between God and man, the clerical opponents of the ordeal had also drawn new lines between man and man.

---

[65] Ed. Marcel Planiol (Rennes, 1896), p. 144.

[66] Fiorelli, *La tortura giudiziaria* (as in n. 54), 1, p. 69.

[67] See H. R. T. Summerson, 'The Early Development of the Peine Forte et Dure' in E. W. Ives and A. H. Manchester (eds.), *Law, Litigants and the Legal Profession* (London, 1983), pp. 116-25.

[68] Hans Fehr, 'Gottesurteil und Folter', pp. 251-2. Fehr's general argument, that the ordeal was a form of exorcism, is not convincing.

Recrudescence

> Ordeal of cold water is to be admitted as a proof in this charge, for it is so difficult to prove.[69]

The crime of witchcraft was difficult to prove. Not only were many of the witches' activities nocturnal, but, more than this, there was a sense in which the offence was invisible. The sick neighbours, the curdled milk, or the secret meetings were only signs of the real crime–*being* a witch. It was proof of this mysterious status that was at issue. We have already seen that trial by ordeal was deemed particularly appropriate for such impenetrable or opaque cases and it is not, therefore, surprising to find relatively early reference to the use of the ordeal in accusations of witchcraft and sorcery. Alongside such inaccessible matters as murder by night or sexual purity, the question of witchcraft and sorcery was sent to God's verdict rather than men's.

Both Carolingian and Anglo-Saxon legislation prescribed trial by ordeal for witchraft. The twelfth-century Norwegian *Borgarthing Law* ordered

if the tools of witchcraft are discovered in anyone's bed or pillow, human hair or nail clippings or frogs' feet or other things which can serve for enchantment, then the bishop's officer may accuse three women who are suspected of it, to answer the charge. They must clear themselves with the iron. If they are clean after the ordeal of iron, then they are free of the accusation; if they are unclean after the ordeal, they are deemed responsible.[70]

On the other side of Europe, at the same time, the hot iron was likewise prescribed in the Spanish *Fuero de Cuenca* for accusations of witchcraft and sorcery.[71]

The disappearance of the ordeal in the thirteenth century had direct repercussions for witchcraft trials. Now that the ordeal was no longer a legal form of proof in ecclesiastical courts, recourse to torture became the natural way of seeking certainty in these, as in other, hard cases. The centrality of torture in the great witch persecutions of the fifteenth, sixteenth, and seventeenth centuries is obvious. Often the authorities felt that witchcraft was a crime in such a special category that even the usual restraints on the application of torture could be abandoned. 'One can repeat torture,' pronounced a French court in

---

[69] Jakob Rickius von Arweiler, *Defensio. . . probae aquae frigidae* (Cologne, 1598), p. 15.

[70] 1.16, ed. with German tr. Rudolf Meissner, *Bruchstücke der Rechtsbücher des Borgarthings und des Eidsivathings* (Weimar, 1942), pp. 44-5.

[71] Caps. 293-4, 296, ed. R. Ureña y Smenjaud (Madrid, 1935), p. 328.

the early seventeenth century, 'because this crime of witchcraft is so extraordinary and so hidden and so secret.'[72] The famous letter written in 1628 by Johannes Junius, burgomaster of Bamberg, shows how essential torture was in the manufacture of witches. Junius had been accused of witchcraft and tortured until he confessed. His letter, written in a hand shaky from his sufferings, and smuggled from prison to his daughter, begins, 'Many hundred thousand good nights, dearly beloved daughter Veronica. Innocent have I come into prison, innocent have I been tortured, innocent must I die. For whoever comes into the witch prison must become a witch or else be tortured until he invents something out of his head . . .'[73] It has been truly said, 'Where there is no torture, there can be little witchcraft.'[74]

There was also, however, another side to the story. Although it is true to speak of the replacement of the ordeal by torture, there survived, too, a tendency to link witchcraft and the ordeal, an under-tow, as it were, of opinion which thought of the ordeal as the right form of proof for this particular offence. A particularly illuminating example occurs in the classic manual of witch-hunters, the *Malleus Maleficiarum*. The authors, the Dominicans Krämer and Sprenger, are discussing the licitness of the ordeal of hot iron: '. . . it is not wonderful that witches are able to undergo this trial by ordeal unscathed with the help of devils . . . Hence even less than other criminals ought witches to be allowed this trial by ordeal, because of their intimate familiarity with the devil; and from the very fact of their appealing to this trial they are to be held as suspected witches.' After this remarkably ingenious piece of argument, they cite as an example the recent case in the diocese of Constance, when the judge, the count of Fürstenberg, 'being young and inexperienced', allowed a suspected witch to appeal to the red-hot iron: 'And she then carried the red-hot iron not only for the stipulated three paces, but for six, and offered to carry it even farther. Then, although they ought to have taken this as manifest proof that she was a witch . . . she was released'.[75] The case they mention,

---

[72] The opinion of the court of Bazuel, in the modern *département* of Nord, 1621, cited in Marie-Sylvie Dupont-Bouchat, Willem Frijhoff and Robert Muchembled, *Prophètes et sorciers dans les Pays-bas*, XVIe-XVIIIe *siècles* (Paris, 1978), p. 210.

[73] Cited in George L. Burr, *The Witch Persecutions* (New York, 1903), pp. 23-8, and E. W. Monter (ed.), *European Witchcraft* (New York, 1969), p. 85.

[74] Pollock and Maitland, *History of English Law* (as in n. 45), 2, p. 555.

[75] Henricus Institoris and Jakob Sprenger, *Malleus Maleficiarum*, 3.17. The work went through dozens of editions between 1486 and 1669; the story was repeated in Ulrich Tengler's *Laienspiegel*, rev. Sebastian Brand (Augsburg, 1509), see Fehr, 'Gottesurteil und Folter', p. 243.

which can be proven to have occurred from documentary sources too,[76] took place in Rothenbach in the Black Forest in 1485.

There is clearly evidence here for a continued association of witchcraft and the ordeal: the red-hot iron, in late fifteenth-century Germany, just as in tenth-century England, and twelfth-century Norway and Spain, seemed, to some people at least, the right tool for the task of unveiling a witch. On the other hand, however, experienced inquisitorial judges rejected the ordeal as a form of proof expressly because it was not sufficiently controllable. The ordeal was, of course, intended to be uncontrollable, to take matters out of men's hands and place them in God's. Krämer and Sprenger feared that the Devil, rather than God, would more likely take charge at this point and hence preferred, in the circumstances, to retain control themselves. They had responsive tools of their own–inquisition and torture–and were thus willing to disavow the use of the ordeal in witchcraft prosecutions.

Nevertheless, despite the objections raised in the *Malleus*, the most remarkable survival of trial by ordeal was to be in witchcraft cases, for the practice of 'swimming' witches, so common in the early modern period, was, of course, a late recrudescence of trial by cold water. Witches had been swum in the Middle Ages (an example is recorded in Bavaria in the 1090s[77]) and there is nothing intrinsically surprising about the application of this form of proof in the sixteenth and seventeenth centuries. Doubts do remain, however, as to whether the early modern spate of swimmings should best be viewed as a survival or a revival, for the normal form of ordeal applied to witches in the later Middle Ages was the hot iron, not the cold water. On the other hand, swimming of witches begins in the sixteenth century in just those areas where trial by ordeal had survived longest. But whether it was survival or revival, this was the form in which trial by ordeal continued to the very verge of living memory.

The 1560s seem to be the decade when the swimming of witches became common enough to attract attention. Johann Weyer, physician to the Duke of Cleves-Jülich, wrote in his *De praestigiis daemonum* of 1563, 'The fact that, when accused witches are thrown into water with their hands and feet bound, they never sink, but swim on the surface, is regarded by magistrates and police in many jurisdictions not as

[76] *Fürstenbergisches UB* (7 vols., Tübingen, 1877–91), 4, p. 42 (1485).
[77] *Annales S. Stephani Frisingensis*, ed. George Waitz, MGH, *SS* 13 (Hanover, 1881), p. 52.

fallacious evidence, but as certain proof'.[78] This seems to be the earliest sixteenth-century reference to the practice. Another author, writing in 1584, regarded the swimming of witches as 'a new custom' (*newen gebrauch*) and associated it especially with Westphalia.[79] This fits together well enough. From the Rhineland and Westphalia the practice spread outwards. By the mid-1580s witches were being swum in France,[80] and French cases recur throughout the seventeenth century, always in the north-eastern regions such as Burgundy, Champagne, and Picardy, regions '*vers la frontière*'.[81] In England the first recorded case of swimming was in 1590,[82] while condemnations of the practice in both the Spanish Netherlands and the United Provinces in the mid-1590s show that it was in use there too.[83] Italy, Spain, and the south and west of France seem not to have been affected.

By 1600 witches were thus being subjected to this form of trial by ordeal in many parts of Europe. The practice continued throughout the seventeenth century and, in some places, into the eighteenth. In colonial Virginia, for example, the ordeal was used judicially as late as 1706,[84] and in Hungary there were official swimmings a generation later than this.[85] However, although scores of witches were swum in this period, the practice always existed in a climate of learned disapproval and opposition from the higher authorities.[86]

---

[78] Johann Weyer, *De Praestigiis daemonum et incantationibus ac veneficiis* (Basel, 1563), pp. 449-50. The work went through many editions and was translated into French and German.

[79] Hermann Neuwald, *Bericht von erforschung, prob und erkentnis der zauberinnen durchs kalte wasser* (Helmstadt, 1584), A3 and B'.

[80] A case is recorded in Champagne in 1584, Robert Mandrou, *Magistrats et sorciers en France au XVIIe siècle* (Paris, 1968), p. 102.

[81] A phrase used by the archbishop of Rheims of the mob swimmings of the 1640s, ibid., p. 356.

[82] Keith Thomas, *Religion and the Decline of Magic* (London, 1971), p. 551. It is doubtful whether the practice spread to Scotland; for one 'unreliable reference' see Christina Larner, *Enemies of God: The Witch-hunt in Scotland* (London, 1981), p. 110.

[83] J. B. Cannaert, *Olim. Procès de sorcières en Belgique sous Philippe II* (Ghent, 1847), pp. 6-9; Johann van Heurne, *Opera omnia* (2 vols., Lyons, 1658), 2, pp. 132-3.

[84] George L. Burr (ed.), *Narratives of the Witchcraft Cases, 1648-1706* (New York, 1914), pp. 441-2.

[85] Wilhelm Soldan, *Geschichte der Hexenprozesse*, rev. Heinrich Heppe, rev. Max Bauer (2 vols., Munich, 1911), 2, pp. 274-5. Muratori also tells how he had heard that the swimming of witches was still practised in Transylvania in his own time, L. A. Muratori, *Antiquitates italicae medii aevi* (2nd edn., 17 vols., Arezzo, 1773-8), 8, col. 132.

[86] For useful bibliography on the learned debate about the swimming of witches, see J. G. T. Grasse, *Bibliotheca magica et pneumatica* (Leipzig, 1843, repr., Hildesheim, 1960), pp. 36-7.

Despite the support of a few learned men, like James VI of Scotland, who wrote 'God hath appointed for a supernatural sign of the monstrous impiety of the witches that the water shall refuse to receive them in her bosom,'[87] the consensus of the learned was against the swimming of witches. On this issue there was a striking unanimity among very diverse thinkers. Jesuits and Puritan clergymen, sceptical physicians and legists, witch-hunters and those who disbelieved in witchcraft, all considered this ordeal to be 'fallacious evidence'. Their reasons were as various as their condemnation was unanimous. Some, like the physician Johann Weyer, thought that suspects might float due to natural causes. In a manner reminiscent of the emperor Frederick II, 350 years earlier, Weyer touched here upon a genuinely materialist critique of trial by ordeal. More common, however, were arguments from religious or legal propriety.

The theological objections were similar to those raised by the reforming clerics of the twelfth century. To many clergymen, both Catholic and Protestant, the swimming of witches seemed as outrageously magical as the witchcraft it was designed to uncover. It was using 'diabolic art to pursue the devil',[88] superstitious, and tempting God. The Puritan divine, William Perkins, called swimming and similar procedures 'after a sort practices of witchcraft, having no power by God's ordinance'.[89] In 1692 the clergy of Connecticut, a colony where swimming was employed, stated 'we cannot but give concurrence with the generality of divines that the endeavour of conviction of witchcraft by swimming is unlawful and sinful.'[90] It was, as some opponents put it, 'a counter magic'.[91]

Strenuous opposition came, in particular, from the higher courts and the university faculties of law. They repeatedly issued condemnations aimed at a form of proof so characteristic of rustics and ignorant inferior judges. In 1591 the jurist Godelmann wrote, 'It is the common opinion of the doctors that the cold water ordeal is nowadays prohibited . . . This common opinion of the doctors is approved by all the faculties of law in the German universities. Judges do wrong who

---

[87] *Daemonologie* (Edinburgh, 1597), 3.6, p. 81.

[88] Louis Servin, *Actions notables et plaidoyez* (2 vols., Rouen, 1629), p. 221.

[89] *A Discourse of the Damned Art of Witchcraft* (Cambridge, 1608), pp. 206-7; he referred to swimming as a custom of 'other countries'.

[90] J. M. Taylor, *The Witchcraft Delusion in Colonial Connecticut* (New York, 1908), pp. 75-6.

[91] Servin, *Actions notables* (as in n. 88), 1, p. 221.

depart from this common opinion.'[92] The Leyden faculties of law and philosophy offered a lengthy and hostile opinion on the subject.[93] Such opposition frequently manifested itself in attempts by higher courts or central authorities to stop lower courts employing or countenancing swimming. One famous clash of wills of this nature occurred in France in the 1590s. Two witches had been swum and condemned by local judges in Champagne. The case went to the Paris *Parlement*, which had superior jurisdiction, and was quashed because of these 'strange procedures'.[94] Eventually, in 1601, an *arrêt* of *Parlement* was issued forbidding the practice in any court within the jurisdiction of the *Parlement*.[95] The repetition of the prohibition in the mid-seventeenth century shows, however, that inferior courts were still breaching the rules set by the *Parlement*.[96]

Friction between superior authorities and lower courts is witnessed elsewhere too. In a mandate to the Council of Flanders in 1595, Philip II's government commanded that witches should be tried 'by law and legitimate judicial procedures', not by swimming, and tried to limit the jurisdiction of inferior courts in witch trials.[97] Swimming was expressly forbidden in the general instructions for witch prosecutions issued by Maximilian I of Bavaria in 1622.[98] In 1677 a local official in Styria was forbidden by the government to use trial by cold water.[99]

It was not only inferior judges who were tempted to resort to swimming a witch; the practice was also common outside the judicial process altogether, among irate peasants or mobs. In Burgundy in 1644, for example, 'everyone, on their own private authority, usurped rights of justice; the lowliest peasants raised themselves up as magistrates . . . they banished all the formalities of justice and wished to rely only upon trial by water'.[100] The great witch persecution

---

[92] Johann Georg Godelmann, *Tractatus de magis, veneficiis et lamiis recte cognoscendis et puniendis* (Nuremberg, 1676) 3.5, pp. 98, 100; the work was first published in Frankfurt in 1591.

[93] Van Heurne (as in n. 83).

[94] Servin, *Actions notables* (as in n. 88), 1, p. 221.

[95] Ibid., pp. 212-32, for a full account; see also Mandrou, *Magistrats et sorciers* (as in n. 80), pp. 181-3; A. Soman, 'Les Procès de sorcellerie au Parlement de Paris (1565-1640)', *Annales*, 32 (1977), pp. 790-814, esp. pp. 809-11.

[96] Mandrou, *Magistrats et sorciers* (as in n. 80), p. 355.

[97] Cannaert, *Olim* (as in n. 83).

[98] Sigmund Riezler, *Geschichte der Hexenprozesse in Bayern* (Stuttgart, 1896), p. 217.

[99] Fritz Byloff, *Hexenglaube und Hexenverfolgung in den österreichischschen Alpenländern* (Berlin and Leipzig, 1934), pp. 120-1.

[100] Jacques d'Autun, *L'incredulité savante* (Lyons, 1671), preface, cited by Mandrou, *Magistrats et sorciers* (as in n. 80), p. 373.

initiated by Matthew Hopkins in the following year in England also saw the use of swimming as an *ad hoc* proof until the criticisms of 'able divines' induced Hopkins to discontinue it.[101] The hysterical Hopkins crusade, launched at a time when the Civil War had disrupted normal judicial operations, was an absolutely characteristic environment for the emergence of the swimming of witches:

> And has he not with in a year
> Hang'd three score of 'em in one Shire?
> Some only for not being drown'd . . .[102]

Most strikingly, swimming was not only a practice that mobs forced unwilling suspects to undergo, but also a mode of proof often voluntarily requested. In 1635, for example, a peasant in Burgundy 'had himself swum twice by his fellows to prove to them his innocence'.[103] In 1696 the judges had to intervene against two parish priests, again in rural Burgundy, who 'organised trial by water as claimed by some peasants, who, accused by their fellows of sorcery, had not found any better method to prove their innocence'.[104] A German author of the early eighteenth century observed, of the cold water ordeal, that 'our women accused of witchcraft are accustomed to appeal to it even today . . .'[105] Hopkins was familiar with this phenomenon too: 'The devil's policy is great, in persuading many to come of their own accord to be tried . . . he advises them to be swum and tells them they shall sink and be cleared that way, then, when they be tried that way and float, they see the devil deceives them.'[106]

It was this combination of the willingness of local judges to employ swimming with the popular esteem for the procedure that made it so difficult to eradicate in the seventeenth century. Moreover, it was awkward to isolate one procedural anomaly from witchcraft prosecution while the prosecution itself continued. So, although the learned and official attack on the swimming of witches obviously inhibited the development of the practice in the seventeenth century, it was only when judges and legislators ceased to credit witchcraft itself that this

---

[101] Matthew Hopkins, *The Discovery of Witchcraft* (London, 1647), pp. 5-7; John Stearne, *A Confirmation and Discovery of Witchcraft* (London, 1648), pp. 18-19.

[102] Samuel Butler, *Hudibras*, 2.3, lines 143-5, ed. John Wilders (Oxford, 1967), p. 156.

[103] Mandrou, *Magistrats et sorciers* (as in n. 80), p. 103.

[104] P. Le Brun, *Histoire critique des pratiques superstitieuses* (Rouen, 1702), pp. 529-30, cited by Mandrou, *Magistrats et sorciers* (as in n. 80), p. 495.

[105] H. A. Meinders, *Unvorgreifliche Gedancken und Monita* (Lemgo, 1716), p. 121.

[106] *Discovery* (as in n. 101).

last vestige of trial by ordeal died away. Eighteenth-century cases of swimming are not hard to find, but they are increasingly limited to the actions of lynch mobs. By the nineteenth century, in England, the normal consequence of a swimming was a charge of assault against the swimmers. In 1864, for example, two people were convicted of assault at Chelmsford Assizes for swimming a witch.[107] Alternatively, enlightened magistrates might head off would-be swimmers before the act. By this period the swimming of witches was, in the eyes of such magistrates, simply a latent popular superstition that could turn vicious if unrestrained.

The swimming of witches in the sixteenth and seventeenth centuries never had as much official sanction as the medieval ordeal commanded in the period before 1200. It was looked down upon. It is not so surprising that, in the early eighteenth century a Protestant writer could condemn it as 'a papistical superstition', in which 'the simple people still secretly have faith',[108] but as early as the 1590s it was explicitly associated with 'the ignorant vulgar'.[109] Herein lies a trap for the modern researcher. The ordeal that survived down to the brink of the present century, the cold water ordeal for witchcraft, was deemed popular, superstitious, even 'papistical', and a product of rural ignorance. By the late eighteenth and nineteenth centuries, swimming was indeed initiated only by uneducated countryfolk. The character of this residual and vestigial form of the ordeal should not, however, influence our picture of the practice in its heyday. The tendency of some scholars to see, in the more isolated rural regions of the modern world, a model of life in the Middle Ages involves a misapprehension. Medieval society was based not only upon small peasant communities, but also upon a military aristocracy and a clerical élite. Between the end of the Middle Ages and the eighteenth or nineteenth centuries, that aristocracy was educated and partly tamed, that élite partly secularized. This new educated secular élite looked down on its charge, the rural population, as, in some sense, the representative of an earlier irrational superstition. The Victorian magistrates who suppressed the villagers' swimming urge, as also the

---

[107] There is an account of the preliminary hearing in *The Times* (of London), Thurs. 24 Sept., 1863, p. 4.

[108] Jacob Brunnemann, *Discours von betrüglichen Kennzeichen der Zauberey* (Stargard, 1708, etc.) (p. 45 in the 1729 Frankfurt edn.), cited by H. C. Lea, *Materials towards a History of Witchcraft*, ed. A. C. Howland (3 vols., Philadelphia, 1939), 3, p. 1427.

[109] Hartwig von Dassel, *Responsum iuris in causa poenali maleficiarum Winsiensium* (Hamburg, 1597, Frankfurt/Oder, 1698), cited Lea, *Materials*, 1, pp. 798-9.

nineteenth-century pioneers in the study of the ordeal, would see continuity between the beliefs and practices of the uneducated countrymen of their own day and those of their medieval ancestors. They had woven a potent image of the past, the popular, the illiterate, the primitive, the ritual, and the rural. The image tells us a great deal about the transformation of class relations and culture in the early modern period. It will not help us understand the medieval judicial ordeal.

8

Further Reflections

THE core of this book contains an argument about the history of trial by ordeal. It has been suggested that the ordeal was a form of proof for the hard cases, in which normal judicial procedures were inapplicable, and that it developed from Frankish origins and spread across Europe in conjunction with Christianity and Christian kingship. It was eventually abolished by a reforming clerical élite in the wake of the intellectual and institutional changes of the twelfth century. In the course of this historical analysis, however, questions of both more general and more theoretical nature inevitably arise. It is the purpose of this final chapter to address some of these broader issues more explicitly and at greater length than would have been appropriate in the strictly historical account.

One important general question is how far it is right to regard trial by ordeal as an essentially pagan practice which contaminated the Church of the early Middle Ages. Such a view would fit in well with one common picture of Christianity as a religion which was, in some ways, subverted by the barbarian invasions and only cleansed by the great reforming movements of the eleventh and twelfth centuries. Both Catholic and Protestant historians can give countenance to this view. To complicate matters, German historians have always seen the issue of the paganism of the ordeal as closely linked with the supposedly Germanic nature of the custom. Writing as recently as 1956, Hermann Nottarp could claim, 'The ordeal, or, more precisely, the belief that underlay it, was especially suited to the Germanic peoples',[1] and the same kind of racialist thinking is revealed by the assertion that the adoption of the ordeal by Christian clerics represented a 'Germanization' of the Church.[2] Indeed, the debate over the pagan or Christian origin of trial by ordeal among German historians has continually tended to become entangled in the wider disagreements between 'Romanist' and 'Germanist'.[3]

[1] *Gottesurteilstudien*, p. 103.
[2] Leitmaier, *Die Kirche*, p. 115.
[3] For the controversy over the Germanic or non-Germanic origins of the ordeal see

Although there is no surviving evidence that the pagan peoples of Europe employed trial by ordeal, the fact that the practice exists, or once existed, among so many non-Christian peoples in so many parts of the world shows that there is no necessary or inevitable link between the ordeal and Christianity. Moreover, the appearance of trial by ordeal in the very earliest recension of the Salic law of *c.* 510 makes it almost certain that the Franks used this form of proof before their conversion to Christianity, for, although the law code dates to the years shortly after the conversion of the Frankish king, Clovis,[4] it is extremely unlikely that the complex and articulated provisions of the Salic law were wholesale innovations of recent, Christian origin. If the Salic law describes, for the most part, the ways of the pagan Franks, trial by cauldron was one of those ways. The ordeal was thus pagan and, as Frankish, Germanic.

If, then, by 'the pagan origin of the ordeal', we mean simply the fact that it was employed by pagans before it was employed by Christians, the ordeal is probably of pagan origin. But such a purely genealogical approach is misleading. Take the analogy of ploughing. Certainly, many non-Christian peoples have the plough, and it is attested for the peoples of Europe before their conversion. This does not make the continued presence of the plough in medieval Europe 'a pagan survival'. Ploughing is a widespread functional and symbolic activity which can be successfully integrated with a number of religious systems. The same is true of the ordeal. It was a method of ascertaining guilt or innocence using the physical elements and it could have pagan or Christian forms. When the ploughman sacrificed to Freya for good harvests, that was pagan ploughing; when he prayed to Our Lord or the saints, then it was Christian ploughing. So too with the ordeal. Anthropologists gave up the habit of labelling customs or practices 'survivals' long ago, and historians should do the same.

The important thing is not the putative descent of some practice or institution, but its function and significance in the living society in which it has a place. From this point of view, trial by ordeal in the central Middle Ages was a Christian institution. 'The ordeal rests on religious belief in the power and will of the deity to perform a miracle, takes place in the church, with the co-operation of the priest and

Erler, 'Der Ursprung', Mayer, 'Der Ursprung', Pappenheim, 'Über die Anfänge'. For an admirable summary of the whole debate amongst these, and other, German scholars, see Iglesia Ferreirós, 'El processo del conde Bera', pp. 1-65.

[4] Whichever of the various favoured dates for that elusive event is chosen.

under the bishop's supervision, after consecration of the material, religious preparation of the proband and the surroundings, Christian oath and mass, involving the participation of the proband in communion, liturgical conjurations and biblical citation.' Here, in Liebermann's admirable summary,[5] are the conditions which made trial by ordeal Christian. It has already been argued that trial by ordeal diffused through Europe as part of the process of conversion and law codes like Ine's or those of twelfth-century Scandinavia, which are, amongst other things, 'conversion codes', give the ordeal an important place.

Nevertheless, modern historians continue to write about trial by ordeal as if it were somehow indelibly pagan and bore the marks of its suspect birth in pre-Christian times throughout its long life. 'Ordeals were originally acts of pagan magic, which were christianized, at least in form,' wrote F. L. Ganshof,[6] implying that their substance was not, while for Charlotte Leitmaier the stronghold of the ordeal was the *Eigenkirche* with its 'superstitious, half-pagan folk and uneducated, dependent priests'.[7] The essential issue, the question of what can be called Christian, is highlighted by this comment of Professor Alan Harding: 'The Church ... very sensibly took over the pagan ordeal and used it for its own purposes, as it had taken over and used the pagan blood-feud.'[8] Now there are some Christians who would say that there can be no 'Christian blood-feud', that there is an unavoidable contradiction in the very phrase. Similarly, it might be claimed that there was in the ordeal, in the expectation of divine judgements regularly and ritually embodied in the physical elements, something inimical and alien to true Christianity.

By the standards of apostolic Christianity these claims may be right. To judge by the standards of apostolic Christianity, however, is to take a stance on what Christian behaviour should be, on what it is to be truly Christian. This is, of course, a necessary activity for Christians and there can thus be no objection to modern Christian historians, advancing and espousing models of true religion, who decry the ordeal as pagan or 'not truly Christian'.[9] By doing so, they are recording how the Church of the early Middle Ages was, in their eyes,

---

[5] *Gesetze*, 2, p. 602.
[6] *La Preuve* 2, p. 74.
[7] *Die Kirche*, p. 122.
[8] *The Law Courts of Medieval England* (London, 1973), p. 27.
[9] Gaudemet in *La Preuve*, p. 103.

a corrupt and contaminated Church. But, for the non-believer or non-Christian, there is obviously no such need to make a judgement on 'true Christianity'. For him, the Church of the early Middle Ages represented as genuine a Christianity–though a different one–as the apostolic community, or the Churches of the Reformation or Counter-Reformation.

The nature of Christianity is not something given or essential. It is a nature that has to be shaped, determined, maintained, challenged, fought over, defined, and redefined in each generation, land, and class. Historically, there are many 'Christianities'. The non-believing historian faces, not a religious or ethical problem, but an historical one. Clearly, from the sixth century until the twelfth the ordeal was Christian, for Christianity countenanced and blessed the practice, despite occasional dissentient voices. Gradually these voices strengthened, and the withdrawal of ecclesiastical approval for the ordeal in the thirteenth century represents a victory for those reformers and critics who claimed that the ordeal was not Christian. The long and heated process of debate over the ordeal from 1050 to 1215 was also a debate over the definition of Christianity.

Just as it was possible for pagan trial by ordeal to become Christian trial by ordeal, so the custom could cease to be Christian. This, indeed, would be a good way of describing what happened in the twelfth and thirteenth centuries, when the reforming clerical élite came to the decision that trial by ordeal was not Christian and then had to persuade or force other ecclesiastics and the lay world to agree with them. By 1300 the ordeal had ceased to be Christian. A new Christianity had emerged, that of later medieval and modern times, in which regular appeal to the deity for judicial purposes was absent or of minimal importance. Other religions have taken different paths and Christianity could have done so too. There is no reason for non-Christian historians of the twentieth century to take the description of Christianity advanced by the reformers of the twelfth century and their heirs as being any more valid or authentic than that of the priests who solemnly officiated at the ordeal in the long centuries before. It is fruitless to ask if the ordeal is essentially pagan, Christian, or superstitious. What is more important is to trace the course of the changes whereby the ordeal, probably the originally pagan ordeal, became the Christian ordeal, and whereby the Christian ordeal became the superstitious and irrational ordeal.

There is some connection between the tendency to see the ordeal as pagan and the habit of referring to it as irrational. Both are formulae for distancing the commentator from an ancient and discredited custom, and both allow for an evolutionist approach in which the twelfth-century reformers emerge as members of a progressive movement with which the modern commentator can identify. There is a very long tradition of denunciation of the ordeal as irrational or superstitious, a tradition which can, indeed, be traced back to some of the medieval critics themselves. This denunciation reached a climax in the self-confident utterances of the Enlightenment: 'Among all the whimsical and absurd institutions which owe their existence to the weakness of human reason, this [i.e. trial by ordeal], which submitted questions that affected the property, the reputation, and the lives of men, to the determination of chance, or of bodily strength and address, appears to be the most extravagant and preposterous.'[10] Such an attitude continues, however, to be standard among legal historians of the present century. Ordeals 'can only be described as irrational', wrote T. F. T. Plucknett.[11] 'Their decline must be viewed in the context of a general move towards more rational legal procedure', claimed Professor Baldwin.[12] Professor van Caenegem, one of the foremost historians of the common law, actually divides the history of proof into two periods, the age of irrational proofs, like the ordeal, and a subsequent age of rational proofs.[13]

Despite this common habit among historians, there has recently been a reaction, involving a questioning of the ease with which we label ancient or alien customs as irrational. Here, again, anthropologists and social scientists addressed the issue earlier and more explicitly than historians. 'Other minds, other cultures, other languages and other theoretical schemes', they suggest, 'call for understanding from within.'[14] This sympathetic and relativist position lies behind the undertakings of medievalists like Dr Hyams and Professor Colman, who have attempted to revise the picture of the ordeal as inherently irrational. In some ways, trial by ordeal offers a perfect issue for testing different approaches to the study of alien practices

[10] William Robertson, *The History of the Reign of the Emperor Charles V* (10th edn., 4 vols., London, 1802), I, sect. I, 'A View of the Progress of Society in Europe', p. 60.
[11] *Edward I and the Criminal Law* (Cambridge, 1959), p. 69.
[12] 'Intellectual Preparation', p. 614.
[13] e.g. *The Birth of the English Common Law* (Cambridge, 1973), p. 63; *La Preuve*, pp. 691-753.
[14] M. Hollis and S. Lukes (eds.), *Rationality and Relativism* (Oxford, 1982), p. 1.

and beliefs–beliefs and practices which, in this case, stem from our own European traditions rather than those of distant or exotic places.

One starting point for a discussion of the rationality of the ordeal is the question, 'Did the ordeal serve a useful purpose?', for, if it 'worked', i.e. achieved certain desirable goals, then it would be hard to deny to the practice, and to its practitioners, a form of, at the least, practical rationality.

To point to the goals or ends of the ordeal is, however, a controversial business. Some functionalists have argued that it had latent functions, that is, that trial by ordeal attained certain ends that were required by the social structure but not perceived by contemporary participants. They have conceived of the ends of the ordeal as general and social, not narrowly legal. Something has been said in argument against this position in Chapter 4 above, but it may be worthwhile to summarize the issue here.

Functionalists work on the following assumptions: an institution or practice like the ordeal had certain desirable effects; something with desirable effects would not be abandoned unless those effects were no longer so desirable or important; therefore, the way to explain such a change as the abolition of the ordeal is to look at the changes which rendered the effects less desirable or important.

Objections can be raised at varying levels of generality. It may be doubted whether the ordeal had the posited effects (as in the case of the 'consensus' theory, above). The term 'desirable' leads us to the question 'desired by whom?' and the chimera of impersonal purpose–'function'. One might wonder whether, indeed, human beings do not sometimes behave 'dysfunctionally', by changing things for the worse–the replacement of the ordeal by torture comes to mind. Finally, the changes which are supposed to render the desired effects less important must be scrutinized: one may doubt if they could have had the consequences claimed for them, or even if they occurred at all. Certainly the general changes so far posited by the functionalists–'population growth', 'better communications', and the rest–have all the appearance of arguments of convenience.

Let us, rather than reopen the issue of the latent function of the ordeal, inspect its overt function, its role in the resolution of disputes. For the ordeal was intended to get legal results. It has, indeed, been argued that its main purpose was to get any result at all in particularly intractable cases. In the clogged and tricky moment when neither testimony nor the oath offered a way forward, trial by ordeal enabled formal judicial process to continue. It enhanced the judicial capacity of the courts and, in the eyes of contemporaries, shed light on obscure issues. In the words of Adam Smith, ordeals 'answered one great end as they put a speedy end to the dispute'.[15] If the desired goal is conceived to be clear determinations of doubtful lawsuits, then the ordeal was indeed a rational means to that end. But so, of course, was torture. Moreover, ordeals would not have had the credibility they did unless they were conceived to be more than the equivalent of tossing a coin. Some forms of duel were, as we have seen, an *Entscheidungsmittel* rather than a *Beweismittel*—a way of getting a result rather than a means of proof—but trial by fire and water could not have survived if this had been its acknowledged role in justice. It is, therefore, true but trivial to say that the main end of the ordeal was to produce a result.

In the simplest sense, trial by ordeal had a very patent and specific purpose, which was to ascertain the judgement of God on the guilt or innocence of a given individual. If one starts by assuming this, then the obvious next step is to ask whether, in fact, it *did* discover guilt or innocence. Here we hit upon a major problem. The ideal way of finding out whether the ordeal gave just results would be to possess accurate and independent information about the guilt or innocence of the accused parties, then to compare this with the outcome of their trials. If the guilty invariably failed the trial, then the ordeal would have proved itself and any explanation would have to take this into account. If the correlation between guilt and failure at the ordeal were purely random, however, then the sceptical, materialist position would be vindicated.

Because of the nature of the case, however, we cannot have such independent information on guilt or innocence. It is not only that at this distance in time we are not able to reopen the files on the long-dead suspects whose fate was determined in this way. The problem lies deeper. For it was only the difficult and intractable cases, the ones where normal evidence failed, that went to the ordeal. It is clear that those who went to trial by ordeal had some presumption against them. Equally clearly, the evidence against them was not decisive. An independent test of the guilt or innocence of ordeal probands is thus impossible by definition.

This is a problem not only for the modern historian, seeking to understand the workings of the ordeal, but also for the critics and

[15] *Lectures on Jurisprudence*, ed. R. L. Meek, D. D. Raphael and P. G. Stein (Oxford, 1978), p. 210.

champions of the ordeal in the Middle Ages. In general, they too were unable to obtain independent evidence of the guilt or innocence of the probands. If such evidence existed, then, *ipso facto*, the ordeal would not be employed.

This is one reason why Peter the Chanter was so delighted when he could cite a patently false ordeal verdict. One case involved a man who was accused of homicide, tried by ordeal, found guilty, and hanged. A few weeks later his 'victim' turned up in the village alive and well.[16] Such cases were unusual. Critics of the ordeal could not normally be so confident that the innocent were being falsely convicted, for the cases that went to the ordeal were the obscure ones.

Thus we cannot make a judgement of the rationality of the ordeal on the basis of its harmony with evidence admitted by men of the Middle Ages. The 'evidence'–the real guilt or innocence of the accused–was inaccessible or controversial to contemporaries, as it is to us. We are not able, indeed, to answer our question empirically. We must content ourselves with asking, in general or hypothetical terms, how the ordeal *could have* revealed guilt or innocence.

There are two ways of giving a positive answer to this question, of claiming that ordeals gave just verdicts. The simpler is to assert that God did intervene and that ordeals were, as they purported to be, *iudicia dei*. This position, obviously held by many in the early and high Middle Ages, would only be a minority opinion in the West today.

The second possible position is to claim that ordeals did give just results but indirectly, not because God intervened, but because ordeals were, in fact, on other grounds, good tests of guilt or innocence. Some historians, concerned to vindicate the rationality of the ordeal, have claimed that, in fact, the relationship between culpability and the outcome of the ordeal was not random, not because God intervened to stigmatize the guilty and protect the innocent, but because physiological aspects of guilt and innocence helped to shape the trial result. For example, it has been claimed that 'As often as not, the guilty party will break down before undergoing the test . . . Alternatively, the terror produced by his belief in the infallibility of the procedure may lead him to fail so simple a test as that of having to swallow some food and drink.'[17] This last phrase refers to the *corsnaed* or 'ordeal of the blessed morsel', which has struck some as the form of ordeal most likely to operate as a lie-detector. 'We can imagine the

---

[16] *Verbum abbreviatum*, 78, *PL* 205, cols. 230-1.
[17] Keith Thomas, *Religion and the Decline of Magic* (London, 1971), p. 260.

tight throat and labored breathing which would make it difficult for the guilty not to choke and splutter.'[18]

Explanations of this lie-detector type seem somewhat strained, however. An individual's sense of guilt is influenced by many things as well as the actual fact of his guilt or innocence. There are guilt-ridden personalities and also cool customers. If physiological factors, such as sweating, dryness of mouth, or tension, really were so important, it would seem that the ordeal was more likely to condemn the nervous than the guilty. There may also be some doubt as to what difference these physiological changes could make. It would require a considerable physiological alteration to have much impact on the experience of picking up a hot iron.

So, since we cannot now know the truth about the individual cases tried by ordeal, we are bound to fall back upon general premises and, if we are not convinced by the 'lie-detector' theory or some variant of it, then we must assert either that God did intervene or He did not. If He did not, then the ordeal indeed 'submitted questions . . . to the determination of chance'.

This coldly sceptical position was occasionally advanced in the twelfth and thirteenth centuries. Frederick II, for example, thought that a man's fate in the ordeal depended entirely on the nature of his body. Peter the Chanter thought that one of the worst things about ordeals was that they often condemned the innocent or vindicated the guilty, because there could only be a random correlation between guilt or innocence and the outcome of the ordeal, since the outcome depended on factors irrelevant to culpability–the callousedness of the hand picking up the iron, the heat of the iron when grasped, and so on.[19] This is also the position of the present writer. Of all the thousands who went to trial by ordeal in the Middle Ages, rather more than half were vindicated, rather less than half condemned. It does not seem likely that all the former were innocent, all the latter guilty.

The heart of this issue of the rationality of the ordeal is the premises upon which men of the Middle Ages operated. In Professor Radding's words,'the ordeal's efficacy . . . depended on a set of beliefs about the world.'[20] The question of rational action thus leads us back to that of rational belief. And rational belief does not mean true belief. It means belief that is in harmony with the evidence and in harmony

---

[18] Colman, 'Reason and Unreason', p. 588.
[19] *Verbum abbreviatum*, 78, *PL* 205, col. 233.
[20] 'Superstition to Science', p. 969.

with other major beliefs. The problem of 'evidence' has been discussed. The crux of the issue is thus the relationship of belief in the efficacy of trial by ordeal with other central premisses of the Middle Ages: 'To say that a belief is rational is to talk about how it stands in relation to other beliefs.'[21] The core belief behind trial by ordeal is that when men are submitted to this form of test according to the proper rituals and invocations, God will reveal their guilt or innocence by changing the natural properties of the elements (i.e. hot iron will not burn, water will not allow a heavy body to sink). Analysed into its components, we find that this belief contains several premisses, in the following order of decreasing generality:

God exists, acts, knows. This would have been openly doubted only at great risk. Nor is there substantial evidence that many did doubt (though the evidence is, of course, biased).

God can change the natural properties of the physical world. Both the highest speculations of the scholastic philosophers and the least articulated beliefs of the shrine-visiting pilgrim took this as axiomatic. The truly materialist objection to trial by ordeal was, as has been stated above, rare. Frederick II is probably an example. Sometimes such a materialism is only apparent. Peter the Chanter, for example, condemned ordeals, among other reasons, on the grounds that they attempted to 'rob the elements of their natural properties through incantations'.[22] This is obviously not a case of sceptical materialism. The Chanter must have believed that some incantations–*Hoc enim est corpus meum*, for example–could 'rob the elements of their natural properties'. It is rather the case that, being convinced, largely on theological grounds, that ordeals were wrong, he was then willing to employ a wide array of arguments against them, including some that would not have had much independent weight. His attempt to discredit the ordeal on naturalistic or materialistic grounds was thus only a belated polemical point bobbing in the wake of his true objections.

God intervenes in the world to dispense justice. This belief requires some further discussion. A recent argument advanced by some scholars, sometimes in the specific context of the ordeal, sometimes more generally, is that the twelfth and thirteenth centuries witnessed a decline in the belief in immanent justice, that is, the belief that God intervened frequently and physically to mete out rewards and

---

[21] Alasdair MacIntyre, 'Rationality and the Explanation of Action', in *Against the Self-Images of the Age* (London, 1971), p. 250.

[22] *Verbum abbreviatum*, 78, *PL* 205, col. 228.

punishments to men according to their deeds. Here, too, is a version of the stadial thesis, which would see men as moving through history from one stage to another, 'stages' defined, in this case, by mentality rather than by material state. Paul Rousset, for example, in his important article, *La Croyance en la justice immanente a l'époque féodale* (The Belief in Immanent Justice in the Feudal Age), invoked Lévy-Bruhl's notion of 'the primitive mind' as a tool of analysis.[23] One of the most recent protagonists of this approach, Charles Radding, has argued that two developments in the twelfth century, a new emphasis on physical causation and the rise of the concept of the fortuitous, had the result that 'God's direction of human activities seemed a little more remote at the end of the twelfth century than it had been at the beginning, and immanent justice appeared less of a ruling force than it had been in previous centuries.'[24]

This claim has to be scrutinized rather carefully. On the one hand, insofar as it relates to the specific case of trial procedure, it is indisputably true. Abolition of the ordeal removed the direct hand of God from the judicial process. Only the oath, a far less direct application of the idea of God's justice, remained. In this sense, then, the end of the ordeal in the thirteenth century limited the field in which immanent justice was expected to operate. The larger issue, however, is whether the impetus to end the ordeal is to be explained by, or, in some way, related to a wider and more general 'decline of belief in immanent justice'.[25] Here, there is more room for doubt. By any obvious criterion, such as the frequency of references to divine intervention or judgement in chroniclers' accounts, or the number of miracles recorded, the thirteenth century was no less fully imbued with a providential view of the world than was the twelfth. Signs of divine grace or punishment, miracles and omens, inspired and directed the friars of the later Middle Ages just as they had guided the religious of earlier centuries. As historical evidence from lay, as distinct from ecclesiastical, sources begins to accumulate in the fourteenth and fifteenth centuries, there may be a slight decrease in overt piety of tone, but this should not delude us into thinking that belief in God's providence was any less active in the later period than the earlier. The real assault on

[23] Paul Rousset, 'La Croyance en la justice immanente a l'époque féodale', *Le Moyen Age*, 54 (1948), pp. 225-48, esp. pp. 243-4.
[24] 'Superstition to Science', p. 964.
[25] Ibid., p. 962.

providentialism was surely a development of the seventeenth and eighteenth centuries.

One curious piece of evidence which shows how hostility to the ordeal and a belief in immanent justice could comfortably coexist is the opinion expressed by Emo, abbot of the Premonstratensian house of Bloemhof near Groningen in the Netherlands. Writing of the floods that inundated Frisia in 1219, he commented that these were doubtless punishments for the sins of the Frisians, especially the failings of the clergy, such as dubious ordinations, the alienation of church endowments, the persistence of clerical marriage, and, most significant for the present purpose, the fact that 'contrary to the canon, ordeal of hot iron is not abolished'.[26] Emo had been given the best scholastic education, being trained in the arts, and canon and Roman law at Paris, Orleans, and Oxford,[27] but his opposition to the ordeal clearly does not come from a declining belief in immanent justice. If, like Emo, men believed that the continued practice of trial by ordeal might be punished by God, it is hard to see how its abolition could reflect a declining belief in immanent justice. In this matter, Emo seems a figure more representative of thirteenth-century attitudes than Frederick II. If there were big changes in mental outlook in the twelfth century that made belief in the ordeal more awkward, these were limited to the new views on the propriety of invocatory ritual, canonical authority, and the priestly role developed by a reforming scholastic and curial élite. For them, the ordeal became irrational. It was lack of harmony with their specialized and novel ideology, not with the outlook of the great majority, that created friction on the subject.

Functionalists are trying to pay the past a misguided compliment when they argue that this bygone and exotic practice did, indeed, make some kind of sense. They argue too weakly. It did not make 'some kind of sense'; it made sense. Intellectually coherent, not contradicted by the available evidence and well-suited to attaining its avowed ends, it invoked a powerful and omniscient deity to manifest justice through the transformation of the physical elements. Every part of this process corresponded well with central beliefs of the age: a powerful God who could be invoked, immanent justice, miraculous change in natural properties. Neither the science nor the theology of

---

[26] Emo, *Chronicle*, ed. L. Weiland, MGH, *SS* 23 (Hanover, 1874), p. 491; the canon he cites is 'Consuluisti', not that of Lateran IV.

[27] Ibid., p. 467, and Menko, *Chronicle*, ibid., pp. 524-32.

the period (insofar as they can be distinguished) contained canons or principles that immediately discredited the ordeal. The central issue of debate in the twelfth century was not whether God *could have* ordained the ordeal but whether he *had in fact* done so. Nowadays we would refute the validity of the ordeal through appeal to the properties of the natural world or, if atheists, through appeal to metaphysical principles. The critics of the twelfth century tried to condemn the ordeal by referring to Scripture and the canons. They argued that the ordeal was wrong, not that it was nonsensical. As has been pointed out above, the ordeal was deemed irrational once the case for its being uncanonical and an illicit tempting of God had been established. The opposite path of argument, from an independent demonstration of the randomness of ordeal results, was not available. Even in the later Middle Ages, the chief objection advanced against trial by ordeal was that it was uncanonical and theologically unacceptable, not that it was irrational.

Here, ultimately, was the problem. If all could agree that, if the proper conditions were fulfilled, invocation could change the physical world to reveal God's dispensation (as in the Eucharist), there was still disagreement as to what those proper conditions were and whether, in the case of the ordeal, they had been fulfilled. This was a debate about authority. For, though the belief underlying the ordeal was certainly not conceptually incoherent, it was open to the query '*How do we know that God will reveal His judgement in this way?*' It was thus the 'charter' for the ordeal that was being debated rather than the possibility of the belief making sense. Indeed, the story of the abolition of trial by ordeal shows how, during the twelfth century, the concept of 'charter' or credentials changed, as certain written authorities assumed an increasingly privileged position, while customary and oral charters lost some of their power.

Modern historians, seeking to judge the rationality or irrationality of the ordeal, will come to different conclusions according to whether they are liberal Christians or atheists. An atheist will presume that God was not manifesting judgement in the ordeal and that therefore the men of the Middle Ages, who believed that He was, were wrong in so thinking. He will also admit, however, that, if one believes in a just, omnipotent, omniscient, and active deity, it is quite rational to believe that He may manifest His will to men on earth in various ways, including, possibly, trial by ordeal. For the atheist, the ordeal was thus rational but mistaken. The liberal Christian, not familiar or comfortable with the crass and interfering God of the Middle Ages, may be tempted to dismiss the ordeal as irrational, but does so at the risk of intellectual incoherence. The providentialism of the Middle Ages was full-blooded and coherent: a powerful God made His will known. Only the emasculation of Christian belief over the last centuries, the tendency to liberalize and demythologise, has made it at all possible for Christians to label belief in the ordeal as irrational.

Select Bibliography

There would be little point in simply listing here all the works mentioned in the footnotes. This list is, instead, intended as a guide to the most important sources of any length and to secondary works bearing directly on the subject of unilateral ordeals. Literature on the duel and on the swimming of witches will be found in the notes to Chapters 6 and 7 above. General legal histories have not been listed; it should be noted that many of them contain helpful discussions of the subject. Although the works of such nineteenth-century pioneers as Lea and Patetta retain their value, the fundamental starting point for study of the ordeal is now Nottarp's encyclopedic book, marred as it is by the infuriating absence of an index. References to trial by ordeal tend to be scattered in a wide variety of sources and hence Browe's anthology of original material will be found very convenient.

Agobard of Lyon, *Liber adversus legem Gundobadi* and *Liber contra judicium dei*, in *Opera omnia*, ed. L. van Acker (Corpus Christianorum, Continuatio Mediaevalis, Turnhout, 1981), pp. 17-49.

Angold, Michael, 'The Interaction of Latins and Byzantines during the Period of the Latin Empire: The Case of the Ordeal', *Actes du XVe Congrès international d'études byzantines*, 4 (Athens, 1980), pp. 1-10.

Baldwin, John W., 'The Intellectual Preparation for the Canon of 1215 against Ordeals, *Speculum*, 36 (1961), pp. 613-36.

Bongert, Y., *Recherches sur les cours laiques du Xe au XIIIe s.* (Paris, 1949), pp. 211-51.

Browe, Peter (ed.), *De ordaliis* (2 vols., Rome, 1932-3).

Brown, Peter, 'Society and the Supernatural: A Medieval Change', *Daedalus*, 104 (1975), pp. 133-51 (reprinted in his *Society and the Holy in Late Antiquity* (Berkeley and Los Angeles, 1982), pp. 302-32).

Colman, Rebecca V., 'Reason and Unreason in Early Medieval Law', *Journal of Interdisciplinary History*, 4 (1974), pp. 571-91.

Conrad, Hermann, 'Das Gottesurteil in den Konstitutionen von Melfi Friedrichs II von Hohenstaufen', in *Festschrift ... W. Schmidt-Rimpler* (Karlsruhe, 1959), pp. 9-21.

Eidelberg, Shlomo, 'Trial by Ordeal in Medieval Jewish History: Laws, Customs and Attitudes', *Proceedings of the American Academy for Jewish Research*, 46-7 (1978-9), pp. 105-20.

Erler, A., 'Der Ursprung der Gottesurteile', *Paideuma. Mitteilungen zur Kulturkunde*, 2 (1941), pp. 44-65.

Fehr, Hans, 'Die Gottesurteile in der deutschen Dichtung', in *Festschrift ... Guido Kisch* (Stuttgart, 1955), pp. 271-81.

Fehr, Hans, 'Gottesurteil und Folter', *Festschrift für Rudolf Stammler* (Berlin and Leipzig, 1926), pp. 231-54.

Fournier, P., 'Quelques observations sur l'histoire des ordalies au moyen âge', *Mélanges Gustave Glotz* (2 vols., Paris, 1932), 1, pp. 367-76.

Geanakoplos, D. J. 'Ordeal by Fire and Judicial Duel at Byzantine Nicaea (1253): Western or Eastern Legal Influence?', *Interaction of the 'Sibling' Byzantine and Western Cultures* (New Haven and London, 1976), pp. 146-55.

Grelewski, S., *La Réaction contre les ordalies en France depuis le IXe siècle jusqu'au Décrét de Gratien* (Rennes, 1924).

Hexter, R. J., *Equivocal Oaths and Ordeals in Medieval Literature* (Cambridge, Mass., 1975).

Hincmar of Rheims, *De divortio Lotharii regis et Tetbergae reginae*, PL 125,cols. 619-772.

Hyams, Paul, 'Trial by Ordeal: The Key to Proof in the Early Common Law', in Morris S. Arnold *et al.* (eds.), *On the Laws and Customs of England. Essays in Honor of Samuel E. Thorne* (Chapel Hill, 1981), pp. 90-126.

Iglesiá Ferreirós, A.,'El proceso del conde Bera y el problema de las ordalías', *Anuario de historia del derecho español*, 51 (1981), pp. 1-221.

Lea, H. C., *Superstition and Force* (4th edn., Philadelphia, 1892), relevant section reissued as *The Ordeal*, ed. Edward Peters (Philadelphia, 1973).

Leicht, P. S., 'Ultime menzione delle ordalie e del duello giudiziario in Italia', in *Festschrift... Ernst Heymann*, 1 (Weimar, 1940), pp. 95-101.

Leitmaier, Charlotte, *Die Kirche und die Gottesurteile* (Vienna, 1953).

Liebermann, Felix (ed.), *Gesetze der Angelsachsen* (3 vols., Halle, 1903-16),esp. 1, pp. 386-9, 401-29; 2, pp. 601-4.

Mayer, E., 'Der Ursprung der germanischen Gottesurteile', *Historische Vierteljahrschrift*, 20 (1920-1), pp. 289-316.

Morris, Colin, '*Judicium Dei*: The Social and Political Significance of the Ordeal in the Eleventh Century', *Studies in Church History*,12 (1975), pp. 95-112.

Nottarp, H., *Gottesurteilstudien* (Munich, 1956).

Pappenheim, M., 'Über die Anfänge des germanischen Gottesurteils', *ZRG, Germanistische Abteilung*, 48 (1928), pp. 136-75.

Patetta, F., *Le ordalie* (Turin, 1890).

La Preuve, 2, *Moyen âge et temps modernes*, Recueils de la Société Jean Bodin pour l'histoire comparative des institutions, 17 (Brussels, 1965).

Radding, Charles M., 'Superstition to Science: Nature, Fortune and the Passing of the Medieval Ordeal', *American Historical Review*, 84 (1979), pp. 945-69.

Regestrum Varadinense, ed. János Karácsonyi and Samu Borovszky (Budapest, 1903).

Roberts, John M., 'Oaths, Autonomic Ordeals and Power', *American Anthropologist*, 67, no. 6, pt. 2 (1965), pp. 186-212.

Schwerin, Claudius von, 'Geschichtliche Gottesurteile', *Forschungen und Fortschritte*, 14 (1938), p. 236.

Schwerin, Claudius von, 'Rituale für Gottesurteile', *Sitzungsberichte der Heidelberger Akademie der Wissenschaften, Philosophische-historische Klasse*, 23/3 (1932-3), pp. 1-66.

Stokes, W., 'The Irish Ordeals', in *Irische Texte*, ed. Stokes, W., and Windisch, E., 3rd ser., 1 (Leipzig, 1891), pp. 183-229.

Szeftel, M., 'Le Jugement de Dieu dans le droit russe ancien', *Archives d'histoire du droit oriental*, 4 (1948), pp. 263-99.

Vacandard, E., 'L'Église et les ordalies', *Études de critique et d'histoire religieuse* (2 vols., Paris, 1905-10), 1, pp. 191-215.

York, E. C., 'Isolt's Ordeal: English Legal Customs in the Medieval Tristan Legend', *Studies in Philology*, 68 (1971), pp. 1-9.

Zajtay, Imre, 'Le Registre de Varad: Un monument judiciaire du début du XIII^c siècle', *Revue historique de droit français et étranger*, 4th ser., 32, (1954), pp. 527-62.

Zeumer, Karl (ed.), *Formulae Merowingici et Karolini aevi*, MGH (Hanover, 1886), pp. 599-722.

Zguta, Russell, 'The Ordeal by Water (Swimming of Witches) in the East Slavic World', *Slavic Review*, 36 (1977), pp. 220-30.

Index

Medieval persons are indexed under first name. Offences and cases tried by ordeal have been indexed under 'ordeal'.

accusatorial procedure, 29, 64
Adalbert, St (d.997), 45
Adalger, partisan of Arnulf of Rheims, 14
adultery, 45; tried by battle, 106; *see also* ordeal, used in cases of; queens accused of adultery
Africa, 2, 36
Agobard, archbishop of Lyons (816–840), 11, 72–3, 75, 84, 117
Alamanni, Alamannic law, 6, 103
Alberic, mentioned in lawsuit (*c.* 1090), 25
Alexander II, king of Scotland (1214–49), 132
Alexander II, pope (1061–73), 50 n. 48, 82
Alexander III, pope (1159–81), 82, 94, 97, 133
Alfonso VI, king of Castile-León (1065–1109), 60–1, 95
Alfonso X the Wise, king of Castile-León (1252–84), 123–4, 126
Alzen (Foix), 133
America, 3, 24
Amiens, 125
amulets, 71
Andalusia, 47
Andernach, battle of (875), 14
Angers, 95
Angers, St Aubin of, 25
Angevin period, 69
Angles, 49
Anglo-French, Anglo-Normans, 47–9
Anglo-Saxons, Anglo-Saxon law, etc. 7, 13, 22 n. 30, 24, 27, 68, 104, 144
Anglo-Scottish borders, 122
Anjou, 50
anstruciones, 4
anthropology, anthropologists, 1, 34, 36, 41, 87, 154, 157
Antoñana, 58–9 (map 3)
Apocryphal Gospels, 84
approvers, 113

Aragon, 96
Aragon, Fueros de, 100
Aragon, kings of, *see* James I
Arians, 21, 71
Arnold, archbishop of Cologne (1138–51), 52
Arnulf, archbishop of Rheims (989–91, 995–1021), 14–15
Arras, 22, 52, 95
arson, tried by battle, 106; *see also* ordeal, used in cases of
Asín, 58–9 (map 3)
assault, 135–6; *see also* ordeal, used in cases of
Assises of Romania, 131 n. 21
Assize of Clarendon (1166), 65, 67–9
Assize of Northampton (1176), 65, 67
Assize of William the Lion, 130
Assizes of Cyprus, 131
Assizes of Henry II, *see* Assize of Clarendon, Assize of Northampton
Assizes of Jerusalem, 29, 46, 131
Astorga, cathedral of, 95
Athelstan, king of England (924–39), 68–9
Athies, 136 n. 38
Atli, king of the Huns, in the *Edda*, 18
Austria, 57
Avitus, bishop of Vienne (*c.*490–*c.*519), 117

Baeza (Andalusia), 47
Baldwin VII, count of Flanders (1111–19), 55
Baldwin, Prof. John, 157
Balkans, 62, 132
Ballard, A., 120
Baltic, 47
Bamberg, 17
Bamberg, burgomeister of, *see* Junius
baptism, 88–9, 91
Bari, 58–9 (map 3)

Barrow, Prof. Geoffrey, 49 n. 41
battle, trial by, 2, 9–10, 16, 26–7, 32–3, 37–8, 44, 49, 54–7, 60–1, 63–4, 72, 73 n. 10, 77, 82, 85, 95–6, 99, 103–26, 131, 159
battles as judgements of God, 14
Bavaria, Bavarian law, etc., 6, 73, 103, 115, 146
Bavaria, dukes of, *see* Henry, Henry the Lion, Maximilian I
Bayeux, 20
Bayeux, Synod of (1300), 130 n. 10
Bazuel (dep. Nord), 145 n. 72
Beaumanoir, Philippe de, Sire de Remi, jurist (d.1296), 109–11, 113–14
Bernard of Clairvaux, St (d.1153), 52–3
Bernedo, 58–9 (map 3)
Berthold of Hamm, count, party to lawsuit (c. 1103), 28
bestiality, *see* ordeal, used in cases of
Beweismittel, 114, 159
Bible, 22, 74, 83, 85, 117, 118
Birger Jarl, regent of Sweden (1248–66), 127
Bischofsheim, *see* Lioba, abbess of
bitter waters, ordeal of, *see* ordeal, types of
Bloemhof near Groningen in the Netherlands, 164
blood, judgements of, 98–9, 118
Bohemia, Bohemian law, etc., 44–6, 93
Bohemia, dukes of, *see* Bretislav I, Sobeslas I (also Přemyslids)
Bohemia, kings of, *see* Ottokar I
Boleslaw (V), duke of Little Poland (1226–79), 36–7
Bologna, 22 n. 31
Bongert, Prof. Y., 26, 34
Borgarthing Law, 144
Bracton, treatise attributed to (13th century), 137
Bratislava, 92
breaches of the peace, *see* ordeal, used in cases of peace-breaking
Brescia, 125
Bretislav I, duke of Bohemia (1034–55), 45
British Isles, 120, 132–3
Brown, Prof. Peter, 34–5, 39–40, 42
Bruges, 32, 61
Bruno of Querfurt, missionary (d.1009), 21
Buda, Synod of (1279), 130 n. 10
Burchard, bishop of Worms (1000–25), canonist, 31, 37–9, 50, 82, 85, 118

burglary, *see* ordeal, used in cases of
Burgundians, Burgundian law, etc., 6, 103, 115
Burgundians, kings of, *see* Gundobad
Burgundy, 125, 147, 149–50
Burgundy, dukes of, *see* Philip
burial of the dead, 45
burial rights, 91–2
Bury St Edmunds, 108
Bury St Edmunds, abbey of, 138
Byzantium, 16, 46, 131
Byzantium, rulers of, *see* Theodore II Lascaris

Caenegem, Prof. R. C. van, 34, 157
Caesarius of Heisterbach, Cistercian writer (d.1240), 80
Calixtus II, pope (1119–24), 28, 51
Cambrai, 52, 80
candle ordeal, *see* ordeal, types of
canon law, 74, 81–3, 85, 98, 117–18, 140, 164
Canterbury, 7 n. 6, 88
Canterbury, archbishop of, 91–2, 94 n. 81
Canute, king of England, etc. (1016–35), 31, 37 n. 9, 64
Caparroso, 58–9 (map 3)
capitulary legislation, 9–11, 24, 31
Capitulary of Quierzy (873), 29
Cardiff, 48
Carolingians, Carolingian influence, etc., 9–13, 16, 24–5, 36, 46, 49, 54, 72, 75, 90, 99, 105, 110, 133, 144; *see also* Charlemagne, Charles the Bald, Charles the Fat, Clovis, Lewis the Pious, Lewis of Saxony, Lothar, Pippin
Cassiodorus, 104
Castile, Castilian law, 19, 47
Castile-León, kings of, *see* Alfonso VI, Alfonso IX, Sancho IV
Catalonia, Catalan law, etc., 27, 50–1, 108–10
Catalonia, council in (1033), 51
Cathars, Catharism, 22 & n., 52–3
cauldron ordeal, *see* ordeal, types of
Celtic countries, 49
Champagne, 147, 149
champions, 10, 13, 52, 57, 112, 121–2, 124
Charlemagne, king of the Franks and emperor (768–814), 9–10, 12–13, 39, 46, in *The Song of Roland*, 106

Charles the Bald, king of the West Franks and emperor (840-77), 13-14
Charles the Fat, king of the East Franks and emperor (876-87), 16-17 & n.
Charles, count of Flanders (1120-27), 78
Charoald, king of the Lombards (626-36), 115
Chelmsford, 151
Chilandar, monastery of, 62 n. 84
Chivalry, Court of, 108
chrism, 71
Christ's passion, 10
Chur, diocese of, 95
Cistercians, 80, 99
civil cases, 101; *see also* ordeal, used in cases of
Clarendon, Assize of, *see* Assize of Clarendon
Cleves-Jülich, duke of, 146
Clovis, king of the Franks (d.511), 154
cohabitation, *see* ordeal, used in cases of
Colman, Prof. Rebecca V., 157
Cologne, 52
Coloman, king of Hungary (1095-1114), 92
compurgation, 26, 30-3, 37, 55, 62, 82, 135-7; *see also* oaths
concealment of treasure trove, *see* ordeal, used in cases of
concubines, 20
confession, 78-81
confession (judicial), 69, 74, 141, 143
Connecticut, 148
'consensus theory', 34-40, 37, 39, 158
conspiracy, effect on legal standing, 31
Constance, diocese of, 145
Constitutions of Melfi or *Liber Augustalis* of 1231, 76, 107, 123-4, 142
Consuluisti, papal ruling of 886-9, 74-5, 164 n. 26
contempt of court, *see* ordeal, used in cases of
conversion to Christianity, 21, 24, 43-7, 46, 87
Corinthians, First Book of, 85
corsnaed, *see* ordeal, types of: blessed morsel
councils, *see* Bayeux, Buda, Catalonia, Gran, Lateran, Leon, Lillebonne, Nablus, Paris, Reisbach, Rheims, Riga, Rouen, Tribur, Valencia, Valladoid, Vich
Coventry, archdeacon of, 94

Coventry, bishop of, 94 n. 81
crime and sin, distinction between, 81
Criseyde, in *Troilus and Criseyde*, 134
criticism of the ordeal, 70-90; *see also* scepticism about the ordeal
cross, ordeal of, *see* ordeal, types of
crowd behaviour, 23, 40, 52
Crusades, crusader law, etc., 16, 22 n. 32, 46-7, 131
Cuenca, 47, 61
Cuenca-Teruel, Fuero de, 19, 47, 61, 144
Cunigunda, wife of Henry II of Germany, 17-18 & nn.
custom, 83, 85-6

Dante Alighieri (d.1321), 122
David (biblical), 118
De divortio Lotharii, work by Hincmar of Rheims, 74
De Monarchia, work by Dante, 122
De praestigiis daemonum, work by Johann Weyer, 146
Decretals of Gregory IX, 83, 85, 98, 119, 130
Decretum of Gratian, *see* Gratian
default of justice, tried by battle, 109
Denmark, Danish law, etc., 21, 44, 76, 100, 120, 127, 132, 138-9
Denmark, kings of, *see* Valdemar I, Valdemar II
devil, 71
Dialogus Ecgberti, 7 n. 6
Dialogus miraculorum, work by Caesarius of Heisterbach, 80
Dieric Bouts, painter (d.1475), 134 n. 36
disputes over territory, *see* ordeal used in cases of
divination, 73, 116, 123-4; *see also* lots; sortilege
Domesday Book, 63 n. 88, 92
Dominic, St (d.1221), 22 n. 31
Dominicans, 123, 145
Dorset, 112
Dublin, 120
duel, *see* battle, trial by
Duncan the Scot, champion (13th century), 112
Dunsaettas, 32, 47 n. 36

Eadmer, monk of Canterbury, historian (d.c. 1130), 7 n. 6, 76
East Frisia, *see* Frisia

eastern Europe, 25, 44, 47, 92, 94, 122
Ebernand von Erfurt, poet (13th century), 17 n. 11
Ebro valley, 61
ecclesiastical cases, *see* ordeal, used in cases of
Edda, 18, 44
Edgar, king of England (959–75), 64
Edmund, St, 107
Edward I, king of England (1272–1307), 133
Edward the Confessor, king of England (1042–66), 17
Edward the Elder, king of England (901–24), 25, 30
Egypt, Sultan of, 21
Eigenkirche, 155
Elsenbach, abbot of, 91
Emma, mother of Edward the Confessor, 17–18 & nn.
Emo, abbot of Bloemhof (1225–37), 164
England, English law, etc., 10, 13, 24–7, 31–2, 35–6, 49, 55–6, 63–9, 93–4, 97, 99–100, 104–5, 108–9, 111–13, 120–22, 125–8, 132–3, 135, 137–8, 142–3, 146–7, 150–1; *see also* Angles; Anglo-French; Anglo-Saxons; Anglo-Scottish
England, kings of, *see* Athelstan, Canute, Edgar, Edward the Elder, Edward the Confessor, Edward I, Ethelred, Henry I, Henry II, Henry III, John, Richard I, William the Conqueror, William Rufus
Enlightenment, 42, 157
Enns (Austria), 29
Entscheidungsmittel, 114, 159
Ephraim ben Jacob, Jewish writer (12th century), 54
Epirus, Epirots, 131–2
Ethelred the Unready, king of England (978–1016), 31
eucharist, 88–9, 165
eucharistic ordeal, *see* ordeal, types of
Eugenius II, pope (824–7), 11
Evesham, 22 n. 30
evidence, 30
Exchequer accounts, 66
exemption, from ordeal, 53–62; clerical, 50, 53–4, 67, 94–7; clerical (from trial by battle), 112, 119; of burgesses from trial by battle, 119–20; of Jews, *see* Jews

exorcisms, 71
Eyjolf, character in *Ljósvetninga saga*, 40–1

false witness, effect on legal standing, 31, *see also* ordeal, used in cases of
fír caire, 5
fír Dé, 5
fír fogerrta, 5
Flanders, 57, 111, 137, 149
Flanders, count of, 15
Flanders, counts of, *see* Baldwin VII, Charles
Flood, 74
Foix, county of, 133
Fontanelle, abbey of, 91
Fontevrault, monastery of, 96
foreigners, oath and ordeal, 32, 37
forest offences, *see* ordeal, used in cases of
forgery, *see* ordeal, used in cases of
fornication, tried by battle, 106; *see also* ordeal, used in cases of
France, French law, etc., 19, 25–7, 49, 51–2, 56, 61, 104, 108–9, 114, 122, 125, 128, 130, 133, 136, 140, 144, 147, 149
France, bishops of, 96
France, king of, 15
France, kings of, *see* Hugh, Louis IX, Louis X, Philip IV, Robert
Francesco Traini, painter (14th century), 22 n. 31
Francis of Assisi, St (d.1226), 21
Franco-Chamavian law, 68–9
Franks, Frankish law, etc., 3–9, 60 n. 79, 68, 103, 115, 131, 133, 153–4; in *The Song of Roland*, 107; *see also* Ripuarian law; Salic law
Franks, kings of, *see* Carolingians, Merovingians
Frederick Barbarossa, king of Germany and emperor (1152–90), 52
Frederick II, king of Germany and Sicily and emperor (1212–50), 76, 107, 119–20, 123–4, 142, 148, 161–2, 164
Frederick of Salm, preceptor of the Rhineland Templars (early 14th century), 16
Freiburg im Breisgau, 57
Freisach in Carinthia, 92
Freising, 73
'Freising poet', 73, 75
Freising, bishop of, 17 n. 12
Freisinger Rechtsbuch (c.1325), 130

Freya, goddess, 154
Frias, 58–9 (map 3)
Fridgerd, character in *Ljósvetninga saga*, 40–1
Frisia, Frisian law, etc. 7–9, 68, 103, 133, 164
Frostathing Law, 19
Fuero de Cuenca, see *Cuenca-Teruel*, *Fuero de Fuero de Logroño*, see *Logroño*, *Fuero de Fueros de Aragon*, see *Aragon*, *Fueros de fueros*, 60, 61, 122; see also Aragon; Cuenca-Teruel; Logroño
functionalists, 34–6, 158, 164
Fürstenberg, count of, 145

Galbert of Bruges, historian (early 12th century), 78–9, 87
Galicia (Spain), 134
Gallo-Roman population, 5
Ganelon, in *The Song of Roland*, 106
Ganshof, F. L., 155
Gaul, 7–8 n. 8, 90
Gautier of Meigné, party to lawsuit (*c*. 1090), 25
Geoffrey Bainard, fought duel (1095), 107
Germanic peoples, etc., 7, 103–5, 153–4
Germany, German law, etc., 20, 25, 38, 44, 52, 54, 107–10, 114, 122, 125, 130–2, 134, 146, 148, 150, 153
Germany, kings of, see Frederick Barbarossa, Frederick II, Henry II, Henry IV, Henry V, Henry (VII), Lewis the Bavarian, Otto I, Rudolf I
Ghent, 61
Glanvill, treatise attributed to, 64–6, 130
Gloucester, earl of, see Robert, earl of Gloucester
Gniezno, 45–6, 51
Godelmann, Johann Georg, German jurist (1559–1611), 148
Goliath, 118
Goths, Gothic Law, 104; see also Ostrogoths; Visigoths
Gottfried of Strassburg, 18–19
Gottschalk, Saxon monk (d.*c*. 868), 21
Grammont, 58–9 (map 3)
Gran, Synod of (1114), 92
Grand Assize, 124–5
Gratian, canonist (12th century), 31, 75, 82–4, 118
Greeks, 131
Gregorian movement, 16, 85, 99–100, 133
Gregory the Great, pope (590–604), 90

Gregory VII, pope (1073–85), 99
Gregory IX, pope (1227–41), 83, 85, 98, 119
Gregory XI, pope (1371–78), 131
Gregory, bishop of Tours (573–94), historian, 4–5, 20–1, 71
Groningen, 164
Gudrun, Atli's queen in the *Edda*, 18, 44
Gudrun, lay of, 44
Guibert, abbot of Nogent, writer (d.1124), 21
Gundeberga, wife of Charoald, king of the Lombards, 115
Gundobad, king of the Burgundians (*c*.480–516), 116 n. 59
Guy (of Steenvoorde), fought duel (1127), 111

Hakon III, king of Norway (1202–4), 20
Hakon IV, king of Norway (1223–62), 20
Hamburg, 98
Hamburg cathedral, dean of, 130
Hamburg-Bremen, archbishop of, 98
Hammurabi, 2
Hanover, 131
Hans Sachs, German dramatist (1494–1576), 134 n. 36
Harding, Prof. Alan, 155
Helsingeland, 127
Henry I, king of England (1100–35), 119
Henry II, king of England (1154–89), 25, 64–5, 67, 119, 124
Henry II, king of Germany and emperor (1002–24), 17
Henry III, king of England (1216–72), 138
Henry IV, king of Germany and emperor (1056–1106), 119
Henry V, king of Germany and emperor (1106–25), 96
Henry (VII), king of Germany (1220–35), 108
Henry of Essex, fought duel (1163), 107
Henry of Ghent, scholastic writer (13th century), 73 n. 10
Henry of Huntingdon, historian (d.1155), 37 n. 9
Henry the Lion, duke of Saxony and Bavaria (d.1195), 77
Henry, duke of Bavaria (948–55), 17 n. 12
Hereford, bishop of, 112
heresy, 84; torture used against, 142; see also ordeal, used in cases of
Hereward of Shoreditch, accused of killing (1214), 56

Herkja, serving woman in the *Edda*, 18
Herman the Iron, fought duel (1127), 111
Hesdin, 136 n. 38
Hildebert, bishop of Le Mans (1096–
    1125), archbishop of Tours (1125–
    33), 95
Hincmar, archbishop of Rheims (845–82),
    13, 53, 74–5, 77, 84–5, 88, 90, 117–18
Historia Scholastica, work by Peter
    Comestor, 84
hólmganga, 105, 114
Holstein, 99
Holy Lance, 22 n. 32
Holyrood abbey, 49 n. 49, 132
homicide and murder, 33, 45, 82, 136, 139;
    secret, torture used against, 142;
    tried by battle, 104, 109, 123, 125; *see
    also* ordeal, used in cases of
Honorius III, pope (1216–27), 47 n. 32
Hopkins, Matthew, 'witchfinder' (d.1647),
    150
horse-stealing, *see* ordeal, used in cases of
Hostiensis, 85–6
Hrut, in *Njal's Saga*, 114
Hugh Capet, king of France (987–96), 14
Hungary, Hungarian law, 30, 44, 63, 92–3,
    128, 130, 147
Hungary, kings of, *see* Coloman
Hyams, Dr Paul, 34–5, 42, 70, 157

Iberian peninsula, 55
Iceland, 2, 40–1, 105, 114
ill fame, ill repute, 30–1, 55, 64, 68; *see
    also* ordeal, used in cases of
immanent justice, 78, 162–4
impotence, *see* ordeal, used in cases of
Indo-European, 6
Ine, king of the West Saxons (c.688–
    c.726), 7–8 & n., 155
Inga of Varteig, mother of Hakon IV, 20
Innocent II, pope (1130–43), 50 n. 48, 96
Innocent III, pope (1198–1216), 13, 53, 82,
    98, 100, 119, 126, 127, 130
Innocent IV, pope (1243–54), 119
inquest, 26, 60–1, 64, 101, 137; *see also
    pesquisa*
inquisition, 140–3, 146
inscrutability of God's judgements, 73, 75,
    117
Inverness, 120
Investiture Conflict, 16
Ireland, Irish law, etc., 5–7, 9, 19–20, 29,
    47–9, 120, 132

Ireland, lords of, *see* John
irrationality of the ordeal, *see* rationality
    of the ordeal
Islam, 47; *see also* Moslems
Isolde, queen, in *Tristan and Isolde*, 18–19
Italy, Italian law, etc., 9–10, 12, 27, 69,
    105–7, 112, 122, 131–2, 140, 147
Ivo, bishop of Chartres (1090–1115),
    canonist, 29, 75, 82, 95–6, 118
Iznatoraf (Andalusia), 47

Jaca, *see* San Pedro
James I, king of Aragon (1213–76), 128
James VI, king of Scotland (1567–1625)
    (James I of England), 148
Japan, 2
Jerusalem, 69
Jesuits, 148
Jews, 11, 21, 53–4, 62, 87, 112
John de Annesley, fought duel (1380), 108
John the Baptist, 88
John, king of England (1199–1216), 66, 69
Jorund, in *Njal's Saga*, 114
Joüon de Longrais, F., 139
Judgement of the Emperor Otto, The, painting
    by Dieric Bouts, 134 n. 36
Judith, widow of Henry, duke of Bavaria,
    17 n. 12
Junius, Johannes, 145
Junius, Veronica, 145
jury, 68, 93, 108, 135, 137–9, 143

Kent, 7–8 n. 8, 91
Kentish law, 7
Kenya, 2
Kidderminster, 113
kingship and ordeal, 36, 69
Krämer (Institoris), Heinrich, Domini-
    can, co-author of the *Malleus malefi-
    ciarum*, 145–6

Labraza, 58–9 (map 3)
Laguardia, 58–9 (map 3)
Lambert le Bègue, reformer (12th
    century), 23
Lambert of Aardenburg, accused of
    treason (1127), 78–9
Landfriede, 52
Lapuebla de Arganzon, 58–9 (map 3)
Lateran Council, Fourth (1215), 35, 53, 89,
    94, 98, 118, 127–8, 130, 133
Latin Empire, 131 n. 21

Launceston, 66
Lea, Henry Charles, 34, 104
Leges Henrici primi, 65
legitimacy, see ordeal, used in cases of legitimacy of doubtful claimants
Leitmaier, Charlotte, 155
León, council of (1288), 130
León, kings of, see Castile-León, kings of
Lerida, 58–9 (map 3)
Lerma, 58–9 (map 3)
Lévy-Bruhl, Lucien, 163
Lewis the Bavarian, king of Germany (1314–47), 134
Lewis the Pious, king of the Franks and emperor (814–40) 9, 11, 54, 104
Lewis, king of Saxony (d. 882), 14
Lex familiae Wormatiensis, 31–2
Leyden, 149
Libellus de bataila facienda, 108, 110
Liber Augustalis, see Constitutions of Melfi
Liber contra iudicium dei, work by Agobard of Lyons, 72
Liber juris civilis of Verona, 139
Liber Papiensis, 106
'lie-detector theory', 160–1
Liebermann, Felix, 7, 155
Liège, 58–9 (map 3)
Liège, church of, 96
Lillebonne, Synod of (1080), 92
Limoges, 54
Lincoln, bishop of, 37
Lincolnshire, 66
Lioba of Bischofsheim (d. 780), 10 n. 13
liturgies for the ordeal, see rituals for the ordeal
Liudprand, king of the Lombards (712–44), 8, 72, 116
Livonia, 47, 56, 69
Ljósvetninga saga, 40–1
Llandaff, 48
Llandaff, bishop of, 47
Logroño, 58–9 (map 3), 60–1
Logroño, Fuero de, 61
Loire valley, 96
Lombards, Lombard law etc., 7–8, 72, 103, 115
Lombards, kings of, see Charoald, Liudprand
London, 55–6, 58–9 (map 3), 65, 120
lordship and ordeal, 36–7, 60
Lorsch, 131
Lothar, king of Lotharingia (855–69), 13
Lotharingia, 13–14, 50

lots, 9, 29, 32, 48, 122; see also divination; sortilege
lottery, 124
Louis IX, king of France (1226–70), 120, 123–5, 140
Louis X, king of France (1314–16), 125
Louvain, 134 n. 36
Lucca, 119
Lucius III, pope (1181–5), 94

magic, used to affect outcome of ordeal, 71, 74, 77; see also ordeal, used in cases of
Magna Carta, 65
Magnus Erikson, Danish noble, 37, 76–7
Magnus VI, king of Norway (1263–80), 128
Magyar law, see Hungary, Hungarian law
Maitland, Fredric W., 69
Malleus Maleficarum, work by Krämer and Sprenger, 71, 145–6
'Manichees', see Cathars
Marcher lords, 47
marital infidelity, see ordeal, used in cases of
Mary, Virgin, 84
matrimonial disputes, see ordeal, used in cases of
Maximilian I, duke of Bavaria (1598–1651), 149
Medina de Pomar, 58–9 (map 3)
Mediterranean, 46, eastern, 132
Melfi, Constitutions of, see Constitutions of Melfi
Mercato San Severino, 58–9 (map 3)
Merovingians, 7
Mid Frisia, see Frisia
Middlesex, 65, 112
Milan, 57, 61
miracles, the miraculous, 86–90, 121–2, 163–4
Miranda de Ebro, 58–9 (map 3)
Mirror of Justices, The, 133
Modena, 134
Monomachiam, papal ruling, 97 n. 90, 118
Montecalvo, 58–9 (map 3)
Montpellier, 56
Mord, in *Njal's Saga*, 114
Morris, Prof. Colin, 16
Moslems, 8, 21; see also Islam
Mozarabic rite, 22
Münster, bishop of, 87

Muratori, L. A., 147 n. 85
murder, *see* ordeal, used in cases of homicide and murder

Nablus, Synod of (1120), 46
Naples, 10
Narbonne, 51
Navarre, 2
Netherlands, *see* Spanish Netherlands, United Provinces
Newcastle, 119–20
Newgate prison, 56
Nicaean emperor, 131
Nicola Pisano, sculptor (13th century), 22 n. 31
Nicolas I, pope (858–67), 118
Nitra, 92
Njal's Saga, 114
Norman Peace (1047), 51
Normans, Normandy, 20, 30, 47–8, 104, 108; *see also* Anglo-French; Anglo-Normans
Normandy, duke of, 15
Normandy, dukes of, *see* Robert Curthose (also England, kings of)
Norse, Old, 89
Norsemen, 114
Northampton, Assize of, *see* Assize of Northampton
Northampton, *see* St Peter's
Norway, Norwegian law, etc., 19–20, 24, 92, 128, 144, 146
Norway, kings of, *see* Hakon III, Hakon IV, Olaf, St.
notariate, 28
Nottarp, Hermann, 55, 153
Novgorod, 69
Numbers, Book of, 82–5

oaths, 14, 24, 26–8, 30–3, 38, 45, 50–1, 55, 63–4, 67, 72–3, 80–1, 85, 92, 96, 105, 108, 110, 115–16, 121–2, 131, 137, 139, 158, 163; *see also* compurgation; foreigners, oath and ordeal
Oesel, bishop of, 47 n. 32
Olaf, saga of St, 15–16
Olaf, St, king of Norway (1016–30), 15–16
Oldenburg-Lübeck, 46
ordeal:
affected by magic, *see* magic
and foreigners, *see* foreigners, oath and ordeal
and kingship, *see* kingship and ordeal
and lordship, *see* lordship and ordeal
and status, *see* slaves; status and ordeal; unfree
'disputed', 41
exemption from, *see* exemption
falsified, 15
rituals, *see* rituals for the ordeal
revenue from, *see* revenue from ordeal
scepticism about, *see* scepticism about the ordeal
types of
battle, *see* battle, trial by
bitter waters (biblical), 82, 84
blessed morsel, 160
candle ordeal, 2
cauldron (specific mentions), 2, 4–9, 11, 13–14, 18–19, 28–9, 32, 38, 44, 48, 50, 54, 56, 60–1, 71–2, 74–5, 82, 88, 95, 130–2, 133 (misunderstood), 154
cold water (specific mentions), 2, 10–11, 13–14, 23–5, 27, 29, 33, 39, 47–8, 51–2, 56–7, 65–7, 74, 76–7, 82, 87–8, 92–4, 98, 116, 121, 131, 135, 144, 146–52, 162
eucharistic ordeal, 17 n. 12, 72, 82, 95
hot axe, 48
hot iron (specific mentions), 1–2, 11, 14–23, 25–7, 29–32, 37, 40, 44, 46–8, 51–3, 55–7, 60–1, 66, 72, 74–6, 78–80, 82, 87, 91–3, 95–6, 98, 100, 121, 130–4, 137, 139, 144–6, 161–2, 164
hot ploughshares, 10, 15–18, 33, 46, 74
ordeal of the cross, 9–10
triple ordeal, 31, 69
used in cases of
adultery, 16–19, 33, 132
arson, 25, 64, 66
assault and wounding, 29, 66, 96, 135
bestiality, 19
burglary, 66–7
civil suits, 25, 27
cohabitation, 9
concealment of treasure trove, 64
contempt of court, 4, 9
disputes over territory, 9
ecclesiastical suits, 9
false witness, 4, 9, 44
forest offences, 131
forgery, 25, 36, 64
fornication, 80
heresy, 21–5, 33, 39–40, 52–3, 57, 69, 80, 95, 142
homicide and murder, 8, 10, 13, 25,

29–30, 33, 38, 46, 64, 66–8, 78, 95, 97, 125, 135–6, 144, 160
horse-stealing, 78
ill fame, 29
impotence, 46
legitimacy of doubtful claimants, 5
magic, 11, 24
marital infidelity, 10
matrimonial disputes, 45–6
paganism, 24
paternity, disputed, 19–20, 33, 40
peace-breaking, 33, 51–2, 92
plotting against the king, 36
poisoning, 10, 33
political charges, 13–16, 37
property disputes, 9, 25, 27–8, 63, 96
rape, 29, 64
rapine, 131
receiving an outlaw, 66
robbery, 64, 67
rustling, 57
sexual offences, 13, 16, 18–20, 24, 33, 144
simony, 16
status disputes, 25
theft, 4, 8–9, 13, 24–5, 30, 32–3, 44, 57, 68, 131
treason, 14, 24, 37, 64, 76, 95
witchcraft, 23–5, 68–9, 71, 134, 144–52
Ordenaunce and Fourme of Fighting within Lists, 110
Orleans, 164
orthodoxy, religious, 20
Ostrogoths, kings of, *see* Theodoric
Otto I, king of Germany and emperor (936–73), 105
Ottokar I, king of Bohemia (1197–1230), 93
Oxford, 55, 58–9 (map 3), 164

Pacific, 36
pagans, paganism, 44, 46, 92, 99; *see also* ordeal, used in cases of: paganism
paganism of the ordeal, 101, 153–7
Palenzuela, 58–9 (map 3)
Pandulf, papal legate (d.1226), 127
Pannonia, 104
Paris, 90, 164
Paris *Parlement*, *see* Parlement
Paris, bishop of, 9
Paris, council at (1213), 99
Parlement of Paris, 149
Passau, bishop of, 55

paternity, disputed, *see* ordeal, used in cases of
Patetta, F., 34
Patrick, St (5th century), 5
Peace of God, 50–2, 69, 92
peace-breaking, *see* ordeal, used in cases of
peine forte et dure, la, 143
perjury, 30–1, 38, 50, 105–6; effect on legal standing, 31, 38; tried by battle, 108
Perkins, William, Puritan clergyman (1558–1602), 148
Péronne, 135–6
pesquisa, 60–1
Peter Comestor (d.c. 1179), 84
Peter Damian (d.1072), 21
Peter the Chanter, scholastic thinker (d.1197), 53, 73, 84, 86–8, 90, 94, 97–8, 121, 160–2
Peter's Pence, 127
Peterborough, abbot of, 125
Peters, Prof. Edward, 140
Philip II, king of Spain (1556–98), 149
Philip IV, king of France (1285–1314), 109–10, 120–1, 124–5
Philip the Good, duke of Burgundy (1419–67), 122
Picardy, 147
Pipe Rolls, 65, 94
Pippin, king of the Franks (751–68), 9, 46
Pisa, 119
Pisa triptych, 22 n. 31
'pit and gallows', franchise of, 48–9, 132
plea rolls, 65–6
plotting against the king, *see* ordeal, used in cases of
ploughshares, ordeal of, *see* ordeal, types of
Plucknett, T. F. T., 157
poisoning, tried by battle, 106, 123; *see also* ordeal, used in cases of
Poland, Poles, 44–5
Polish duke, 45; *see also* Boleslas (V)
political charges, *see* ordeal, used in cases of
polygamy, 45
Polynesia, 2
Poppo, missionary (10th century), 21, 44
Portugal, 69
Přemyslids, Bohemian ducal family, 44–6
'primitive mind' (Lévy-Bruhl's concept), 163

property cases, tried by battle, 105–6, 108; *see also* ordeal, used in cases of property disputes
Prüm, abbot of, party to lawsuit (*c.* 1103), 28
Puritan clergyman, 148

queens accused of adultery, 17, 24
Quierzy, capitulary of (873), *see* Capitulary of Quierzy
Quo Warranto, 125

Radding, Prof. Charles, 161, 163
Rainald, bishop of Como (1061–92), 50 n. 48
Ralf fitzHugh, accused of robbery (1214), 56
rape, *see* ordeal, used in cases of
rapine, *see* ordeal, used in cases of
rationality of the ordeal, 34–5, 61, 85–6, 157–66
receiving an outlaw, *see* ordeal, used in cases of
Red Sea, parting of, 74
Regiam majestatem, 130
Regino, abbot of Prüm, canonist (d.915), 31, 82, 118
Reisbach, Council of (800), 11
relics, 22, 51, 121–2
revenue from ordeal, 93–4
Rheims, 14
Rheims, archbishop of, 147
Rheims, council of (1119), 51
Rheims, council of (1157), 53
Rhineland, 52, 54, 131–2, 147
Richard I, king of England (1189–99), 66
Richardis, wife of Charles the Fat, 16–18 & nn.
Riga, 56, 58–9 (map 3)
Riga, bishop of, 56
Riga, Synod of (1428), 134
Rioja, 61
Ripuarian law, 4, 9, 32
ritual, 81, 88–90, 116–17
rituals and duel, 121
rituals for the ordeal, 10–11, 19, 21, 25, 65, 71, 88, 97, 120–1, 131, 162
robbery, *see* ordeal, used in cases of
Robert, king of France (996–131), 72
Robert of Arbrissel, founder of Fontevrault (d.1117), 96
Robert Bloet, bishop of Lincoln (1094–1123), 37 n. 9

Robert Curthose, duke of Normandy (1087–1106), 20
Robert, earl of Gloucester (d.1147), 47
Robert of Jumièges, archbishop of Canterbury (1051–2), 17
Robert de Montfort, fought duel (1163), 107
Robert Pullan, theologian (d.1146), 97
Robert, son of Patrick, approver (13th century), 113
Roger Bacon, Franciscan scholar (d.*c.* 1292), 133
Roland, in *The Song of Roland*, 106
Roman church, 100, 118, 127
Roman Law, 27, 85, 121, 123, 140, 142, 164
Roman version of ordeal ritual, 11
Romano-canonical law, 100, 141
Rome, 11
Rothenbach in the Black Forest, 146
Rouen, archbishop of, 91
Rouen, council at (1214), 99
Rousset, Paul, 163
Rudolf I, king of Germany (1273–91), 124
Rumania, 63
Ruprecht of Freising, author of the *Freisinger Rechtsbuch* (*c.* 1325), 130
Russia, Russian law, 21, 29
Russkaia Pravda, 93
rustling, *see* ordeal, used in cases of

Sachsenspiegel, German law book (*c.* 1225), 26, 110, 112, 131
sacraments, 79–80, 87–9
Saga of Saint Olaf, 15–16
sagas, 15–16, 40–1, 105, 114
Sahagún, 58–9 (map 3)
St Alban's, 93
St Aubin of Angers, 25
St Denis, 9
St Eulalia, cathedral of (Elne), 51
St Gaudens, 108
St George, Skoplje, monastery of, 62 n. 84
St John's church (Salzburg diocese), 91
St Mary's Mount (Salzburg diocese), 91
St Michael Archangel, monastery of, 62 n. 84
St Omer, 57
St Peter's cathedral, Cologne, 52
St Peter's, Northampton, 91
St Pölten, 55, 57, 58–9 (map 3)
Salic Law, 4, 9–10, 26, 28, 103, 154
Salisbury, 107
Salzburg, archbishop of, 91

Samson, archbishop of Rheims (1140–61), 53, 98
San Pedro de Jaca, 96
San Pedro, cathedral of (Vich), 51
Sancho IV, king of Castile-León (1284–95), 137 n. 40
Sant'Angelo in Theodice, 58–9 (map 3)
Santacara, 58–9 (map 3)
Santo Domingo de la Calzada in the Rioja, 61
Santo Domingo de Silos, 58–9 (map 3)
Sardinian magnate, 98
Savonarola, Girolamo (d.1498), 22 n. 32
Saxi, 'the southern king' in the 'Lay of Gudrun', 44
Saxo Grammaticus, historian (12th century), 105
Saxons, Saxon law, etc., 7–9 & n., 12, 21, 68, 103
Scandinavia, Scandinavian law, etc., 19–20, 25, 43–4, 47, 105, 114, 133, 155; *see also* Denmark; Norway; Sweden
scepticism about the ordeal, 12, 19, 62, 68–9, 71–2, 75–7, 87, 159, 161; *see also* criticism of the ordeal
scepticism about trial by battle, 116–17
scepticism about witchcraft, 146
scholasticism, scholastic thinkers, etc., 82, 87–9, 164
Schwentner, Bernhard, 117
Scone, 49 n. 49
Scotland, Scottish law, etc., 36, 39, 47–9, 69, 108, 119–20, 127, 130, 132, 147
Scotland, kings of, *see* Alexander II, James VI, William the Lion
Sens cathedral, 93
Serbs, Serbian law, 62, 132
Severus, bishop of Prague (1030–67), 45
sexual offences, tried by battle, 106; *see also* ordeal, used in cases of
Shadrach, Meshach and Abednego, 21
Sicily, 127, 133, 142
Siegburg on the Rhine, abbey of, party to lawsuit (1152), 25
Siete Partidas, 123, 126
Sigurth Thorlakson, in *Saga of Saint Olaf*, 15–16, 41
simony, *see* ordeal, used in cases of
sin and crime, distinction between, 81
Skoplje, 62 n. 84
slaves, 4, 8–9, 32, 140; *see also* unfree
Slavnik dynasty, 45
Slavs, 46, 131

Smith, Adam, economist (1723–90), 159
Sobeslas I, duke of Bohemia (1125–40), 37
Soissons, 23, 52
sorcery, *see* ordeal, used in cases of magic
sortilege, 116; *see also* divination; lots
Spain, Spanish law, etc., 8, 20, 24–5, 28, 47, 57, 60–1, 105, 122, 128, 130, 134, 144, 146–7; *see also* Aragon; Castile-León
Spain, kings of, *see* Philip II
Spanish Netherlands, 147
Speyer, 54
Sprenger, Jakob, Dominican, co-author of the *Malleus maleficiarum*, 145–6
stage, historical, 163
stage, social, 34
status, and oaths, 30; and ordeal, 32–3, 68; and trial by battle, 109–11, 125; *see also* ordeal, used in cases of status disputes; slaves; unfree
Stephan Dushan, king of Serbia (1331–55), 132
Stephen V, pope (885–91), 74–5
Strassburg, 52
Strassburg, bishop of, 53
Styria, 149
Suffolk, 108
Summa confessorum, work by Thomas of Chobham, 80
Summa Monacensis, 97
Sundays, respect for, 45
Sweden, 127, 133
Sweden, rulers of, *see* Birger Jarl, 127
swimming of witches, *see* ordeal, types of: cold water ordeal, used in cases of witchcraft
Swithun, Saint, 18
synods, *see* councils

Tafalla, 58–9 (map 3)
Tait, James, 120
Taunton, 92
Templars, 16
tempting God, 86, 97, 100, 123, 134
Teruel, 61
testimony, 14, 24, 27–9, 31, 63, 72, 106, 158; *see also* witness; written evidence
Teutberga, wife of Lothar, king of Lotharingia, 13–14, 16, 118
Thames valley, 7–8 n. 8
theft, 113; effect on legal standing, 31; tried by battle, 104, 106, 109; *see also* ordeal, used in cases of

Theodore II Lascaris, emperor of Nicaea (1254–8), 16
Theodoric, king of the Ostrogoths (d.526), 104
Thierry, in *The Song of Roland*, 106–7
Thietmar, bishop of Merseburg (975–1018), historian, 17 n. 12
Thomas Aquinas, St (d.1274), 87, 122
Thomas Caterton, fought duel (1380), 108
Thomas of Bruges, champion (13th century), 112
Thomas of Chobham, author of *Summa confessorum* (early 13th century), 80
Thomas of Woodstock, 110
Thorkel, character in *Ljósvetninga saga*, 40–1
Thrace, 132
Thuringians, Thuringian law, 10, 103
torture, 75, 101, 135, 139–46, 158–9
Tournai, 29, 135–6
transubstantiation, 83, 89–90
Transylvania, 147 n. 85
treason, torture used against, 142; tried by battle, 106–8, 115, 119, 123, 126; *see also* ordeal, used in cases of
Très ancienne coutume de Bretagne, 143
'trial of faith', 21–2, 33
Tribur, Council of (895), 31, 85
Troia, 58–9 (map 3)
Troilus, in *Troilus and Criseyde*, 134

unfree, 29, 33, 36–7, 52, 66, 95, 125; and trial by battle, 109; *see also* slaves
United Provinces, 147
universities, 89
Uppsala, archbishop of, 133
Urban, bishop of Llandaff (1107–33), 47
Usatges of Barcelona, 51
Utrecht, diocese of, 80

Valdemar I, king of Denmark (1157–82), 37
Valdemar II, king of Denmark (1202–41), 100, 138
Valencia, council of (1255), 130
Valenciennes, 121–2
Valladolid, council of (1322), 130
Varad (modern Oradea in Rumania), 63, 128–30
Venetian service, 132
Vermandois, 125
Verona, 139
Vézelay, 39–41
Vich, council of (1068), 51

Victorian magistrates, 151
Vincennes, 111
violation of truces, tried by battle, 108
Virginia, 147
Visigoths, Visigothic law, etc., 7–8, 104; *see also* Goths
Visigoths, kings of, *see* Wittiza
Vitoria, 58–9 (map 3)
'vouching to warranty', 109

Wales, Welsh law, etc., 32, 47–9, 107
Webster, John, Jacobean dramatist, 10
Welbeck, abbot of, 94 n. 81
Wends, 92, 99
Wessex, *see* West Saxons
West Frisia, *see* Frisia
West Saxons, 7–8 & n.
West Saxons, kings of, *see* Ine
Westfield (Sussex), 92
Westminster, 107
Westphalia, 147
Weyer, Johann, physician and writer (1515–88), 146, 148
Widukind of Corvey, historian (10th century), 21, 44
William de Vescy, challenged to duel (1294), 107
William of Eu, fought duel (1095), 107
William Rufus, king of England (1087–1100), 76–7, 95, 107
William the Conqueror, king of England (1066–87), 37, 91, 99, 104
William the Lion, king of Scotland (1165–1214), 36, 39, 120, 130
Winchester, 111
Winchester Annals, 17
witchcraft, torture used against, 142; *see also* ordeal, used in cases of
witness, 24, 26–30, 32–3, 50, 73, 75, 85, 109, 115, 135–6, 140–1; *see also* testimony
Wittiza, king of the Visigoths (702–10), 8
Wormald, Patrick, 7 n. 7
Worms, 54, 95
Worms, bishop of, 50 n. 48
wounding, *see* ordeal, used in cases of assault and wounding
written authority, 86, 165
written evidence, 26–8, 101, 105–6

York, 121
York Minster, 121
York, province of, 119
Ypres, 23, 52, 55, 57, 58–9 (map 3), 79

www.ingramcontent.com/pod-product-compliance
Lightning Source LLC
Chambersburg PA
CBHW030528100426
42813CB00001B/182